Mixing Music

by Michael Miller

A member of Penguin Random House LLC

Publisher: Mike Sanders
Associate Publisher: Billy Fields
Acquisitions Editor: Jan Lynn
Cover Designer: Lindsay Dobbs
Book Designer: William Thomas
Compositor: Ayanna Lacey
Proofreader: Lisa Starnes
Indexer: Tonya Heard

This book is dedicated to my six wonderful grandchildren—in chronological order, Collin, Alethia, Hayley, Judah, Lael, and Jackson. Together, they provide an interesting mix in my life.

First American Edition, 2016
Published in the United States by DK Publishing
6081 E. 82nd Street, Indianapolis, Indiana 46250

Published in the United States by Dorling Kindersley Limited.

IDIOT'S GUIDES and Design are trademarks of Penguin Random House LLC

ISBN: 9781465454638
Library of Congress Catalog Card Number: 2016935175

Note: This publication contains the opinions and ideas of its author(s). It is intended to provide helpful and informative material on the subject matter covered. It is sold with the understanding that the author(s) and publisher are not engaged in rendering professional services in the book. If the reader requires personal assistance or advice, a competent professional should be consulted. The author(s) and publisher specifically disclaim any responsibility for any liability, loss, or risk, personal or otherwise, which is incurred as a consequence, directly or indirectly, of the use and application of any of the contents of this book.

Trademarks: All terms mentioned in this book that are known to be or are suspected of being trademarks or service marks have been appropriately capitalized. Alpha Books, DK, and Penguin Random House LLC cannot attest to the accuracy of this information. Use of a term in this book should not be regarded as affecting the validity of any trademark or service mark.

DK books are available at special discounts when purchased in bulk for sales promotions, premiums, fund-raising, or educational use. For details, contact: DK Publishing Special Markets, 345 Hudson Street, New York, New York 10014 or SpecialSales@dk.com.

Printed and bound in the United States of America

idiotsguides.com

Contents

Introduction

I love playing and listening to music. I'm a drummer by nature, although I also can plink out a few chords on a piano and strum a little on the guitar. I've done some composing and arranging in my day, and I've written a fair number of books about these and other music-related topics. (Check them all out at my website, millerwriter.com.)

I also happen to know my way around the recording studio. I'm a bit of an aficionado of the classic days of studio recording and of the recording and mixing engineers who made those golden sounds happen—with far fewer resources than we have today. There was a lot of magic in the mixing back then, whether we're talking the "live" mixing of a Frank Sinatra recording, the groundbreaking manipulation of four- and eight-track machines for The Beatles and The Beach Boys during the 1960s, or the more polished sounds from the multitrack sessions of the 1970s and 1980s with performers such as Steely Dan and Michael Jackson.

Of course, recording and mixing has changed a lot since then. The glory days of recording in a big (and expensive) professional recording studio are long gone, as are the days of magnetic recording tape and huge analog mixing boards. Today, recording is, as often as not, done in a small or even home studio, one or two tracks at a time on a personal computer running sophisticated multitrack recording software. This same setup—hardware and software—is typically used to mix those recorded tracks, which means the entire process can be done by just about anyone with a personal computer, an audio interface box, and a microphone or two.

As much as I revere and respect those golden days of studio recording, technology really has democratized the recording process, enabling artists without much, if any, budget to produce (and distribute) professional-sounding CDs and digital tracks. That's a good thing.

However, even when you have all the necessary technology at your fingertips, skill is still involved in making and mixing those recordings. Just because you have access to a PC or Mac and a copy of Pro Tools or Logic Pro doesn't mean you have the knowledge or skills required to create a commercial recording. There's a lot you need to know and do to turn those recorded tracks into a quality final product.

Although the recording itself is important (and worthy of its own book), much of the magic happens during the mixing stage. You need to select which tracks to keep and which to dump, edit those tracks if necessary (and it's often necessary; musicians both pro and amateur aren't always perfect), and then throw all the tracks together in a way that sounds pleasing to the ear and gets across the vision of the artist. And it's not just setting the levels for each track; you need to pan the tracks across the stereo soundstage; cut and paste tracks and sections to create the final arrangement; and apply equalization, compression, reverb, and other effects to shape the sound of each voice and instrument. A skilled mixing engineer can make a huge impact on a project and is every bit as important as the band's lead guitarist or bass player.

Not everyone who has access to a recording/mixing setup has these necessary skills, however. Every budding mixing engineer has to start somewhere, and facing a screen full of virtual sliders, plug-ins, and equalizers can be daunting. What do you need to know to create a pleasing and powerful mix? And just how do you re-create the sounds you hear in your head—and on other recordings?

Learning at the elbows of a skilled engineer is always desirable, but you might not have the luxury of interning at a big recording studio. (That's if there are any big studios left in your area and if they accept interns.) You might not even have the time or money to take courses in mixing, which are available at many fine music schools across the land. You need to learn mixing now, on your own terms—and, quite possibly, on a limited budget.

Which is why you picked up this book.

Idiot's Guides: Mixing Music teaches you everything you need to know to start mixing your own recording projects. Whether you're mixing tracks you've personally recorded or been engaged by a producer or artist to mix their previously recorded tracks, this book leads you step by step through what you need to do and how you need to do it. There's a lot to learn about the mixing process, but this book is a great place to start. You learn the basics and a little more—enough to set you on the road to creating great-sounding recordings.

How This Book Is Organized

As noted, mixing is a complex topic, and there are lots of aspects to learn. As such, I've arranged the contents of this book in a way that leads you through the underlying concepts into the individual components of the mixing process, with lots of hands-on advice along the way.

Idiot's Guides: Mixing Music is composed of 20 chapters, each covering an important aspect of the mixing process. These chapters are organized into six general parts, as follows:

Part 1, Introduction to Recording and Mixing, describes what mixing is and how it works and helps you understand how it fits within the overall recording/production process.

Part 2, Building Your Mixing Studio, walks you through everything you need to know to construct your own home or small mixing studio. You learn how to choose and set up your mixing space, select the right mixing hardware, find the best DAW software program, and choose and set up the right monitor speakers.

Part 3, Before You Mix, describes everything you need to do before you actually start mixing. You learn how to record tracks for better mixing results, prep the recorded tracks for mixing, and plan out your musical arrangement in advance.

Part 4, Creating the Mix, is all about mixing your recorded tracks. You learn all about the mechanics of the mixing process, including how to balance the levels of your tracks and position voices and instruments in the stereo soundstage.

Part 5, Enhancing the Mix, goes beyond setting levels to focus on applying dynamic and spatial effects, such as compression, equalization, gating, reverb, and delay.

Part 6, Creating Better Mixes, presents real-world advice for mixing your projects. You learn advanced techniques such as pitch correction, timing correction, automation, and mixing for mobile listeners. You also learn tips for mixing specific types of tracks—vocals, instruments, and drums. (Yes, I know drums are instruments, but they require special attention different from any other instrument.) There's even a chapter on what happens when you're done mixing. (Spoiler alert: it's mastering!)

In addition, I've included a glossary of terms and a useful list of mixing resources at the back of the book. All in all, there's a lot here for your immediate learning and future reference.

What You Need to Use This Book

Any aspiring mixing engineer can learn the basic mixing techniques from *Idiot's Guides: Mixing Music*. You don't need any prior knowledge or experience to get started, although it helps—but is not essential—if you understand a little bit about music and know your way around the recording studio.

At some point, you'll want to put the theory into operation, which means you'll need access to some or all of the equipment and software discussed in Part 2. In particular, you'll want a personal computer with your digital audio workstation (DAW) program of choice installed. It's what you need to start mixing.

How to Get the Most Out of This Book

To get the most from this book, you should know how it is designed. I've tried to put things together in such a way to make learning how to mix both rewarding and fun—using easy-to-understand language and real-world examples.

Supplementing the main text are a number of sidebars that present additional advice and information. These elements enhance your knowledge or point out important pitfalls to avoid. Here are the types of sidebars you'll see scattered throughout the book:

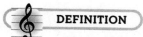

These sidebars contain definitions of terms pertaining to aspects of music theory.

These sidebars contain additional information about the topic at hand.

These sidebars contain advice about how best to use the theory presented in the text.

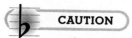

These sidebars contain cautions about what to avoid when you're reading and writing music.

The First Rule of Mixing: There Are No Rules

As you can see, there's a lot of useful information between the front and back covers of this book. (At least I hope you find it useful!) All that said, there's one general rule you need to keep in mind before you get started:

> In the world of mixing, there are no rules.

That is, all the advice and suggestions you read here and elsewhere are just recommendations. What works for one project might not work for another. A given song might require a different approach, or a particular artist or producer might demand something beyond the expected. That's part and parcel of the game. You need to work with the specific tracks, instruments, performers, and personnel to make the most of every project you handle.

You'll also find that every engineer has his or her own unique approach—specific EQ settings, plug-ins, and such that they rely on from project to project. The way one engineer EQs the snare drum is going to be at least slightly different from the way another engineer does it. It's worthwhile to seek advice from other experienced engineers—but then filter that advice for your own projects.

So take the advice given in this book as a starting point, a general recommendation, one way to approach a given situation. It's not the final word, and other engineers are likely to quibble with some of the specifics. That's okay. You need to learn to make your own choices.

In the world of mixing, nobody's wrong and everything's right—given the right circumstances, of course.

Let Me Know What You Think

If you want to learn more about me and my other books (I've written about a lot of music-related topics, including music theory, music history, and music composition), check out my personal website at millerwriter.com. Search or click through to find the page for this book to find any corrections or clarifications we've posted.

You also can use the contact form on my website to contact me with questions or comments. I always love to hear from my readers. I can't promise I'll answer every message, but I do promise that I'll read each one!

It's Time to Start Mixing

There's a lot to learn about mixing music, so let's get started. Turn the page and get ready to learn!

Acknowledgments

I had assistance from many people in the creation of this book and would like to thank them all collectively and individually. In particular, thanks to Jan Lynn, Christy Wagner, Mike Sanders, and everyone else at Alpha Books for turning my manuscript into the book you're reading.

Introduction to Recording and Mixing

What is mixing, anyway? Part 1 shows you what mixing is all about and how it fits within the overall recording/mixing/mastering process. In the following chapters, you learn the difference between live and studio mixing and discover just what a mixing engineer does.

Understanding the Recording Process

Mixing is just one part—albeit a very important one—of the overall recording/production process. Before we get into the details of mixing, you need to know where mixing fits into the entire process—the better to understand how it works and why it's important.

How Recording Has Changed Over the Years

Recording today is quite a bit different from what it was back when I was growing up in the 1960s and 1970s—or even just a few short years ago. The recording industry has progressed from primitive direct-to-acetate single-mic recording, to 24-track tape recording, to today's unlimited tracks recorded (and mixed) digitally. What used to require the rental of professional studio space and a massive mixing board (and the high costs associated with each) can now be accomplished on a consumer-grade personal computer in the comfort of your own basement or bedroom. Professional-grade results can be had on even the most limited of budgets, which means practically any artist can record and produce his or her own compact discs or digital files ready for distribution and playback.

The reality is that all parts of the recording process have changed substantially over the 100 or so years we've had recorded music. Let's take a quick look at how things used to be, how they've changed, and where we are today.

Early Recording: It's All Mechanical

The very first recordings, starting with Thomas Edison's groundbreaking recordings in the late 1870s, were all mechanical in nature—and all, essentially, direct-to-disc (or cylinder). The electrical microphone had not yet been invented, so sound was typically captured via one or more large cone-shaped horns, kind of like the opposite of the gramophone horns used for playback during the same era. The musicians played or sang directly into the horn, which in turn vibrated a diaphragm connected to a stylus. The stylus then cut a groove into a soft recording medium rotating beneath it.

The earliest recordings were made on tinfoil cylinders. Later recordings were made on wax cylinders or discs. As you might suspect, the resulting audio was decidedly lo-fi, capturing only frequencies in a narrow 250- to 2,500-hertz (Hz) range. No low bass, no airy highs, just the mid-range tinny sound.

Because we're talking direct-to-disc recording with a single sound source (the horn), no mixing was involved. There was no amplification in the process, so volume levels were set by moving performers closer to or farther away from the horn. You couldn't go back to rerecord individual parts, and there was no way to "fix it in the mix." The disc or cylinder picked up exactly what was being played (within that narrow frequency range), in all its unfiltered and unamplified glory.

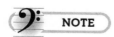 **NOTE**

The limitations of these early acoustic recording methods caused engineers to favor louder instruments, such as trumpets and trombones, as well as singers with louder voices. Softer instruments and voices were difficult to capture.

The Second Wave: Recording Goes Electric

The acoustic recording era lasted until the mid-1920s, when electrical microphones, signal amplifiers, and disc-cutting machines became common. Western Electric was the company behind the innovations that significantly changed the entire recording process.

The invention of the microphone was the most important change in the process. The microphone translated sound waves into electrical signals, which could then be amplified, filtered, and balanced electronically. Over time, engineers began to use multiple microphones to more accurately capture larger groups of musicians.

The adoption of the microphone also ushered in the rise of less-bombastic performers. Whereas the old "sing into the horn" process favored brassy instruments and brassy vocalists, amplified microphones fit softer instruments into the mix and also encouraged more intimate vocal performances. (Compare the over-the-top older recordings of Al Jolson with the newer, softer crooning of Bing Crosby; Crosby exploited the warmth of the mic in ways that simply weren't possible before.)

Equally important, this new recording era required a new class of professional, the *audio engineer*. The engineer mixed (live) signals from multiple microphones, adjusting levels on the fly to capture the best results direct-to-disc. For the first time in recording (and recorded) history, a nonperformer assumed a critical role in the creative process.

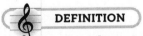 **DEFINITION**

An **audio engineer** is an individual who records, mixes, or masters an audio recording.

This new electrical/electronic recording (and the introduction of the engineer into the process) resulted in substantially improved fidelity. The resulting frequency range was much broader, reproducing signals from 60 to 6,000 Hz.

Unfortunately, the actual recording was still mechanical and direct-to-disc (either wax or metal); magnetic tape was still several years in the future. The disc-cutting machine created a master disc that was then used to mass-produce shellac or vinyl discs for consumers.

The Magnetic Era: Get It on Tape

Recording direct-to-disc, of course, has its limitations, not the least of which is that you can't go back and edit anything. It's a one-shot deal, even if you can mix sounds from different microphones as you're recording in real time.

Thus we come to our third era of sound recording—what many have dubbed the "magnetic era." Beginning in 1945 and continuing through the 1980s (and still in some studios today), this era is distinguished by the ability to record to *magnetic tape*, which meant multiple tracks could be recorded and edited to create the recorded product.

DEFINITION

Magnetic tape is a medium for audio or video recording that incorporates a thin magnetic coating on a narrow strip of plastic film.

Magnetic tape recording was invented by the Germans in the 1930s, but the dawning of World War II restricted its use to that country alone. It wasn't until after the war that singer, radio star, and avid golfer Bing Crosby famously purchased two Ampex Model 2000 recorders so he could prerecord his radio shows and give himself more time on the links. Similar Ampex recorders quickly made their way into the recording studios of the day, and a new way of recording music (and radio shows, of course) was born.

With magnetic tape, a live performance is captured via one or more microphones and then stored magnetically on large reels of audiotape. Magnetic tape provides a much improved frequency response over previous mechanical recording technologies, delivering true high-fidelity sound.

Even better, magnetic tape can be edited—crudely, by cutting and splicing pieces of tape together, or in a more sophisticated fashion by sending signals from one tape recorder to another, choosing which tracks to highlight or silence in the process. The first tape recorders were mono affairs, but later models let engineers record first 2, then 4, then 8, 16, and 24 tracks on ever-widening tapes.

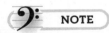

NOTE

More tracks resulted from the use of wider tape. One-, two-, and three-track recorders typically used ¼-inch-wide tapes, 4-track machines used ½-inch-wide tapes, some 8-track machines used 1-inch-wide tapes (some used ¼-inch tapes), and 16- and 24-track recorders used 2-inch-wide tapes. So-called Sel-Sync (Selective Synchronous) technology provided the ability to record different tracks on the same tape at different times, thus enabling synchronized overdubbing.

Let's consider the original single-track recorders. One or more mics were mixed "live" to the single track, which was then used to produce monophonic records or "transcribed" (i.e., prerecorded) radio shows. Simple enough.

In the 1950s, two-track recorders became common. You might think these were used to make basic right/left stereo recordings, but in fact, stereo records and record players were not yet widely available to the general public. Instead, many engineers used one track to record instruments and the other to record vocals and then mixed the two tracks down to one track for mono release. This let engineers record vocals separate from the backing instruments (while listening to the instrumental track via headphones), affording more desirable recording conditions for vocalists. In some instances, engineers recorded the whole shebang live on the first track and used the second track for overdubs.

Ampex introduced its first three-track recorder in 1960. This machine was the one engineers used for stereo projects. Backing instruments were recorded in stereo on the first two tracks (right and left), with vocals isolated on the third track. This third track would then be mixed toward the center for more pleasing results.

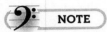

NOTE

Most of Phil Spector's "Wall of Sound" recordings were done on three-track machines. He recorded the backing musicians and singers "live" to two-track stereo and used the third track to record the lead vocals.

Four-track machines followed a few years later. Even though some engineers wondered what in the world they'd do with that extra track (three was enough?), they soon found use for it in the recording process. Engineers learned to use separate tracks to record individual instruments or sections, in some cases giving each instrument its own track on the tape. Consider a typical three-piece plus vocals rock band—put the drums on one track, bass on another, guitar(s) on a third, and vocals on the fourth. All four tracks could then be mixed down to either mono or stereo, as desired.

Musicians, producers, and engineers soon began clamoring for even more tracks to create more sophisticated recordings. When four-track recording was the norm, additional tracks could be created by mixing two or more existing tracks to a single track on another recorder mid-process. So for example, you might record the basic rhythm section tracks on the first four-track tape and then mix that down to a single track on another machine, freeing up three tracks for overdubs, vocals, more instruments, and the like. The only problem with this technique was that it introduced a not insubstantial amount of noise into the process, especially when used multiple times on a single project. But that was a small price to pay for the increased creative freedom.

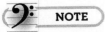

NOTE

"Bouncing" tracks from one recorder to another was how The Beatles created some of their biggest hits, including *Revolver* and *Sgt. Pepper's Lonely Hearts Club Band,* when Abbey Road Studios only had four-track recorders. In the four- and eight-track recording years, this track-bouncing moved at least part of the mixing process into the recording phase of things—the "premixing" of bounced tracks was done well before the final mix was made.

Commercial 8-track recorders were introduced in 1966, and by 1970, 16-track machines were increasingly common. Most studios switched to 24-track machines when they became available in the mid-1970s, and that's where analog tape recording maxed out. Most of the big albums of the late 1970s, 1980s, and early 1990s were recorded on 24-track machines, which afforded ample recording space for multiple instruments and vocals. With so many tracks available, engineers could devote separate tracks to individual drums in a drum kit; each background vocalist in the chorus; individual instruments in string sections; and every tambourine, shaker, and cowbell in the percussionist's arsenal. This led to increasingly complex *mixing* sessions, as all those tracks had to be mixed down to stereo for the final master.

The necessity of mixing down multiple tracks led to the creation of yet another new production position, the *mixing engineer*. (That's separate from the *recording engineer,* who is responsible for the recording of the original tracks.) With so many tracks recorded, the role of the mixing engineer becomes essential; it's this new part of the process that emphasizes which takes are included, which tracks get prominence, and where each individual instrument or voice appears in the final mix.

DEFINITION

Mixing is the process of putting together all the tracks in a recording project to make a pleasing overall recording. The **recording engineer** runs the recording board and supervises the recording process. The **mixing engineer** supervises the postrecording mixing process.

Recording Today: It's All Digital

Acoustic, electric, and magnetic recording are all *analog* processes. That is, the recording exactly mirrors in shape or form the original *sound wave,* without any breaks. In fact, if you look at a typical sound, of any type, using an oscilloscope, you see an unbroken wave, like that in the accompanying figure.

DEFINITION

A **sound wave** is a physical wave that pulses through the air, the changing pressure of which creates a distinct sound. **Analog recording** captures the sound wave while maintaining the general shape of the original waveform.

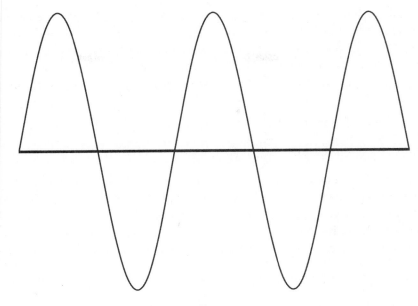

An analog waveform.

The first century of recorded sound captured and reproduced performances in this analog fashion. The goal was to mirror the original sound as accurately as possible, capturing all the subtleties and nuances of the original. Take, for example, the acoustic era, where recording machines used a sound-collecting horn attached to a sharp needle; sounds were collected in the horn, which vibrated the needle, which scratched a path onto a rotating tinfoil cylinder or wax disc. The needle moved up and down according to the pitch and volume (*amplitude*) of the sound, approximating the original soundwave.

Something similar happens when recording to magnetic tape. The recording heads of the tape recorder rearrange the magnetic particles on the tape to approximate the original soundwave. It's an exact reproduction—or as exact as the recording medium allows.

You see, one of the issues with analog recording is that, no matter how thin the needle or sophisticated the tape recorder, it can't reproduce the original music *exactly*. The *waveform* associated with live music is rather complex and has a large *dynamic range*—the difference between the loudest and softest passages. This means that even the best analog recording equipment can't make a 100 percent accurate reproduction of the original.

Further, analog recordings are difficult to edit. Splicing into the middle of a soundwave (or multiple soundwaves, on a multitrack recording) is an imprecise science, and it's difficult if not impossible to reach into a track on tape and pull out the soundwave of an individual voice or instrument.

There's also the issue of how many tracks you have to work with. Analog recording technology pretty much maxed out at 24 tracks on 2-inch magnetic tape. (Although you could bounce tracks from machine to machine or even synch two machines together to record in tandem—both Rube Goldberg–type approaches.) With artists clamoring for more control over their recordings—and wanting to record multiple takes of multiple instruments—those 24 tracks often didn't seem generous enough.

This leads us to *digital recording,* which is what we use today. Digital audio takes a much different approach than analog reproduction. Instead of trying to produce an exact image of an analog sound, digital audio uses small bursts of information—digital bits in the form of 1s and 0s—to represent pieces of the analog sound wave. When the bits of digital information are small enough, and when there are enough of them, an extremely accurate picture of the original sound emerges.

DEFINITION

Amplitude is the height of the sound wave; the larger the amplitude, the louder the sound. A **waveform** is a graph of the sound wave, illustrating the audio signal's sound pressure over time. **Dynamic range** is the difference between the loudest and softest passages of sound in music. **Digital recording** represents the original analog waveform as a series of digital ones and zeros. **Sampling** is the process of digitally encoding a sound.

All digital recordings are made by creating digital samples of the original sound, recorded either to tape or to a computer's hard disk. An analog-to-digital converter (ADC) "listens" to the original analog signal and takes a digital snapshot of the music at a particular point in time. This process is called *sampling,* and you can see how it works in the accompanying figure. Each digital "snapshot" captures a specific section of the original sound.

NOTE

The quality of the digital recording depends on how many samples are taken per second. The more samples taken (the higher the *sampling rate*), the more accurate the snapshot of the original sound. The other quality factor is the length of the sample taken, measured in bits. The smaller the sample size, the more accurate the recording.

With quality equipment (and accompanying software), digital recording can approach or sometimes surpass the fidelity of an analog recording, especially when you consider that digital allows less noise into the process. (Tape and discs have an inherent noise floor—plus new noise is introduced on each pass through the process.)

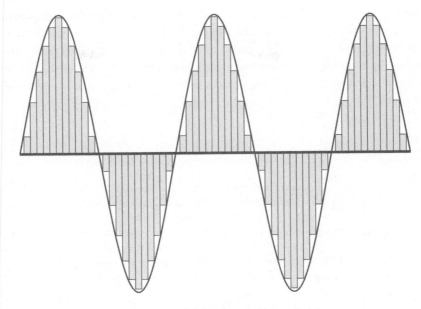

Digital sampling of an analog sound.

The big advantage of digital, however, is its editability. It's a lot easier to reach into a digital file to pull out or replace digital bits than it is to edit an analog waveform on tape. You can edit digital audio files on literally a bit-by-bit basis, which lets you punch in replacement parts when somebody hits a wrong note, change the pitch of notes (great for singers with less-than-perfect pitch), and even change the length and timing of individual notes to create a more rock-solid beat. You don't have to live with what was originally recorded.

And you get this improved editability at very low cost. All the fancy editing you can do with digital can be done on consumer-grade personal computers. You don't need expensive professional recording or editing equipment; any old laptop or desktop PC or Mac, along with relatively affordable digital audio workstation (DAW) software, will do the job.

In addition, because digital recording today is done to hard disk instead of magnetic tape, you're not limited to a set number of tracks. Unlike 2-inch tapes that hold only 24 recorded tracks, your computer's hard disk can hold hundreds of tracks—really, an infinite number. You're limited only by the size of your hard disk.

Digital recording came into existence in the late 1970s and really took off throughout the 1980s. Originally, digital recording equipment was high priced, hard to use, and often less than reliable. But things improved and the cost came down, to the point that digital recording is well within the budget of any working musician. You no longer need to go into a professional recording studio to get professional results.

So here's how it works in the digital era: you record the performers as they play or sing, typically dedicating an individual track for each instrument or voice. (In the case of a drum kit, you might have a dozen or so tracks, one for each drum and cymbal.) The individual tracks do not have to be recorded at the same time or place; you can record individual performers at their convenience and copy those digital tracks to the other tracks in your project. Engineers also might record multiple takes of the same performer and then digitally select bits and pieces from different takes to create a master track.

NOTE

Some session musicians record their tracks in their own home studios, using their own recording equipment and programs, and email or otherwise digitally transmit those digital files to the project's producer or engineer. (They typically have a rough mix or click track to play to when recording.) The engineer then inserts those files into the master project, synching up tempo and key and such digitally. A single project might include tracks from a dozen musicians, none of whom ever meet face to face.

When all the individual tracks have been recorded, the mixing process begins. In today's recording environment, mixing often involves editing (or "fixing") individual tracks, sometimes in a note-by-note fashion. It also entails selecting which tracks and takes to use; balancing those tracks both within the mix and within the stereo *soundstage;* and applying equalization, reverb, and other special effects to make everything sound better. The result is that the mixing engineer plays a huge role in creating the final product. The choices you make when mixing determine what the listener ultimately hears.

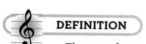

DEFINITION

The **soundstage,** or *soundfield,* is the physical or virtual space in which sounds reside. The stereo soundstage defines the left-to-right presence of individual sounds.

The Three Parts of the Process

Back in the first era of acoustic recording, the entire recording/production process was a single step. The musicians played or sang into the horn, and the master cylinder or disc was created in real time.

In the second era of recording, they still created the master disc in real time, but the recording engineer had more to do, thanks to the use of multiple microphones. The engineer did rudimentary mixing in real time, adjusting the levels between mics to create the mono signal that got sent to the master disc.

The process changed substantially during the era of magnetic tape, which introduced the three-phase process common today. The first phase was the recording itself, presided over by the recording engineer. The second phase of the process was the mixing of the recorded tracks down to a single mono or two stereo master tracks. The third phase of the process, enabled by automated disc-cutting machines, was the mastering of that final mix into a format best suited to the distribution media (vinyl discs, audiocassettes, and the like).

Today's digital recording era uses this same three-phase process. Although some of the phases might overlap to some degree on some projects, it basically looks like the following figure.

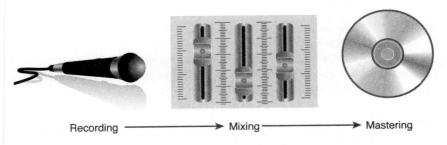

Recording ⟶ Mixing ⟶ Mastering

The three phases of the modern recording process.

In essence, the process starts with the digital recording of the various pieces and parts of a song. These pieces and parts are then cobbled together into a distinct whole during the mixing process. In the end, the final mix is turned into a finished product, ready for digital or physical distribution, during the mastering process. Each part is dependent on the others yet distinct in terms of what it accomplishes.

Recording

The first part of the recording process (ignoring any preproduction work, of course) is the recording itself. This involves the recording of all the necessary tracks, typically in digital fashion. (You also can record to tape and then transfer the tape to digital files, but that's not within the province of home recorders.)

How you record your digital tracks varies from project to project, producer to producer, and artist to artist. A solo artist might painstakingly record each individual track himself, building up a song by layering vocals over instruments one track at a time. A band might record the instrumental tracks live as a single unit and record the vocals afterward. Some artists record some tracks live but then use session musicians to add other tracks at their leisure. An orchestra, jazz band, or choir might record an entire performance live in a single tape, with no overdubs. Like I said, it varies.

What's common is that you end up with a series of recorded tracks that then have to be mixed together, which leads us to the next phase of the process.

Mixing

The mixing process today is more involved and more essential than it ever has been. Even if you do nothing more than mix down the multiple recorded tracks to a two-track stereo master, there's a lot of work to do, thanks to the proliferation of tracks enabled by digital recording. Mixing 16 or 24 tracks to stereo was hard enough, but now you might have 50 or 100 original tracks to deal with. (Thanks, digital recording!)

But there's more involved than just that. You have to pick which tracks and takes (or pieces of takes) to use, which really involves shaping the final product. The mixing engineer (often in conjunction with the artist and producer—but sometimes on his own) can determine which guitar line listeners hear, whether the chorus repeats after the second verse or the third, which drum beat is played, and more. It's a truly creative role, not just a reactive one.

The mixing engineer also has to make each track, as well as the final mix, sound as good as possible. That might mean "fixing" wrong notes or misplaced rhythms, replacing individual parts one measure or note at a time, or even wiping entire tracks that don't work. You also get to "sweeten" the sound by applying equalization, reverb, compression, and other audio *effects,* either on a track-by-track basis or to the final mix. This is especially important when tracks are recorded "dry" (without any effects), as most tracks are today. You determine how each voice and instrument sounds.

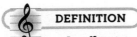

DEFINITION

An **effect** is any device or software plug-in that changes or processes the sound of a recording in any way other than equalization or volume level.

You also determine where each voice or instrument "sits" in the mix. That is, which voice or instrument is prominent in each part of the song, whether the rhythm guitar or horn section or backup vocals are up front in the mix or fade into the background. You also get to place each instrument in the stereo soundfield—center, left, right, or anywhere in between. It's how you build the final sound.

When you're done mixing, you're left with (typically) a two-track stereo mix. This isn't what gets sold on iTunes or pressed to CD, however, which brings us to the final part of the process.

Mastering

The final mix created by the mixing engineer now has to be *mastered* for final distribution. This can be done by the mixing engineer or by a separate *mastering engineer.* By this point, you've already placed all the vocals and instruments in the mix and the soundfield and applied effects to individual tracks. The mastering process, then, applies levels and effects to the entire mix, not to individual tracks. The goal is to make the final mix sound as good as possible on the various distribution media.

> **DEFINITION**
>
> **Mastering** is the process of readying a final mix for distribution on other media. The **mastering engineer** supervises the mastering process.

And then you're done. The master you create is used to press CDs, sent to iTunes and other online stores for digital download, and sent to Spotify and other music services for online streaming. Time for the next project!

The Least You Need to Know

- Recorded music has gone through four distinct eras: the acoustic era (before microphones), the electric era (now with microphones), the magnetic era (recording to multitrack magnetic tape), and the digital era (recording digital files on computers).
- Today's digital recording enables professional-quality results from affordable home computers and recording/mixing software.
- The recording process is done in three phases: recording, mixing, and mastering.
- Mixing involves the combination of multiple recorded tracks into a two-channel stereo mix, along with the editing and sweetening of individual parts.

Understanding the Mixing Process

You've recorded all your instrumental and vocal tracks, and they're saved in your digital audio workstation (DAW) program of choice on your computer's hard disk. Now it's time to start thinking about turning all those tracks into a finished recording.

Transforming a collection of recorded tracks into a finished product is what the mixing process is all about. You need to edit and combine those tracks to get the overall sound you want, complete with any necessary processing and equalization. Your final mix can then be mastered into the product that consumers listen to.

In this chapter, we review the basics of the mixing process, which is a lot more involved that it sounds at first blush. In subsequent chapters, we work through more specific mixing techniques, including adding equalization and plug-in effects. But you need to know what you're doing before you start doing it—and that's what this chapter is all about.

In This Chapter

- What is mixing all about—and why is it important?
- Differences between live and studio mixing
- What a mixing engineer does—and how to become good at it

What Mixing Is—and Why It's Important

Mixing, at its most basic, takes the multiple audio (and, depending on the project, MIDI) tracks you've recorded and blends them together into a sonic whole. But there's more to it than that.

What's Involved in the Mixing Process

A lot is involved in moving from multiple recorded tracks to a finished two-track stereo mix. As the mixing engineer, you have to perform some or all of these related operations:

- Set the relative volume levels between tracks so some instruments or voices are more or less prominent in the mix.

- Set the position of individual instruments and vocals right or left in the mix, which creates a wider stereo soundfield and allows breathing space for those instruments and vocals.

- Apply equalization to the individual tracks, to bring out the desired tonal ranges of specific instruments and vocals.

- Apply any necessary audio effects or processing to individual tracks, such as reverb, delay, compression, and so on, to create a more pleasing or appropriate sound.

Depending on the project, you also may have to perform more sophisticated editing of the tracks. Track editing is sometimes regarded as part of the recording process, but I include it in the mixing phase because it technically happens postrecording. This type of track editing might include any or all of the following:

- Choose between multiple takes of a given voice or instrument, when a given part was recorded more than once.

- Splice pieces of multiple takes together to get a more perfect "take."

- Edit in replacement notes—or edit out unwanted notes—to correct performance mistakes.

- Change or correct the pitch of a voice or instrument to correct off-pitch performances or just for creative effect.

- Change or correct the timing and placement of individual notes to ensure a more accurate or steady rhythm.

You do all this on your computer, from within *Pro Tools* or similar *DAW* software. (Most engineers use the same software for mixing as they do for recording.) You can use your keyboard and mouse to make the appropriate adjustments or connect an external mixing console to interface with the DAW program. You may incorporate outboard effects boxes or software-based effects. You'll probably utilize your DAW program's automation function to change levels and apply effects on a "real-time" basis throughout the mix.

Naturally, you need to hear what you're doing, so having appropriate *monitor speakers* is a necessity. You can mix with headphones (and I discuss this in Chapter 6), but you'll better hear what you're doing through a good pair of studio monitors.

> **DEFINITION**
>
> **Digital audio workstation,** or **DAW,** software is a type of software program that offers audio recording and mixing capabilities. **Pro Tools** is the most popular DAW program among professional recording and mixing engineers. **Monitor speakers,** sometimes called *studio monitors,* are small, powered speakers optimized for use in the small rooms typical of recording and mixing booths.

You don't need a fancy professional studio to make your mix, although having some degree of isolation from outside noise is desirable. Some great recordings have been mixed in bedrooms and basements—although the pros will insist on a more acoustically appropriate space for their work.

How long does it take to make a mix? It depends on the individual song, what was recorded, and what you want the end mix to sound like. If you're mixing a live-to-computer recording of a choir or small group, it might be a quick and simple matter to level the tracks, apply a little equalization (EQ) and reverb, and be done with it. If, on the other hand, you're dealing with a complex project with dozens of individual tracks recorded at different times and places, it may take weeks to edit, level, and process everything to get it sounding good. (Naturally, the skill and experience of the mixing engineer comes into play here, as well. The more often you've done this, the faster you'll be at it.)

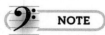

> **NOTE**
>
> It's possible that when you're mixing the tracks, you'll find that you need a little something more than was what recorded, maybe a different guitar solo, an added percussion instrument, or a new backing vocal. In this case, you'll need to return to the recording studio, call in the appropriate musicians, and record what you need. You can then insert the new track(s) into your project and continue mixing.

Why Mixing Matters

As you can see, there's a lot involved in the modern mixing process. Mixing was, perhaps, a little less complicated back in the days of four- and eight-track recording, simply because you had fewer tracks to deal with. But with today's digital recording, you might have 40 or 50 or more individual tracks, some of them multiple takes from the same instrument or voice, and just mixing them down to stereo is a major undertaking. Add the job of applying effects and processing, necessary because most tracks today are recorded relatively "dry" (without any processing or effects), as well as the frequent need to "fix" mistakes made during recording, and you see just how complex the mixing process truly is.

Without mixing, all you'd have would be a collection of individual tracks, recorded at different levels and with different room conditions, all played together at the same time. Most of the tracks would be dead center in the stereo field, mushed together in a way that you couldn't tell one instrument from another. Some instruments would be too loud, and others not loud enough. Most wouldn't sound anything like what they're supposed to, due to the lack of EQ and processing. And you'd be left with all the little mistakes that make it into the recording process today. In short, you'd have an unlistenable mess.

Making that unlistenable mess listenable is why mixing is so essential. Think of it like cooking. A chef assembles all the raw components of a recipe, from eggs to flour to seasonings. But just throwing all those ingredients into a bowl doesn't make for a finished dish. The chef has to combine the ingredients in the right proportions, in the right order, and then stir and sift and do whatever else necessary to get the dish ready for the oven. You can't just serve a mashup of raw ingredients.

Audio mixing is much the same. All the recorded tracks are your raw ingredients. Serve them to the listener as is, and you have an unappetizing mess. But mix them together in the right order with the right levels and the right audio seasoning, and you get something quite tasty indeed. It's just like cooking, but with audio.

Like cooking, mixing also is a creative process. It's not *just* about making all the pieces and parts sound good together. You also can get artistic with those ingredients to help shape the final song. You might not play the instruments or sing the vocals, but you can determine which instruments are prominent; which vocal takes are used; even when to add or repeat a verse, chorus, or solo in the song. A good mixing engineer is as much an arranger as he is a technologist. It's more than just twiddling knobs or sliding sliders; it's about using your ears, your mind, and your heart to help artists realize their creative visions.

Mixing Live and in the Studio

There are actually two types of mixing today. One involves mixing music live as it's being performed, and the other involves mixing music that's already been recorded. Many of the same techniques apply to both, but each is unique in its own fashion.

Live Mixing

Sound mixing is very important for live performances. Whether it's a couple of acoustic guitarists at the local coffeehouse, a praise band playing a Sunday morning church service, or a rock and roll or country band playing onstage for thousands of cheering fans, somebody has to make those musicians sound good. This is the job of the "sound guy," the mixing engineer behind the soundboard.

Live sound mixing is just like mixing in the studio, except it's all done in real time. The mixing engineer has to set the levels (and in some cases, the stereo positioning) of every microphone and electric instrument onstage and keep those levels appropriate throughout the entire performance. You can adjust EQ, add processing and effects (pretty much the same effects as you would in the studio), and ensure the overall volume levels are appropriate for the venue. (That's a big deal in small rooms and churches, where someone will always say "It's too loud!"—even if it's not.)

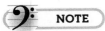 **NOTE**

> What you can't do in live mixing is edit any of the sound sources; you just can't do that in real time. About the most you can do is apply Auto-Tune to the vocals, and even that's tricky. If someone plays a wrong note, that's what the audience will hear.

Live sound can be mixed on computers or traditional mixing consoles—or a combination of both, where the mixing board controls the live sound program on the computer. The mixing engineer is typically responsible for both the front-of-house sound and what the musicians hear in their stage monitors. You also may be responsible for feeding a live mix for recording, if the artist or house does that.

To make all this happen live, you need to do some work ahead of time, in the form of a preshow sound check. Be sure all the mics and inputs are working, set the levels appropriately, and apply all the necessary EQ and effects, and you'll be ready to go when the band hits the stage. Sure, things can still go sideways when you're dealing with live performances, but a solid sound check helps minimize unnecessary surprises.

Bottom line: the skills you need for live sound mixing are a substantial subset of the skills you need for mixing in the studio. If you can do one, you're well on your way to doing the other.

Studio Mixing

Studio mixing, although similar to live sound mixing, takes place in a much different environment. The big difference is that you're not under the same time constraints. In the studio, you have more time to make your decisions and apply your options. When you're mixing live, you have to do most of your work on the fly. In the studio, you have more time to breathe.

You'll need the extra time, however, because the results are much more critical for recordings than for live performances. Audiences will give you a break—or not even notice—if you don't have the bass drum gated enough for a few bars or if the background vocals are a little low in the mix during the first chorus. Even the most minor errors won't fly in the studio, however; any mistake you or the performers make is captured on a recording for all of history. Studio mixing engineers have to be extremely detail focused and willing to go back and do it over if necessary. The live sound guys get a little bit of a pass on this.

Studio mixing is also a little more involved, in that you're assembling a song from multiple passes and options. Live, the song is already in place, so the engineer is less a part of the creative process. In the studio, mixing can involve a fair amount of editing, sometimes on a note-by-note basis. Live sound guys don't have to bother with this.

All that said, if you have experience with live sound, you'll feel right at home in the studio. You can learn the additional editing skills that are part and parcel of today's studio scene and build on the techniques you've learned from mixing live. Yes, it's a little more work, but you'll have the time to learn.

 **NOTE**

This book, of course, is all about studio mixing. A lot of what I discuss here is also applicable for mixing live performances, but if you're a live sound guy, you'll want to supplement this text with information specific to live sound reinforcement.

Understanding the Role of the Mixing Engineer

The basic mechanics of studio mixing can be learned. (Which is why you're reading this book, I assume.) But mixing is as much an art form as it is a science. You need the requisite technical skills, of course, but you also need a good set of ears, a thorough understanding of how music works (that's music theory), experience listening to and playing various types of music, your own musical ideas, and good interpersonal skills.

What a Mixing Engineer Does

Your first role, of course, is combining all the different recorded elements into a final version of the song. The producer organizes the session (including contracting musicians and, in many cases, selecting the songs to record), the musicians play the music, and the recording engineer records the initial tracks, but it's up to you, the mixing engineer, to make sense of all that's been recorded. You have to set the levels of each instrument and voice and, at the same time, pan each element across the stereo soundfield so all the component parts combine into an aurally pleasing whole.

In addition, you have to "sweeten" the sound by applying EQ, processing, and other effects to each individual track. It's your job to make each track sound its best—alone and particularly in conjunction with the other tracks. This can be a lot of work, and it requires a really good set of ears and knowledge of all the processing options available to you.

In some instances, you'll be called upon to edit the recorded tracks. This typically involves cutting and pasting sections from one track to another or, in some cases, punching in new sections. (A section can be as long as an entire verse or chorus or as short as an individual eighth note.) You also may need to change the pitch of a specific voice or instrument (using Auto-Tune or similar plug-ins) or make notes longer or shorter to correct someone playing not quite on the beat. It's a lot of painstaking detail work, but it's your job to do it.

It's also possible you'll be called upon to make major creative decisions. I'm talking things like choosing between multiple takes of the lead vocal, determining which version of a guitar solo is best, altering the sound of a given instrument to better fit the overall feel of a song, even deciding to cut or add whole verses or choruses in a song. I'll be honest: being part of the creative process like this is fun and exciting, but it's also a little nerve-wracking. You have to get inside the heads of the artists and producers to make this happen.

What You Need to Become a Successful Mixing Engineer

How do you become a successful mixing engineer? There are several things you can and should do. Let's look at them.

Get some training in engineering   Professional mixing engineers typically have some sort of formal training. Many schools offer courses and degrees in audio engineering or recording, and you'll learn a lot from this experience. If you want to do this full-time, taking some (or a lot of) classes is essential.

Get some training in music   Learning about mixing and engineering is key, but it's also important to have a good, solid music background. You need to know the difference between a verse and a chorus, a half note and a quarter note, a B-flat and an A-sharp. (Okay, that last one's a trick question—B-flat and A-sharp are the same note—which you'd know if you had the proper musical training!)

It also helps if you can play one or more musical instruments. This makes it easier for you to communicate with the musicians you'll be working with. The more you know, the more you'll be able to contribute to the creative process.

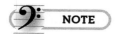

NOTE

If you need some basic music background, check out my companion book *Idiot's Guides: Music Theory, Third Edition* (Alpha Books, 2016), available where you found this one.

Listen to a lot of music   The best way to learn what makes a good mix is to listen to some good mixes. Listen to songs in the categories you work in; listen to songs across other categories; listen to classic recordings; listen to all the new stuff. In a nutshell, listen to as much music as you can—and listen critically. Try to figure out what's behind the best-sounding recordings, why they sound that way, and what the mixing engineer did that was special. The more you hear, the more you'll be able to apply what you've heard.

By the way, it's not just about listening; it also helps if you really like the music you hear. It's tough to do your job if you don't enjoy the music you're working with.

Learn how to use the most popular DAW programs   Engineers today typically do their mixing on computers running DAW software such as Pro Tools, Cubase, and Logic Pro. If you're working on your own, you can probably choose which of these you want to use and then learn it inside out. If you're working in a pro studio, you'll have to learn the DAW software the studio uses. You also may be called upon to use other programs as requested by the artists you work with. Most of these DAW programs work in pretty much the same fashion, but you still need to know what buttons to click and menus to choose to get the job done.

Keep abreast of the latest technological developments   The area of audio recording—especially small studio and home recording—is one of rapid change; the technology is being constantly updated and refined. You need to keep in touch with new hardware, new software, new plug-ins, new techniques, and new approaches. It's easy to be left behind technologically; to stay relevant in this ever-changing industry, you need to be aware of and willing to experiment with all the new stuff that comes along on almost a weekly basis.

Learn how to get along with others   To get ahead in the music business, you need to be a people person. You have to be able to get along with pushy producers, prima donna divas, strung-out guitarists, terminally laid-back bassists, wild and crazy drummers, and a whole lot more. Musicians are creative types, and creative types are often interesting to work with. Musicians are sometimes egotistical, sometimes nervous and full of performance anxiety, and quite often under pressure to perform under a strict time schedule. They sometimes drink a little too much, do more drugs than they should, or like to have their egos stroked. Sometimes they just have bad days.

You have to be able to deal with all this while at the same time telling the singer that a particular take was a little flat, informing the guitarist that a particular effect doesn't quite fit, or letting the drummer know that he's rushing his fills. You have to be friendly and diplomatic, which isn't always easy. But the better you can get along with others—the more pleasing your professional personality—the more people will respect your work and call you again for future projects.

As legendary studio drummer Hal Blaine once told me, "If you grin, you're in. If you pout, you're out."

Keep learning   Whether we're talking recording technology, musical trends, or just dealing with people, you need to keep learning. You're never done; there's always something new to learn that will make you a better mixing engineer. Keep an open mind, and learn from everything you experience. Read all you can, listen to all you can, and especially learn from everyone you meet. You can never know it all, but you can always keep trying.

By the way, note I didn't write that you need an expensive, high-end studio to be a successful mixing engineer. It's more about what you know than the equipment you have to work with. Even the least-expensive software today can create great-sounding mixes, as long as the right person is behind the controls. Master the necessary techniques, keep your ears open, and keep learning— that's how you'll become successful.

The Least You Need to Know

- Mixing involves combining individual recorded tracks into a single finished product.
- A mixing engineer also needs to apply equalization, audio effects, and processing—and, in some cases, edit individual notes and parts.
- Mixing live sound is similar to studio mixing, but it's done in real time—and without any editing along the way.
- To become a successful mixing engineer, you need to have the proper training, a solid background in and a love of music, a familiarity with the most popular DAW programs, an awareness of the latest technological developments, and the ability to get along well with others.

PART 2

Building Your Mixing Studio

Now it's time to get serious. What do you need to do to build your own mixing studio? Discover what type of room works best, learn how to furnish your studio, choose the right mixing hardware and software, and find the best monitor speakers for your space. It's all about getting set up and ready to go.

Setting Up Your Mixing Space

Before you begin your journey into the mixing process, you have to put together your own mixing studio. This can be as basic as a computer setup in a spare bedroom or den or as fancy as a dedicated room in a larger recording studio.

The space you dedicate to mixing (or share between mixing and recording) affects the mixing process. A more comfortable and ergonomic space makes mixing easier; a cramped or shared space with poor acoustics not only makes mixing more work, it also may affect the quality of the end result.

Of course, your mixing studio will contain all the various pieces of equipment you need to complete your tasks: a computer (with the proper software installed), a digital audio interface, monitor speakers, a mixing board, outboard processors, and the like. I cover those items in detail in subsequent chapters; for now, let's focus on the mixing space itself.

In This Chapter

- Selecting the most appropriate room for mixing
- The equipment and furniture you need in your mixing room
- Setting up your mixing studio
- Dealing with common issues

Choosing the Right Mixing Space

Where should you do your mixing? It all depends on your particular situation. If you work for a professional recording studio, it probably has a dedicated mixing room, so you'll use that. It's also possible you'll use the main recording control room for mixing as well as recording, although you won't need the attached recording studio.

If you're building your own small or home mixing studio, you have some choices to make.

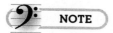 **NOTE**

> If you're setting up a complete home recording studio, your recording space will probably also be your mixing space. Your recording equipment will also be your mixing equipment, so be sure the space you choose equally suits both parts of the process.

Size

Many engineers set up their recording and mixing spaces in a spare bedroom, den, or garage, which works just fine for the engineering parts of the process.

You really don't need a lot of space for mixing. How much space do you need? You just need enough space to fit your mixing desk and monitor speakers—and your chair, of course. A closet might be a little too cramped, but all or part of a spare bedroom should suffice. You want to be able to walk in, sit down, swivel your chair, and get to work.

That said, if you have a bigger space available, use it. You don't want to be too cramped when you're working, and it's always nice to have extra space to host anyone else who might need to listen in. If you have a big enough room to hold both your mixing area and a couch or a couple chairs, that's the room to choose.

In addition, if you need to do any overdubbing during the mixing process, you want to have the room for a guitarist to plug in or a singer to stand up and do their thing. You may even want a spare keyboard in the room—you never know when you need to insert a spare note here or there, and it's easier to do from the mixing console than a separate recording room.

Ambient Noise

When you're mixing, you don't want extraneous noise to interfere with the process. You have to focus exclusively on the music, in fine detail, and if outside noises seep in, you'll get distracted and also produce a less-effective mix.

This argues, of course, for the quietest room you can find. You want to be able to close the door and block all other noises from the house—fish tanks, air conditioners, dishwashers, running water, you name it. (I once had a recording/mixing space right underneath the house's main water pipes. Every time somebody flushed a toilet, I blew a take.) Also be sure you won't pick up any outdoor noise. Listen for birds and crickets and wind and rain, none of which you probably want on your recordings.

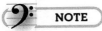 **NOTE**

> When listening for noise in a room, do so via a microphone. A good mic will pick up noise you might not hear with your bare ears, so be sure any noise you have around you is low enough the mic won't hear it.

If you do have a little noise in an otherwise desirable room, consider the use of soundproofing material—which also can improve the sound you hear while monitoring your mix, as I discuss next.

Acoustics

Most bedrooms, basements, and garages are not, by default, acoustically ideal. You don't want a room with a lot of *reflections* and echoes, as you're likely to find in a garage or basement with concrete floors. Nor do you want a room that's completely *dead,* as some bedrooms tend to be. No matter what type of room you choose, you probably need to do some work to bring it up to spec, acoustically.

I discuss acoustic treatments later in this chapter. But for now, when you're considering a room for your mixing space, keep these acoustics-related points in mind:

- Hard floors and walls create unwanted reflections and *reverberation.*
- Uncovered windows also created unwanted reflections and reverberation.
- Thick carpets absorb high frequencies—but not low frequencies.
- Small rooms with low ceilings and parallel walls can create standing waves, which result in increased or decreased sound levels at certain frequencies in certain spots.

All these things argue for a larger rather than a smaller room, and one with a minimum number of windows. In a larger room, acoustical issues tend to work themselves out with minimum treatment. In a smaller room, you may need to physically compensate for the effects of bad acoustics.

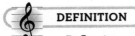

> **DEFINITION**
>
> **Reflections** are sound waves that reach the listener after bouncing off one or more surfaces, such as ceilings and walls. **Reverberation** is the persistence of sound in a room after the original sound has ended, caused by reflections. A **dead** or **dry** room has little if any reflected sound.

Furnishing Your Studio

Once you've chosen your room, you need to furnish it with everything you need to complete your mixing duties.

Computer System

The first item to focus on is the computer on which you'll be doing your mixing. You can use either a Windows or Mac computer, either a desktop or laptop model. Whatever you choose, you'll want at least one fairly large widescreen computer monitor. The more screen space you have, the more tracks and effects and such you can view at a time.

I discuss what type of computer to use in Chapter 4, so turn there to learn more.

DAW Software

When you have your computer set up, you can install the software you'll use for your mixing. I'm talking digital audio workstation (DAW) programs, such as Pro Tools or Cubase. You have lots of applications to choose from here, and they all have similar functionality. Turn to Chapter 5 to learn more.

Monitor Speakers

You could, in theory, use a set of standard computer speakers to listen to the music as you mix, but that is a less-than-ideal solution. Instead, you need a pair of dedicated studio monitor speakers.

Studio monitors are higher-quality speakers than what you typically find connected to a computer—or even to a living room audio system—and are designed to represent recorded sound as cleanly and accurately as possible. Unlike consumer or computer speakers, monitor speakers do not color the sound in any way, so you get a clear, sonic picture of what was actually recorded.

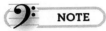

NOTE

Some home mixing engineers use headphones instead of monitor speakers. If you want to go this way, you can, although I don't necessarily recommend it (see Chapter 6).

I talk a lot more about monitor speakers (and headphones, too) in Chapter 6.

Audio Interface

Speaking of monitor speakers, you need a way to drive those speakers from your computer, and the standard speaker outputs probably won't do the job. Nor, for that matter, can you connect studio microphones, electric instruments, MIDI controllers, and the like to a standard, consumer-grade computer.

To connect all these professional inputs and outputs, you need something called an *audio interface*. This is an outboard unit that connects to your computer, typically via USB, and provides the necessary inputs and outputs for your recording and mixing work.

DEFINITION

An **audio interface** is an outboard box or internal card that connects microphones and musical instruments to a computer, often replacing the computer's built-in sound card.

Some audio interfaces are relatively simple, offering right/left speaker and headphone outputs, one or more ¼-inch inputs, and one or more XLR microphone inputs. These simple boxes are just fine for most mixing purposes and run under $100.

If, on the other hand, you use your rig for both recording and mixing and have a lot of recording inputs, you'll need a more sophisticated audio interface. Look for one with as many (and as many different types) of inputs as you need. Naturally, expect to spend more money on this type of unit.

Mixing Console

The next piece of equipment is one you *can* add, although you might not *need* to add. Many home and small studio mixing engineers are comfortable doing their mixing directly on the computer screen, using a mouse and keyboard. Others, however, prefer the feel and flexibility of a traditional mixing console, with physical knobs and sliders for each channel.

If you're an old-school guy, then by all means add a mixing console or control surface to your mixing studio. You can go with small boards that handle only a few (4 to 8) tracks at a time or opt for larger professional boards that can handle 24 or more tracks simultaneously. Obviously, a larger board will set you back more money.

Whatever type of console you choose, it connects to your computer (typically via USB) and lets you control your DAW program from the console. Instead of clicking and dragging onscreen sliders, you push a physical slider with your hand.

Outboard Processing and Effects Boxes

In the course of your mixing activities, you will find yourself applying various processing and effects to your recorded tracks. You can do this via software plug-ins, of which there are tons to choose from, or via outboard processing and effects boxes. Going the physical route is a bit old school, of course, but many seasoned engineers have particular outboard boxes they swear by and use on every project.

If you want to go the outboard route, be sure you have the space and the means to connect all the boxes to your computer or mixing board. It's relatively easy to send a track's signal from the DAW program to an outboard connection and back in again.

Mixing Desk/Workstation

Now, where do you put all this equipment in your mixing room? You need some sort of desk or other piece of furniture that can hold one or more computer monitors, a pair of monitor speakers, an audio interface box, perhaps a few outboard effects boxes, a keyboard, a mouse, and maybe even a small mixing console. If you're using a desktop computer, it can sit on the floor underneath or beside the desk; if you're using a notebook computer, you'll need room for that on the desktop, too.

A mixing desk can be a literal desk, of course. You might need to raise the computer monitors a little higher for better visibility, but a real desk can do the job.

If you're on a budget, you can make your own desk by laying a wooden door (without the handles) on top of two small filing cabinets. Just be sure you get it at the right height; there's nothing worse than having the desktop too high or too low for comfortable keyboarding and mousing.

Dedicated studio desks and workstations are sold, designed just for your mixing and engineering needs. These are typically multilevel affairs so you can put your computer monitor(s) and monitor speakers above the mixing console, keyboard, and mouse. These units run anywhere from a few hundred to a few thousand dollars, so shop carefully.

A typical studio desk/workstation for mixing use, from Omnirax (omnirax.com).

Furniture

Finally, you need someplace to sit when you're mixing—which means you need to get some sort of comfortable chair where you can park your derriere. That's typically a desk chair, not an over-stuffed side chair or recliner.

Because you'll be spending a lot of hours in this chair, consider an ergonomic model with good back support. You probably want armrests, although a model with movable (and removable) armrests might be a good idea. An office chair with a mesh back is nice because it won't get all sweaty when you've been sitting in it for a while.

 TIP

I'm a big fan of Herman Miller Aeron chairs. Although somewhat pricy, they feature a superior ergonomic design that is quite comfortable during long mixing sessions.

If you're in a larger room, you'll also want seating for anyone else who might be listening to your mixes—producers, artists, and other visitors. I've seen a lot of mixing rooms with large leather couches; you also could make two or more comfy chairs work. Basically, you want something that will make your guests comfortable while they're listening.

Setting Up Your Mixing Studio

Now that you know what room you are using and what equipment you need, it's time to get everything set up. Let's look at what to do.

Dealing with Room Acoustics

It's highly unlikely that the room you choose is acoustically perfect for your needs. You're going to have reflections and reverberations, dead spots and live spots, and various other sonic issues you'll need to address. Fortunately, most acoustic issues can be dealt with at minimal cost and with relative ease. You don't have to build a perfectly acoustically isolated room to get acceptable mixing results.

The first thing you need to do is minimize any noise from outside the room. That means ensuring your room has a good solid door and that it shuts tight.

Next, you want to reduce or remove any reverberation or reflections. Be sure the windows have fabric drapes (not just blinds) and that they're drawn to cover the glass. If the floor is already carpeted, fine. If not, you can install a relatively short/thin carpet or simply place a few area rugs or oriental rugs on the floor. The rug approach actually works better than thicker carpet. You don't need to cover the entire hard floor, just enough to break up the reflections.

You'll probably want to place something sound-absorbent on the room's hard walls. You could hang a few dense blankets here and there, or you could splurge for acoustic foam panels. For that matter, a few painting-size frames covered with cloth or fabric will do the trick, too.

Next, be sure you've removed all the excess junk from the room. Look for anything that might rattle, and get rid of it. And it goes without saying that you don't want a fish tank or small refrigerator in the room while you're working.

Finally, be sure your chair and desk don't squeak. The last thing you want to do when completing a tricky mix is to get distracted by noisy furniture!

Setting Up Your Mixing Desk

Now that you've got an empty room with great acoustics, it's time to start filling it with gear.

You'll place all your mixing equipment, including your computer and monitor speakers, on your mixing desk. But where do you place the mixing desk?

For the best sound from your monitor speakers, place the mixing desk on the shortest wall on the room. (If your room is perfectly square, ignore this advice.) You want the mixing desk centered on this wall. Positioning in the middle of the shortest side of a rectangle helps cancel out the effect of any reflections—the bounce back should be evenly distributed, providing a more accurate stereo image from your speakers.

Don't position your desk in a corner, as this will create uneven reflections from different-length walls. Same thing with positioning it off-center on a wall; don't do it.

You also don't want the desk (and your speakers) right up against the wall. Once you have the mixing desk positioned, pull it away from the wall by 1 or 2 feet. Acoustically, having speakers backed up against a flat surface results in unnaturally boomy bass, which will affect your mixes. You'll hear too much artificial bass and, therefore, put too little real bass into your mix.

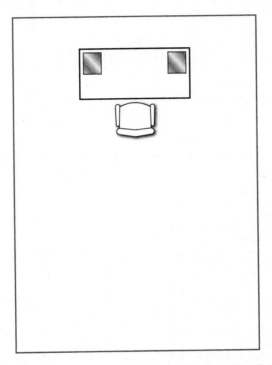

The ideal placement for a mixing desk—centered on the shortest wall, pulled out a few feet.

Now you get to arrange all your gear on your mixing desk. One way to do this is to organize your desk into two surfaces—a raised surface along the back half and a desk-height surface at the front.

Place your monitor speakers to the far left and right on the raised back surface. Place your computer monitor(s) in the middle of the raised back surface.

Place your keyboard, mouse, and (optional) mixing console/control surface in the middle of the lower front surface. (Some workstation furniture has an even lower front section just for the keyboard.) You can use the far sides of the lower front surface to host any other outboard equipment you may have.

A typical mixing desk layout.

These are rough suggestions, of course. You'll want to arrange your gear in a way that feels best to you and offers the best workflow for your mixing tasks.

Positioning Your Monitors

Let's pay a little more attention to the placement of your monitor speakers. Yes, you want them positioned on the back left and right corners of your mixing desk (or on separate floor stands to the left and right of the desk), but there's more to it than that.

Specifically, you want to focus on the *angles* of the speakers. Just placing them parallel to the back wall won't result in an accurate sound reaching your ears.

Start by turning in each speaker at a 45-degree angle. Now, sit down at your mixing desk and fine-tune the speaker angles so they're aimed right at your ears. You want a direct line from the left and right speaker to your left and right ears. This is the correct position.

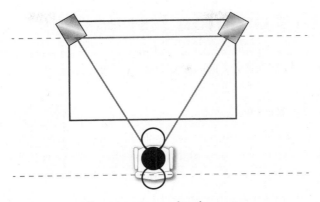

Proper monitor speaker placement.

TIP

You can check your speaker alignment by sitting in between the two speakers and playing a mono (not stereo) recording. The sound should appear to be coming from directly in front of you. If it sounds like it's coming from one side or another, adjust your speakers accordingly.

You also want to get the height right. Be sure each speaker is sitting upright, with the smaller tweeter on the top and the larger woofer on the bottom, and then raise or lower the speakers so the top tweeters are at the same height as your ears when you're sitting at your desk.

In addition, you probably want to place your monitors on foam insulation pads. Foam pads help decouple your speakers from the surface of the desk or stand, which provides more accurate low-frequency reproduction. In other words, the sound will be less muddy than otherwise.

Foam monitor insulation pads from Auralex Acoustics (auralex.com).

Dealing with Common Issues

When you're setting up your mixing room, you may run into an issue or two. Let's look at some of the more common problems and what you can do to minimize them.

Uneven or Boomy Bass

This typically results when the speakers are positioned on the wrong (long) wall in a rectangular room. Reposition your mixing desk and speakers along the shortest wall so the speakers are aimed down the longest wall.

If you're in a square room, especially a smaller one, the solution is trickier. About the only thing you can do is try moving the speakers back or forward, or even closer together or farther apart, until you get a better sound.

Room Is Too Bright or Has Too Much Reverb

This results from too many reflections from hard surfaces. Put some acoustical treatment on the walls—hang a drape or an area rug or something to absorb some of that unwanted sound.

If the simple solution doesn't work, mount acoustic foam tiles on the walls. Use thicker foam to further dampen the low frequencies.

Not Enough High Frequencies

This can happen if the floor is completely covered in a thick carpet, which absorbs those highs. About the only solution here is to pull up the old carpet and go with something thinner—or just a plain wood floor with a few strategically placed area rugs.

Electrical Hum

This is a grounding problem, specifically something called ground-loop hum. (Don't worry about the technicalities; you'll know it when you hear it.) Working with electrical components is always tricky, but you can often minimize this issue by running all your equipment off a single outlet with a multiple-outlet power strip.

The Least You Need to Know

- Just about any room can be converted into a mixing studio, although larger rooms are better than smaller rooms.
- Cover glass windows with fabric drapes and hang drapes, rugs, or acoustic treatment on bare walls to minimize reflections.
- Place all your mixing equipment, including your monitor speakers, on a mixing desk or workstation, and position the mixing desk on the shortest wall in the room.
- Position your speakers at least 1 foot away from the back wall, facing in at approximately 45-degree angles to aim directly at your ears.

Choosing the Right Mixing Hardware

Mixing in the digital era takes place on computers, using sophisticated digital audio workstation (DAW) software. What type of computer you use depends a little on the DAW program you use—although most DAW applications run on all types of computer systems.

In This Chapter

- Selecting the right computer system
- Adding an external audio interface
- Using an external mixing console or control surface
- Connecting other external equipment

Choosing a Computer System

Here's the deal: if you already have a computer, desktop or laptop, you can probably use it for your home mixing studio. Most DAW programs run on most computers made in the past several years, so you're probably good to go.

But what if you're not? What if you want a dedicated computer for your mixing studio, or your current computer is too old or slow to use for your mixing needs?

Then it's time to look for a new computer—one with more than enough "oomph" to handle your recording and mixing tasks.

Windows or Mac?

The first decision you need to make is whether you want a Windows PC or an Apple Mac. In years past, many music professionals automatically opted for Macs because most early recording/mixing software was designed to run on the Apple platform exclusively. That's no longer the case, and you'll find that almost all DAW programs are available for both Windows and Mac operating systems (OSs).

Which type of computer you choose, then, is a matter of personal choice. If you like the Mac OS, go with a Mac. If you like Windows, go with a Windows PC. You'll get similar performance from either platform—even though you'll pay a lot more for a Mac than a Windows PC with similar specs.

Desktop or Laptop?

Your next decision is whether to go with a desktop or laptop computer. Again, this is a matter of personal choice. Today's laptops are every bit as powerful as their desktop cousins, and all DAW software runs equally well on desktop or laptop models.

Some engineers prefer laptops for their portability. You can take a laptop anywhere you want to work on your mixes or even do live recording. You can't do that with a desktop.

A desktop PC is often easier to position and deal with in your mixing studio. Place the system unit on the floor to free up desk space and then use whatever keyboard or mouse (or track ball—more on that later) is most comfortable to you; you're not limited to the laptop's built-in keyboard and trackpad. You also can connect more and larger computer monitors, which lets you see a larger workspace than a laptop's typical 15-inch (or smaller) screen. (You also can, of course, connect external computer monitors, keyboards, and mics to a laptop computer.)

Bottom line: choose whichever type of computer you're most comfortable with.

Pro Tools running on a MacBook Pro laptop. (Photo courtesy of Avid, avid.com.)

How Much Power Do You Need?

Whichever operating system and form factor you choose, you need to be sure your computer has the necessary "oomph" to run your DAW application without bogging down at critical moments. As in many things, more power is better.

Here's the deal: if you're serious about the work you do, you'll want to invest in the most powerful computer you can afford. Processing digital audio files is CPU-intensive work, and the faster and more powerful your computer's microprocessor, the easier things will be.

This is particularly important in the recording part of the process. With an underpowered computer, you'll experience long wait times while processing files and, more importantly, unacceptable latency when using MIDI and virtual instruments, and when monitoring your playback. This *latency*—a slight delay between what you play and what you hear—makes it extremely difficult to play and record in real time. You can diminish the latency effect by using a computer with a relatively fast processor; lots of random access memory (RAM); and a big, relatively fast hard disk.

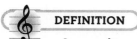

DEFINITION

In an audio system, **latency** is the amount of time between a signal arriving at an input and when it is sent from an output.

So when you're looking at new computers, look at each machine's processing power (the CPU) and memory (the RAM). The more of each, the better. A faster CPU lets you run more plug-ins without bogging down your system. More RAM lets you store and run more virtual instruments and libraries—and handle more tracks in your mix.

> **TIP**
>
> Also important is the hard drive on which you store your project files. Consider add-ing an external hard drive to your system, dedicated solely to storing your audio files, which should result in faster performance. (You also can use multiple external hard drives to store multiple projects.)

Specifications are important, however; you need to ensure your computer can run the DAW software you want to use. Now, every software package has its own unique hardware require-ments, so you'll want to check your program's specs against the performance of your personal computer. If your computer isn't up to snuff, the DAW program may freeze up or run slowly, if at all.

Just to give you an idea of what to aim for, let's take a look at the hardware requirements for Pro Tools, one of the most used—and most demanding—DAW programs available today. Here are the minimum hardware specs you need:

- **Apple operating system:** Mac OS X 10.8.5, 10.9.0 to 10.9.5, 10.10.0 to 10.10.5, or 10.11 to 10.11.1

- **Windows operating system:** Windows 7 64-bit (Home Premium, Professional, and Ultimate Editions) or Windows 8/8.1 (Standard and Pro Editions)

- **Processor:** Intel Core i5

- **Memory:** 4GB RAM (8GB or more required for video playback)

- **Disk space:** 15GB needed for installation

Note that these are the minimum requirements; the software will run faster and more smoothly if you have more RAM and a faster processor, of course. Also know that other DAW programs may have different requirements, so check on the manufacturers' websites before you buy.

> **TIP**
>
> You should always back up your files when recording and mixing. You don't want to lose your work if something happens to your main computer or storage device. You can back up to an external hard drive or a cloud-based backup service.

How Many Screens?

You do a lot of work on your computer screen, even if you have a traditional mixing console. You look to your computer monitor to view all the recorded tracks, the mixing controls, plug-ins, and the like. Obviously, the more screen real estate you have, the more elements you can see at the same time.

If you only have a single computer monitor, make it a big one—24-inch diagonal or larger. Smaller screens simply don't let you put enough elements onscreen at the same time, which makes it difficult to perform your mixing tasks. (This is a particular issue with laptop PCs, which typically have screens in the 15-inch range or smaller.)

Even better, consider going with a dual-monitor setup. This way, you can display the project window and recorded tracks on one monitor and a separate mixer window on the other. Most PCs have more than one monitor output, so this should be easy enough to setup and then configure in your DAW program.

Bitwig Studio running on dual monitors—mixer on the left, track editing on the right. (Photo courtesy of Bitwig, bitwig.com.)

Mouse or Trackball?

Most of us are used to controlling our computers with a mouse—or, on a laptop, via the touch-sensitive touchpad. For fine detail work, however, like what you get into with onscreen mixing, something a little more precise might be better.

For that reason, some professional mixing engineers prefer to use a trackball instead. A trackball looks a little like an upside-down mouse; you roll the ball with your hand instead of pushing a mouse around your desktop. You may find that a trackball offers more precision than a mouse. If so, go that route.

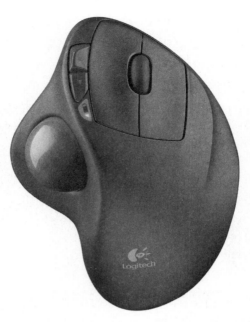

A Logitech trackball controller, preferred by some recording engineers (logitech.com).

Choosing an Audio Interface

All computers come with a built-in sound card or audio adapter, which translates the computer's signals into audio signals that are then fed to your speakers. When doing professional mixing, you do *not* want to use your computer's onboard sound card.

Built-in computer sound cards are simply not designed for professional audio recording. Most consumer-grade sound cards are noisy and don't offer enough dynamic range—they're not professional grade. In addition, you don't get a lot of inputs and outputs, they don't support balanced signals, they don't generate phantom power for microphones, and on and on and on.

Instead, you want to replace your computer's onboard sound card with an external audio interface. Pro-quality audio interfaces provide much higher audio quality, for both recording and playback, and offer all the professional inputs and outputs you need for your small recording/mixing studio. When you connect an audio interface box to your computer, it overrides your PC's internal sound card.

All sorts of audio interfaces are available for both home and professional setups. For mixing-only purposes, or for recording one track at a time, you can get by with a simple interface that offers two speaker outputs, a headphone output, and a ¼-inch and/or XLR input for instruments and mics. The box connects to your computer via USB and then you connect your speakers, head-phones, and mics or instruments directly to the box. You can find lots of simple audio interfaces in the $100 to $200 range—some even less.

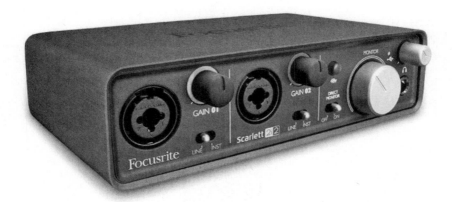

A simple two-input audio interface from Focusrite (us.focusrite.com).

Because you're probably using this same computer to record your projects, if you plan on record-ing multiple instruments or vocalists at the same time (even if it's just multiple mics on a drum set), you need to go with an audio interface box with more inputs—typically four or more XLR and four or more ¼-inch jacks. Some interface boxes also let you connect MIDI instruments. Expect to pay more for this added connectivity, but if that's what you need, that's what you need.

Adding a Mixing Console/Control Surface

You may be comfortable doing your mixing exclusively on your computer screen. You move the onscreen sliders and push the onscreen buttons with your mouse, and that works fine for you.

Others, however, may prefer the old-school feel of a physical mixing console. It's just a different experience tweaking the sliders by hand and pushing the buttons with your finger.

If you prefer a more physical mixing experience, several options are available.

For most home or small studios, you can add an external *control surface* to your computer system. This type of controller looks like a traditional mixing board, albeit on a smaller scale, and connects to your computer via USB. You can then use the physical controller to operate the sliders in your DAW program the old-fashioned way.

DEFINITION

A **control surface** is an outboard mixing board or controller that interfaces with a computer-based DAW program.

All sorts of DAW controllers are available. Some use touch-control sliders, while others have more traditional physical sliders. The simplest control surfaces only control 4 or 8 channels at a time, although you can find larger ones with up to 24 sliders.

An 8-channel digital control surface from Behringer (behringer.com).

For large studio use, you can go with a more traditional mixing console. Most modern mixing consoles have USB ports to connect to your computer; once connected, you use the mixing console to control your DAW software. The advantage of these larger mixing consoles is that they have all the necessary inputs and outputs to connect outboard effects and processors, if that's your thing.

Obviously, the bigger consoles cost a lot more than the smaller control surfaces—the difference between a few hundred bucks and a few thousand—so choose carefully.

CAUTION

Not all control surfaces work with all DAW programs. Check the specs on your DAW software to see which control surfaces it is compatible with.

Using Other Outboard Equipment

You may want to add other outboard equipment to your mixing studio. Most DAWs let you use various software-based plug-ins for effects and processing, but you also can use external boxes for specific effects. For example, you may have a favorite outboard reverb box or compressor you want to use in the digital realm.

Fortunately, most DAW programs make adding outboard processors fairly easy. You have to send the signal from the program to an external *bus* and then connect the outboard box to that bus. This is easier when your audio interface has a large number of inputs and outputs, of course.

DEFINITION

A **bus** is a signal path that feeds into or out of a program or device.

So if you want to use external processing, you can probably do it. Just be sure your DAW program supports outboard effects and that you have the appropriate inputs and outputs on your audio interface.

TIP

If you're shopping for recording equipment, some popular online retailers include Musician's Friend (musiciansfriend.com), Pro Audio Solutions (proaudiosolutions. com), Sweetwater Sound (sweetwater.com), and zZounds Music (zzounds.com).

The Least You Need to Know

- You can use any type of computer—Windows or Mac, desktop or laptop—for digital mixing.
- If you're shopping for a new computer, get the fastest CPU and most RAM your budget can afford.
- For mixing, connect an outboard audio interface to your computer to replace the built-in sound card.
- If you like, connect an external mixing console or control interface to operate your DAW program physically.
- You also can connect outboard effects boxes to your computer and DAW program.

Choosing the Right Mixing Software

When you're working in a home or small studio—and in most pro studios today, too—you do your mixing on a computer, using a digital audio workstation (DAW) software program. DAW programs, such as Pro Tools and Cubase, let you record, edit, mix, and master your projects and save the resulting output in distributable digital audio files.

The challenge, then, is choosing the right DAW program for your mixing needs. Many good options are available at various price points; the one you choose depends on the type of projects you do and how you like to organize your own personal workflow.

Understanding DAW and Mixing Software

A DAW program is essentially a computerized recording and mixing console. Connect an audio interface box to your computer, plug in the necessary microphones and instruments, and use the DAW to record your music. The tracks you record are saved digitally, which means you can then edit and tweak them on your computer to your heart's content.

You then use the DAW program to mix down your tracks to a mono, stereo, or surround sound file. That final mix also can be mastered for final distribution, again using the DAW program.

Most DAW programs function in much the same way. You have a project or edit window in which all the tracks you are recording or have recorded appear. Each track "lane" can contain multiple audio clips, so you can assemble a track from multiple takes or loops. Tracks can be either audio tracks recorded via microphone or direct injection or MIDI tracks captured from a MIDI keyboard.

This window is also where you edit your project. You can rearrange tracks, move around clips on a track, even edit individual clips (typically by clicking on a clip to open it in a separate editing window). You also can apply EQ, processing, and effects directly to tracks in the project window.

The other main window in most DAW programs is the mixing window. This window looks pretty much like a traditional mixing board, with individual mixing strips for each track in your project. Each mixing strip includes a fader; mute and solo buttons; and controls to add EQ, processing, and effects.

You'll also see master transport controls, which you use to initiate playback, recording, and the like. How you arrange all these windows within the master DAW application window is purely a matter of choice.

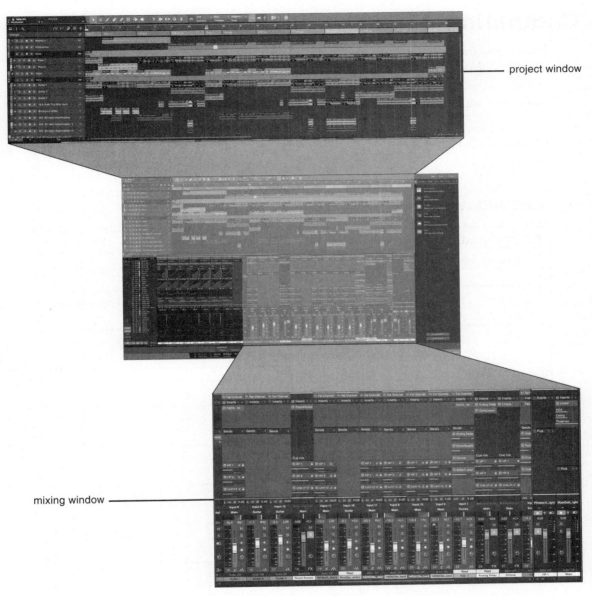

project window

mixing window

In the PreSonus Studio One workspace, the project window is at the top, and the mixing window is at the bottom right.

Comparing Popular DAW Programs

More than a dozen DAW programs are available for you to use to mix your audio products. These programs typically do both recording and mixing, and some of the higher-priced versions provide virtual instruments and plug-ins that play more in the recording space. (This means sometimes, but not always, the lower-priced version is the better deal if all you're doing is mixing.)

I discuss each of the programs separately, but let's get things started with a table that compares the major packages.

Popular DAW/Mixing Software

Software	Manufacturer	Website	Price	Tracks	Platforms
Ableton Live Intro	Ableton	ableton.com	$100	16	OS X, Windows
Ableton Live Standard	Ableton	ableton.com	$450	Unlimited	OS X, Windows
ACID Pro	Sony Creative Software	sonycreativesoftware .com/acidpro	$150	Unlimited	Windows
Bitwig Studio	Bitwig	bitwig.com	$300	Unlimited	Linux, OS X, Windows
Cubase Elements	Steinberg	steinberg.net	$100	48 audio/64 MIDI	OS X, Windows
Cubase Artist	Steinberg	steinberg.net	$300	64 audio/128 MIDI	OS X, Windows
Cubase Pro	Steinberg	steinberg.net	$550	Unlimited	OS X, Windows
Digital Performer	MOTU	motu.com	$500	Unlimited	OS X, Windows
Logic Pro X	Apple	apple.com/logic-pro	$200	255	OS X
Nuendo	Steinberg	steinberg.net	$1,800	Unlimited	OS X, Windows
Pro Tools First	Avid	avid.com/Pro-Tools	Free	16	OS X, Windows

Software	Manufacturer	Website	Price	Tracks	Platforms
Pro Tools Express	Avid	avid.com/Pro-Tools	Bundled with many hardware devices	16	OS X, Windows
Pro Tools	Avid	avid.com/Pro-Tools	$600	128	OS X, Windows
REAPER	Cockos Incorporated	reaper.fm	$60	512	OS X, Windows
Reason Essentials	Propellerhead Software	propellerheads.se/reason	$70	Unlimited	OS X, Windows
Reason	Propellerhead Software	propellerheads.se/reason	$400	Unlimited	OS X, Windows
SONAR Artist	Cakewalk	cakewalk.com/products/SONAR	$100	Unlimited	Windows
SONAR Professional	Cakewalk	cakewalk.com/products/SONAR	$200	Unlimited	Windows
SONAR Platinum	Cakewalk	cakewalk.com/products/SONAR	$500	Unlimited	Windows
Studio One Prime	PreSonus	studioone.presonus.com	Free	Unlimited	OS X, Windows
Studio One Artist	PreSonus	studioone.presonus.com	$100	Unlimited	OS X, Windows
Studio One Professional	PreSonus	studioone.presonus.com	$400	Unlimited	OS X, Windows

As you can see, DAW and mixing programs are available for every budget, from free to more than $1,000, and for every type of project. Read on to learn more about each individual program.

Ableton Live

Ableton Live is a DAW and music-sequencing program popular in the electronic dance music (EDM) community. It has a lot of functionality for live performances (hence the *Live* part of its name) and is used by a lot of DJs and EDM musicians in live settings as well as for creating new music in the studio.

Mixing in Ableton Live.

If you're into the EDM scene, you can use Ableton Live not only to create loop-based music, but also to mix it. If you're into more traditional rock and pop recording, Live is a little less useful, especially for mixing. It lets you do basic stuff, but there are more powerful DAWs out there.

Ableton sells two versions of Live. The Intro version lets you use 16 tracks and costs $100; if you need an unlimited number of tracks, go with the $450 Standard version.

ACID Pro

Like Ableton Live, Sony's ACID Pro is targeted at loop-based recording, and it's good at it. Also like Live, ACID Pro's mixing capabilities are fine for loop-based and EDM projects, but they come up a little short for audio recording and mixing.

One of the nice things about ACID Pro is the price. At $150, it's one of the more affordable DAW programs out there, especially considering it offers an unlimited number of tracks for that price. If you make your own beats for EDM or hip-hop music, you probably already know about it.

Bitwig Studio

Bitwig Studio is an up-and-coming DAW program that offers loop- and clip-based recording, similar to Ableton Live, but with more robust audio recording and mixing capabilities. As a newer program, it features a more modern-feeling interface than other DAWs, and it's getting a lot of attention from established Live users who like the more modern look and feel. If you're into EDM and loop-based projects, at $300 it's worth a look.

Cubase

Steinberg's Cubase is a much different beast from the three DAWs we've discussed so far. This program has been around for more than 25 years now, and it offers a full-featured recording/ mixing/mastering experience that appeals to both professional and home-based engineers.

Cubase offers powerful and versatile recording features, for any combination of audio recording, loops and clips, and MIDI instruments. You can even compose directly in Cubase, using any number of built-in or third-party virtual instrument libraries.

For mixing purposes, Cubase is hard to beat. The latest versions incorporate many useful features found in Steinberg's high-end Nuendo dedicated mixing software (discussed later in this chapter), especially in terms of automation and effects routing. The higher-priced versions include tons of virtual instruments, processors, and effects—more useful for recording, probably, but still nice to have. Cubase is also one of the best DAWs available for mixing video soundtracks and surround-sound projects.

Cubase's mixing window gives you everything you need for mixing, all in one place.

Steinberg currently offers three different versions of Cubase. Cubase Elements is the entry-level version, at $100, and gives you 48 audio tracks to work with. Cubase Artist is the version most suited for small and home studios, priced at $300 with 64 tracks available. The aptly named Cubase Pro is for professional studios, offering an unlimited number of tracks for $550.

For professional engineers, Cubase Pro competes head-to-head with Pro Tools. (You learn about Pro Tools a bit later in the chapter.) For home and small studio engineers, either the Artist or Pro version does everything you need it to do—at a price, of course, and with a fairly steep learning curve. Cubase is a great program, however, for whatever your mixing needs might be.

Digital Performer

MOTU's Digital Performer is a full-featured DAW program that competes with Cubase and Pro Tools in the high-end space. It offers a combination of Live-like loop recording and traditional recording, but with traditional mixing capabilities. Of particular interest is Digital Performer's Mix Mode, which lets you create alternate mixes with relative ease; you can experiment to your heart's content and then choose the mix you like best.

MOTU offers just a single version of Digital Performer, at $500. This is a full-featured version, with unlimited track capability.

Logic Pro X

Apple's Logic Pro X is a midrange DAW program particularly suited to loop-based and EDM productions. If you're used to Apple's GarageBand app, Logic Pro will feel like a natural step up from that. It's a little limited for traditional audio-based recording and mixing, but it works for a lot of folks.

As an Apple product, it's no surprise that Logic Pro is a Mac-only app; there's no Windows version available. At $200, it's an affordable option for many home and small studios.

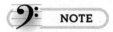 **NOTE**

One unique feature of Logic Pro is its companion Logic Remote app for the iPad. You can use the app to control Logic's transport, mixer, and Smart Controls directly from your tablet, over Wi-Fi.

Nuendo

Here's the weird bird in the mix. Not only is Steinberg's Nuendo considerably more expensive than the other programs discussed here, it's also the only one focusing solely on mixing and mastering. As such, it's a popular program among professional mixing engineers and one you'll find used in a lot of big studios.

As a postproduction platform, Nuendo can't be beat. Whether you're mixing and mastering traditional music recordings, audio voiceovers, movie or TV soundtracks, music for computer and video games, or even surround-sound projects, Nuendo offers more functionality and options than you'll find in any of the other programs discussed here—even Pro Tools.

It's not hard to see why Nuendo is the audio postproduction program of the pros—especially those in the video field. All this functionality comes at a price, however; at $1,800, Nuendo ain't cheap. You probably won't use Nuendo for your small and home studio mixing, but if you graduate to the pro level, it's the one to choose.

Pro Tools

Now we finally come to Pro Tools. This is the DAW everybody knows, even if they don't personally use it. In recording studios around the world, the name *Pro Tools* is synonymous with digital recording, mixing, and mastering. If you do more than record and mix your own performances in your basement or bedroom, it's likely that you'll encounter Pro Tools—it's that ubiquitous in the industry.

The Pro Tools Mix window is where you'll do most of your mixing.

Pro Tools was created in 1984, under the name Sound Designer, as a sound editor for the E-mu Emulator sampling keyboard. The name changed to Sound Tools in 1989, and it was renamed to Pro Tools in 1991. That first version of Pro Tools could record and mix just 4 tracks, and it sold for $6,000. Fortunately, the program has gained more functionality and lowered its price considerably since then.

During the 1990s, many professional studios switched to digital recording and standardized on Pro Tools as their DAW software. Fun fact: The first #1 record totally recorded, mixed, and mastered from within Pro Tools was Ricky Martin's *Livin' la Vida Loca,* in 1999. It was just the first of many pro recordings made with Pro Tools.

Today, most major studios in the United States and around the globe use Pro Tools. (Those that don't use Pro Tools typically use Cubase instead.) Pro Tools is less ubiquitous in small and home studios, probably for cost reasons; going all in with Pro Tools software and hardware is an expensive proposition. Still, Avid has always pursued the home recording market with lower-priced (and lower-functionality) versions of its software, so it's easy enough for you to use Pro Tools if you're building a studio on a budget.

What you get with Pro Tools is a tried-and-tested recording/mixing environment, as well as compatibility with the largest number of projects out there, both pro and otherwise. Pro Tools does just about anything you need it to do, and a huge number of effects plug-ins, virtual instruments, and the like have been designed just for the Pro Tools environment. Yes, Pro Tools (like Cubase and similar high-end DAWs) has a fairly steep learning curve, but there's not much this program won't do. It's also the industry default, so it's hard to go wrong choosing Pro Tools for your DAW.

Avid offers several different versions of Pro Tools. There's a limited-functionality free version, called Pro Tools First, which is great for beginners. You also may run across Pro Tools Express, which is essentially the same as Pro Tools First but bundled with various hardware devices from third-party manufacturers. For full-featured functionality, there's the $600 package simply called Pro Tools. And for professionals with large budgets, Pro Tools HD comes bundled with various combinations of Pro Tools–compatible hardware.

Most home or small studio engineers go with the standard $600 Pro Tools package. If you want to get a taste of the Pro Tools environment before committing, download the free Pro Tools First version from apps.avid.com/ProToolsFirst.

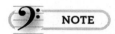 **NOTE**

A whole subindustry has been built around Pro Tools, especially for professional use. Avid and other manufacturers sell Pro Tools-compatible control surfaces, audio interfaces, computer acceleration cards, and more. Some of Avid's Pro Tools HDX hardware/software bundles run $10,000 or more—definitely targeted at professional studios.

REAPER

At just $60, REAPER is at the opposite end of the affordability scale from Pro Tools. It's not near as flexible (or ubiquitous) as Pro Tools, but its mixing capabilities are more than adequate for most small projects. It's especially popular for home recordists and engineers on a budget.

Reason

Propellerhead's Reason has been around for a while and has many loyal supporters, especially among home engineers. Its mixing capabilities are enhanced by uniquely large and functional mixing controls, which more resemble a traditional physical mixing console than those in other programs. That said, it isn't as flexible for mixing as Pro Tools or Cubase, so you don't see it used much by the pros.

Reason is available in two versions, the $70 Reason Essentials, with limited flexibility and add-ins, and the more robust $400 Reason version.

SONAR

Cakewalk's SONAR is another old-timer in the mixing world. It's also one of the few not available on the Mac; it's a Windows-only DAW. It has a lot of long-term adherents, even if it hasn't really broken into the professional studios. Of particular note is its ability to save and recall different mixes of the same project with its Mix Recall feature.

SONAR is available in three different flavors: Artist ($100), Professional ($200), and Platinum ($500). The main differences are the plug-ins and virtual instruments included. For basic mixing, the Artist version probably suffices.

Studio One

One final DAW to consider is Studio One from PreSonus. Studio One is a newer program that offers a Cubase-like workspace and workflow. It doesn't have the compatibility with legacy plug-ins and virtual instruments, however, so that might be an issue. As far as mixing goes, it should be a familiar option for Cubase users who want to try something new. It's available in a single $400 version.

Which Software Should You Use?

Recommending a DAW program is a lot like recommending a car—just because I like to drive a certain model doesn't mean you'll like it, too. Choosing a DAW is as much about finding one you're comfortable with and handles the projects you do as it is about anything else. It's a personal choice.

In terms of workflow and performance, most DAW programs work in much the same fashion and produce similar quality results. The details may vary a bit from program to program, especially in terms of workflow and plug-ins available, but if you're familiar with one, you can easily use another.

That's not to say engineers and producers don't have their favorites. There's a strong distinction between DAWs used for loop-based projects, such as hip-hop and EDM recordings, and those used for more traditional recording projects. There also are those programs that directly target professionals and, thus, found in most pro studios.

With that in mind, consider the following:

- If you're into loop-based recording and EDM, consider Ableton Live, ACID Pro, or Bitwig Studio.

- If you work on more traditional recording projects but have a limited budget, consider REAPER, Reason, or SONAR.

- If you want the most functionality and budget isn't an issue, go with Pro Tools or Cubase. These are the programs the pros use, and you can't go wrong with them.

Of course, out in the real world, you might not have a choice in which DAW program you use. If you're working for a big studio, you'll use the DAW it's standardized on—probably Pro Tools. If you're working in someone else's small studio, you'll use the software they have installed. So it's good to be flexible.

In addition, because most small studios do all their recording and mixing in the same program (and sometimes on the same computer!), it's likely that whatever software you use for recording is also the one you use for mixing. That's fine; most DAWs have more than satisfactory mixing capabilities. It's just a matter of shifting your brain from recording to mixing modes and utilizing the appropriate features of the DAW program.

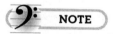
NOTE

It's possible to record in one program and transfer your recorded tracks to another DAW for mixing. Digital files are digital files, and it's easy enough for any DAW to import and work with individual tracks saved as digital audio files in any other DAW.

The Least You Need to Know

- DAW programs let you record, mix, and master projects on a personal computer.
- Most DAW programs offer a project or edit window that displays all the clips and tracks recorded as well as a mixing window with traditional faders and mixing controls.
- The most popular DAW program, especially among professionals, is Pro Tools.
- Other popular DAW programs include Ableton Live, Cubase, REAPER, and SONAR.

Choosing the Right Monitor Speakers

To be a successful mixing engineer, you need the requisite mixing skills, of course, and a good set of ears. You also need to ensure that those ears are hearing an accurate reproduction of what was recorded and what you're mixing. That's where monitor speakers come in—and the better the monitors, the better your mixes will be.

In This Chapter

- A look at studio monitors and why you need them
- The various types of studio monitors
- Choosing the right studio monitors for your budget
- Can or should you use headphones instead of monitor speakers?

Understanding Studio Monitors

There's no more important piece of equipment in your mixing studio than your monitor speakers. If your monitors aren't up to snuff, you won't hear exactly what was recorded. And if you don't hear an accurate reproduction of what was recorded, you won't know how to process those tracks—you won't set the right levels, you won't get the equalization right, you won't apply the right reverb, and you won't insert the right effects.

To do your job as a mixing engineer, you need to hear precisely what was recorded and how you're processing those recordings. You don't want the sound to be colored in any way; you need a flat, clean response without any artificial bass or treble boost.

Unfortunately, you won't find this kind of clean response with the typical speakers hooked up to your computer system or in your laptop PC. Computer speakers, with very few exceptions, are small and underpowered and have very poor fidelity. They might sound okay listening to streaming music or low-quality MP3s, but they simply cannot deliver the fidelity you need for your monitoring and mixing purposes.

Nor, for that matter, are typical consumer loudspeakers that much better. Yes, a good set of floor-standing or bookshelf speakers sound better than the tinny speakers connected to your computer system, but it's likely their sound is colored in subtle ways that can adversely impact your mix. More importantly, consumer loudspeakers are designed for use in large rooms and offer the best listening experience for those sitting 10 or 12 feet away. You're not sitting that far away in your mixing studio. Even the best audiophile speakers just aren't designed for studio use.

Studio monitor speakers are often called *nearfield* monitors because they're optimized for listening at relatively close quarters—that is, you're sitting very near the speakers, not halfway across the living room. The audio qualities of nearfield monitors are necessarily different from traditional floor-standing or bookshelf speakers used in home audio systems.

That is why you need to invest in a pair of studio-quality nearfield monitor speakers to be a successful mixer. Monitor speakers are bigger and better than typical computer speakers; they reproduce the full *dynamic range* of your music as accurately as possible, without any distracting shadings.

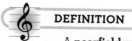 **DEFINITION**

A **nearfield monitor** is designed for listening at close range, no more than a few feet away from the speaker. **Dynamic range** describes the ratio of the softest sound to the loudest sound. A larger dynamic range is better.

By the way, most monitor speakers are powered speakers, just like your computer's normal speakers. That means you don't need an external power amplifier; the amplifier is built into each speaker cabinet. You connect your monitor speakers to your computer's normal speaker output connections and then plug them into a nearby power outlet.

From this description, you've probably gotten the impression that studio monitors are expensive. Well, they are—at least compared to the cheap computer speakers on sale at your local big-box electronics store. But they're no more expensive than bookshelf speakers you might see in a typical home audio system; in fact, the bang per buck you get with studio monitors is actually quite impressive.

You connect your monitor speakers to the audio interface connected to your computer, typically using ¼-inch cables. You can place the speakers on your mixing desk or workstation, although you'll probably want them raised a bit so they're at or close to ear level. As discussed in Chapter 3, you want to position your studio monitors on either side of your computer monitor, angled inward at about 45 degrees. The goal is to have each monitor aimed as directly as possible at your right and left ears.

So how much do studio monitors cost? There's a wide range, and you can spend anywhere from $100 to $1,500 and up for a good pair of powered monitor speakers. Naturally, the more you spend, the better the sound quality—although even the lowest-priced studio monitors deliver better sound than you're used to hearing from your computer.

How Many Speakers Do You Need?

How many monitor speakers do you need in your mixing studio? The snap answer is two, but that might not be the right number for your particular needs.

Mono Versus Stereo

Back in the days of two- and four-track recording, when most listeners had monophonic record players, engineers mixed down to a single channel for the final mix. And when you're mixing to mono, all you need is a single speaker to monitor your mix. (Hey, if it was good enough for Phil Spector and Brian Wilson, right?)

These days, you're not likely to run into a lot of mono projects, unless you're working with clearly retro artists. (And there are some around. The James Hunter Six's 2016 recording "Hold On!" was released on mono. Really!) The folks who listen to your recordings seldom listen in mono; whether they're listening in a car, with a smartphone or MP3 player, on a computer, or on a real audio system, they all pretty much have two speakers.

For these reasons, you probably want to go with a two-speaker setup. There's just not a lot of call for mono these days.

Subwoofers

Depending on the speakers you use, you might want to augment their sound with a *subwoofer*. If your main monitors are smaller and don't quite have enough oomph in the bass, a subwoofer adds the bass that's missing.

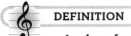

> **DEFINITION**
>
> A **subwoofer** is a freestanding speaker designed to reproduce very low bass notes.

Most subwoofers have a single large speaker—typically 8 to 12 inches—and sit directly on the floor. Low-frequency bass notes are not directional so the subwoofer can be placed anywhere in your mixing room.

A 10-inch subwoofer from Behringer (behringer.com).

Surround-Sound Monitoring

When might two speakers not be enough? If you're mixing audio for a movie, TV, or videogame soundtrack, chances are you're working in a *surround-sound* environment. That means mixing more than just two channels of sound. Some surround-sound formats offer eight or more discrete channels (front, side, and rear—plus subwoofer) for you to work with.

> **DEFINITION**
>
> **Surround sound** envelops the listener from speakers positioned both in front of and behind the audience. The most common surround-sound format is a 5.1 mix, with three speakers in front (left, center, and right), two on the side (left and right), and a sixth (.1) subwoofer channel.

If you're mixing soundtracks for video projects, just assume you'll have to provide a surround-sound mix. (Most higher-end DAW programs offer surround sound–mixing capability.) That means you'll need to have as many monitor speakers as you have surround channels. For a typical 5.1-channel mix, that means five monitors plus a subwoofer; for a 7.1-channel mix, that's seven monitors plus a subwoofer. And of course, you'll need stands (and cables and foam pads) for all of them, too.

Other Speakers for Other Listeners

You need the cleanest-sounding speakers possible to perform your mixing duties. But most consumers won't be listening to high-fidelity studio monitors. The real people who listen to your recordings listen through middling-quality bookshelf audio systems, low-priced surround-sound systems (including those ubiquitous sound bars) designed more for video than for audio, tiny and tinny computer speakers, car audio systems, and, more often than not, standard-issue earbuds connected to their smartphones and MP3 players. None of these listening environments come close to the pristine sound you get in the studio.

For this reason, it's a good idea to listen to your mix through a variety of speakers and listening devices. You still need high-quality studio monitors to do the mixing, but you also want to hear how your mix sounds in different environments.

Back in the "Wall of Sound" days, Phil Spector used to run his mix through a tiny car speaker because that was how his teenaged listeners would likely hear it while cruising the local strip. It's no different today; you want to hear how your listeners are going to hear your mix.

That argues, of course, for connecting different types of speakers to your mixing system. Yes, you need your main studio monitors, but you also might want to connect a pair of cheap computer speakers, wireless Bluetooth speakers, and maybe even one of those surround-system soundbars. For that matter, you'll get a lot of insight by listening to your mix through a set of earbuds, too.

You get the idea. You need to hear your mix under the best possible conditions (using studio monitors) and the worst possible conditions (cheap speakers and earbuds). Yes, your mix needs to sound good in the studio monitors, but it also has to sound good the way most of your listeners will hear it. The more speakers, the merrier!

What to Look for in Monitor Speakers

Many options are available when it comes to monitor speakers. You need to choose between active and passive speakers, different types of drivers, different speaker sizes, and more. It can be a bit confusing.

Active Versus Passive

The first choice you want to make is between *active* and *passive* monitors. Most lower-priced monitors are active, which means they're powered speakers—they include their own power amplifiers, and you have to plug them into a wall outlet for them to work. Passive monitors, on the other hand, require external amplification. As you might expect, you'll spend a lot more money on the extra amps needed for this sort of setup.

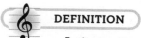

DEFINITION

Active monitors have their own built-in amplifiers. **Passive** monitors require external amplification.

There's really no inherent advantage to either type of speaker. Active monitors can sound just as good as passive ones—typically at a lower cost and with less equipment (external amplifiers) to deal with.

Number of Drivers

Most studio monitors include two internal speakers (called *drivers*): a *tweeter* for high frequencies and a *woofer* for midrange and low frequencies. This is called a *two-way* system; a *three-way* system adds a separate midrange driver to the mix, with only the lowest frequencies sent to the woofer.

A quality two-way system can sound every bit as good as a more expensive three-way system. It's more about the sound reproduced than the means used to make that sound.

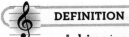

A **driver** is a separate speaker within a larger speaker enclosure. A **tweeter** is a small driver designed to reproduce high frequencies. A **woofer** is a larger driver designed reproduce lower frequencies. A **two-way** speaker system includes two drivers—a tweeter and a woofer. A **three-way** speaker system includes three drivers—a tweeter, a midrange, and a woofer.

Power

When we talk about speaker power, we could be talking about two things. With active speakers, power (measured in *watts*) typically refers to the power of the built-in amplifier. With passive speakers, power refers to the amount of power the speaker can handle from an external amplifier.

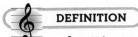

A **watt** is a measurement of power in electrical devices.

The more powerful the amplifier, in either an active or passive speaker system, the louder the sounds the speaker can reproduce. That's fine, but it's only part of the power equation. More power also provides for cleaner sound, as you can play it louder without pushing the amplifier or speaker to its limits. That typically results in a wider dynamic range, more headroom, less distortion, and more overall detail to the sound.

In practice, if you compare two speakers played at the same volume level, the one with the higher wattage amplifier sounds better.

Ported Versus Closed Cabinet

Monitor speakers come in both *ported* and nonported versions. A ported cabinet—one with a small hole in it—can help extend the speaker's low-frequency response. You typically find ported cabinets in smaller speakers to compensate for the smaller woofers in those units.

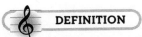

A **port** is a small opening in a speaker cabinet designed to enhance bass response.

Unfortunately, ported speakers don't always reproduce accurate bass. They sound boomier, but the bass isn't precise. In general, you get more accurate bass from a speaker with a larger woofer than from one with a ported cabinet.

A ported speaker from PreSonus; the port is the small slit along the bottom (presonus.com).

Size

How big do you need your monitors to be? Although size matters to some degree, you don't want to overdo it. You want the size of your monitors to be appropriate for the size of your room. If your mixing room is on the smallish side, go with smaller monitors.

EQ Adjustment

Some studio monitors let you adjust their frequency response via some sort of EQ knob or knobs. Turn one knob to boost or cut the highs and another to boost or cut the lows. This type of adjustment can help compensate for any acoustic deficiencies in your mixing room, but it's probably better to leave the controls flat and work on the room itself.

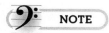

NOTE

You won't find studio monitor speakers at your local computer or consumer electronics store. Instead, you'll need to visit a music store that specializes in recording and sound reinforcement products or shop at a similar online retailer. Popular speaker brands include ADAM Audio, Alesis, Behringer, Event Electronics, Genelec, JBL, KRK, M-Audio, Mackie, PreSonus, Roland, Samson, and Yamaha.

Selecting the Best Monitors for Your Budget

How do you select the best monitor speakers for your mixing studio? It comes down to choosing the type you want, using your ears, and paying attention to your budget.

Once you've decided on the basic type of speaker (active versus passive, and so forth), the most important thing is to find a speaker that truthfully reproduces the recorded sound. It's not how the speakers sound in your room; it's how accurately the speakers reproduce sound from the original source.

You don't want your speakers to lie to you; you don't want them to boost or cut the bass, the mids, or the high frequencies. The speakers shouldn't sound bright, they shouldn't sound boomy, and they shouldn't sound dull. The sound reproduction should be as flat as possible.

Your speakers also must be clean. That is, you want speakers with a wide dynamic range and a low noise level. Ideally, you want to close your eyes and not be able to tell if you're listening to speakers or to live musicians.

Of course, you need to purchase monitor speakers that fit within your overall budget. You might find the absolute best, most honest-sounding monitors, but if they're in the $2,000 range and your budget is in the $200s, you'll need to compromise a little. To that end, I have some suggestions for speakers for various budgets. You'd be surprised at the sound you can get with even the most affordable studio monitors!

NOTE

In addition to the cost of the speakers themselves, you may need to purchase stands to elevate the speakers for ear-level listening. It's also a good idea to isolate your speakers by placing them on foam pads. That adds a few bucks to your budget, too.

Budget Monitors

Most home and small studios don't have big equipment budgets. Fortunately, when it comes to studio monitors, $500 goes a long way.

With a $500 budget, you're looking at a pair of speakers that cost no more than $250 each. This typically gets you a two-way active system, with or without ports.

If your budget is really tight, you can find quite a few monitors in the $100/pair range, from Alesis, M-Audio, Samson, and others. These are okay monitors, better than typical computer monitors, but they're on the smallish side with limited low-end response. I'm talking two-way systems with tiny 3-inch woofers and 1-inch tweeters and power in the 20- to 30-watt range. If this is all your budget allows, fine, but you can get better performance for not a whole lot more money.

A pair of budget monitors from M-Audio—$100 for the pair (m-audio.com).

Move up to the $150 per speaker ($300/pair) range, and you have a lot more options. Speakers in this range, by all the major manufacturers, typically have larger (5- or 6-inch) woofers and more powerful (100-watt or more) amplifiers.

Spend a little bit more ($200 to $250 per speaker), and you get even larger woofers (8 inches and up) with cleaner response. You get a lot of bang for your buck at this level.

$150 buys you this studio monitor from Samson—$300 for a pair (samsontech.com).

 **NOTE**

There are also passive monitors in the budget and mid-price ranges, but remember, you'll have to purchase an amplifier in addition to those speakers—which adds several hundred dollars more to your budget.

Mid-Price Monitors

What if your budget is bigger, say, in the $1,000 range? Many great options are available here.

When you're spending $500 or so per speaker, you're typically looking at two-way systems with 150 watts or more of power. Speaker sizes remain the same as with the previous level, but the construction of the speakers is better and typically offers wider dynamic range. In general, speakers at this level just sound better.

A mid-price monitor with an 8-inch woofer from Mackie (mackie.com).

Pro-Quality Monitors

Have an unlimited (or nearly unlimited) budget? If the sky's the limit, you have some truly great studio monitors to choose from.

In active monitors, once you get into the $1,000 per speaker range, you start getting into real power—400 watts or more. Many of these more-expensive models also have three speakers instead of two, with a separate midrange speaker.

When you get into this range you also start seeing more passive monitors. These typically feature larger and more exotic speakers, but they also require you to buy separate power amplifiers. These monitors are found only in higher-end professional studios.

A three-way passive monitor from JBL (jbl.com).

What About Headphones?

Then there's the issue of headphones. Do you even need expensive monitor speakers when you have a perfectly good set of headphones?

Headphones Versus Monitors: Pros and Cons

First, know that, yes, you can mix with headphones. Some people do it. Not a lot, but some.

You might choose to monitor your mix via headphones for a number of practical reasons. Maybe you don't have or can't afford a good set of studio monitors. Using headphones for mixing is a better option than relying on standard-grade computer speakers.

Or maybe you're in a volume-limited environment. For whatever reasons (sleeping children, complaining neighbors, you name it), you can't turn up the volume loud enough on your speakers to do your job. Listening via headphones is quieter.

It's also possible that your mixing environment might be too noisy for studio monitors. If you have too much ambient noise seeping into your mixing room (from kids, neighbors, planes, trains, etc.), putting on a set of headphones can block much of that noise.

Perhaps your mixing room has severe acoustic issues. If the bass is too boomy or there are too many reflections, switching to headphones might be a viable option.

If you're mixing on the go, not in your home studio, headphones are handy. When you're trying to get a mix done and you're away from the studio (or in a different studio), headphones help you maintain conformity in unfamiliar or sonically unfriendly surroundings.

In addition, headphones work well when you're doing a lot of noise reduction or audio restoration. They bring out the background noise better than speakers, so you can more easily hear things you might have missed otherwise.

Finally, if you need to fine-tune the reverb, you might want to consider headphones. Because of their extremely close-in nature, it's easier to hear reverb on headphones than on speakers.

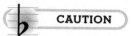

CAUTION

Because you more easily hear reverb on headphones, beware of using too little reverb because it's so apparent.

There are also several good reasons *not* to use headphones for mixing:

Even the lowest-cost studio monitors reproduce sound more accurately than most headphones. You simply get better sound for mixing through speakers.

Also, stereo imaging is easier to hear on monitors than it is on headphones. With headphones, because the right and left channels are fed directly to your right and left ears, it sounds as if the music is coming from either side of you (or even from inside your head) rather than in front of you. This results in an apparently wider and more separated stereo soundfield, which can cause issues when it comes to placing elements in the soundfield. You don't have these issues when listening to monitors.

And remember, most of your listeners will be listening via speakers, not headphones. Always mix for your listeners.

For most engineers, the cons of headphone use outweigh the pros. That doesn't mean you can't or shouldn't mix with headphones, just that most engineers don't.

Of course, you always have the option of mixing with both speakers and headphones. That is, you use your normal studio monitors to create your main mix but then check the mix on headphones. Sometimes you can hear things on 'phones you can't hear on speakers. In any case, you want to be sure your mix sounds good for headphone listeners, too.

CAUTION

Headphones can be a viable alternative to studio monitors, but earbuds are not. Earbuds simply don't deliver the quality or type of sound reproduction you need for accurate mixing.

Evaluating Headphone Types

If you do decide to use headphones while mixing, there are two main types of phones you can use—closed back and open backed. Each has advantages and disadvantages.

Closed-back headphones completely surround the ear to create a soundproof seal. This type of headphone is most often used when recording because they offer the best isolation from external noise. Recording musicians use closed-back phones so the monitor mix doesn't bleed into their microphones.

These closed-back studio headphones are from Sennheiser (sennheiser.com).

DEFINITION

Closed-back headphones surround the ear and provide maximum isolation. **Open-back** headphones sit on top of the ear and provide better sound quality.

Open-back headphones, on the other hand, sit more on top of your ears rather than fully surrounding them. As such, they're not as isolated. Sound from the headphones will leak into the room, and you'll be able to hear room noise while wearing them.

These open-back monitoring headphones are from AKG (akg.com).

Open-back headphones don't provide the sound isolation like their closed-back cousins, but they do provide better sound quality. That's why open-back headphones are the type most often found in mixing studios; they simply sound better. When mixing, it's the sound quality that matters, which is why mixing engineers prefer this type of headphone.

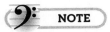 **NOTE**

Open-back headphones are more comfortable than closed-back phones, which is important during long mixing sessions.

Whatever type of headphone you go with, the more you pay the better they'll sound. Just as with studio monitors, higher-priced headphones deliver better fidelity than lower-priced models. Choose the type of headphone you want, set your budget, and get the best model available within your price range.

The Least You Need to Know

- Studio monitors are speakers designed for close-up use in recording and mixing studios and provide highly accurate sound reproduction.
- Most studio monitors are active speakers with built-in amplifiers.
- You can find many good-quality studio monitors for less than $500 a pair—although you can spend (a lot) more if you want.
- Some engineers choose to use headphones for mixing; although the sound isn't as good as with studio monitors, headphones enable you to do your mixing in a variety of less-than-ideal conditions.
- The best headphones for mixing are open-back models because they provide more accurate sound reproduction and are more comfortable to wear.

Before You Mix

Ready to mix? Not quite yet. In Part 3, you discover which recording techniques result in the best mixes, learn how to prepare your recorded tracks for mixing, and find out how to build an arrangement during the mixing process.

Recording for Mixing

Before you begin the mixing process, you need to have something to mix. Recording is the first part of the entire process and where you get the raw material to create the perfect mix.

How and what you record affect the mixing process. Depending on what happens during the recording phase, things can be made easier for the mixing engineer or much, much more difficult. Ideally, you want the recording engineer (which could be you, too) to plan ahead for the mixing process, recording all the tracks with mixing in mind.

In This Chapter

- How recording affects mixing
- The basics of the recording process
- Considering the mixing process while recording
- Setting the proper recording quality and file format

Recording Versus Mixing: Why Each Is Important

Recording captures the raw performances. Whether those performances are by an entire group "live" in the studio or by individual musicians tracking one by one over a period of time, they're the creative material you, as the mixing engineer, have to work with when assembling the final version of the project.

Put another way, mixing doesn't matter if there's nothing good to mix. You need solid performances, captured as accurately as possible, to work with in the mixing room. If there's nothing good recorded, there's not much you can do in terms of mixing.

So it's important that you start with strong performances by the musicians, captured as accurately as possible during the recording process. It doesn't matter how good the recording or mixing engineers are; if the initial performances are subpar, you'll end up with a subpar product. Yes, there are those who think you can "fix it in the mix" (and, yes, there are some things you can do in the mixing process to compensate for substandard performances), but it's much, much easier if you're working with good performances from beginning. When you record a great performance, your mixing job is a lot easier; all you have to do is ensure that the great performance gets heard in the final product. A great performance makes a great recording.

On the other hand, there's only so much you can do to make a poor performance sound better. Depending on how bad the performance is, you may never get it to sound good, let alone great. It's the old "garbage in, garbage out" thing—a poor performance cannot be turned into a great recording, no matter how talented the mixing engineer is. There just aren't enough tricks in the box to turn horse dung into caviar. It just can't happen.

That's why the recording process is so important. The recording engineer can't magically make artists give stellar performances in the studio, but he can ensure that their performances are captured at the best quality possible. A good recording engineer can make any voice or instrument sound better, just by the way its recorded. It's a matter of choosing the right microphone, placing it correctly, using the studio space in the best possible way, feeding the right monitor mix into the performers' headphones, encouraging the performers over multiple takes, setting the right levels, and more.

The better the recorded tracks, both in terms of performance and recording quality, the easier the mixing process. A good mixing engineer can set levels, place items in the stereo soundfield, apply EQ, and use various processing and effects to make middling recordings sound good, good recordings sound great, and great recordings sound like the hits they deserve to be. If the raw materials aren't that good, the mixing engineer has several tricks he can use to make them sound better. If the raw materials are stellar—well, then it's a lot of fun making them sound the very best they can be.

So recording is important because that's how the individual raw performances are captured. Mixing is important because it turns those individual performances into a great-sounding whole. You can't have one without the other.

Understanding Recording Basics

The recording part of the process can be as simple as pressing the red Record button or as complex as recording and assembling tracks from multiple artists in multiple locations. It involves setting up the studio, choosing microphones and input methods, setting levels, and riding the faders during the performance. It's all in service of the recording itself, which these days is made direct to a computer's hard disk using Pro Tools or a similar DAW program.

 **NOTE**

> Most studios use the same DAW program for recording and mixing. So familiarity with Pro Tools, Cubase, or whatever program serves you well in both the recording and mixing processes. (You also can transfer recorded tracks from one DAW program to another for mixing, which I discuss in Chapter 8.)

Let's consider a few different recording projects.

Recording a Large Ensemble Live

First, there's the "live" recording of a big band, choir, or orchestra—maybe a student, church, or community group. You bring all the singers or musicians into the studio, position them the same as they'd be onstage, and set up a few mics in front of them to capture the entire group sound. You don't have numerous microphones to deal with because you're not individually mic'ing each singer or instrument; the key thing is to capture the sound of the entire ensemble. So you position two mics (for stereo) in front of the group, maybe a mic or two overhead, and maybe a mic or two elsewhere in the studio to capture the room ambience.

Once everything's set up, the conductor counts down from four, you press the Record button, and you capture the performance in a single take. No overdubs, no multitracking, just a simple live performance captured to a few recorded tracks.

What you get for mixing are these simple recorded tracks. You don't have a lot to work with, so your job is mainly to get a decent mix between the front sound and any ambient sound. You can EQ as necessary, or maybe add a little reverb to make it sound like it was recorded in a bigger, livelier room, but that's about it. Mixing is easier because the recording was simple; you don't have to deal with a ton of different elements.

Recording a Multitracked Performance

More common is the typical rock, pop, country, or R&B record of today. You have to record all the backing instruments—guitars, keyboards, bass, drums, maybe more—the backing vocalists, and the lead vocals. The rhythm section may perform "live" as a group, but it's more likely that you'll be recording one or two instruments at a time and multitracking one on top of another. Then you'll record the backing vocalists (probably singing together but in different mics) and add the lead vocals on top of that. There may even be some overdubs and sweetening with synths, strings, and whatnot.

In other words, there's a lot of recording involved. Not only will you record multiple instruments and vocals, you also may record multiple takes from each individual. The thinking in some studios and by some artists is to record as much raw material as possible so the mixing engineer has more options to work with.

This means employing several different mics and *direct injection* (*DI*) boxes, creating several different preliminary monitor mixes for the artists to listen to while recording, and ensuring everybody's in tune and playing at the same tempo. It also may involve shipping out a rough mix to other musicians in other locations so they can record their contributions on their own equipment and ship them back to you. This type of project is long, involved, and quite complicated. It also creates numerous tracks for the mixing engineer to work with.

 DEFINITION

With **direct injection (DI)**, electric instruments such as guitars or keyboards are plugged directly into the mixing board or recording console instead of being recorded via microphone.

Mixing for this type of project is equally complicated. The mixing engineer has to deal with a plethora of tracks, including some for multiple takes of the same voice or instrument, that don't always match up sonically. A lot of work is involved just getting all the different tracks, sometimes recorded in different studios, to fit together. Then there's the EQ, processing, and effects you need to apply to each track individually. And that's before you start mixing everything together—setting the levels, placing the elements in the soundfield, and working on the overall mix.

For both the mixing and recording engineers, recording a multitracked performance is not a simple process.

Recording a Solo Artist

Many artists today, in popular music and especially in the electronic dance music (EDM) and hip-hop fields, like to record everything themselves, either on live instruments or via MIDI, loops, or whatever. They start by recording a basic synth or bass track, add a drum loop, layer on more synths and clips, and build the recording from the ground up.

Some of these artists record themselves, in their own home studios. (Or let's be honest, in their bedrooms or living rooms.) Others enlist the aid of a recording engineer, either in a home or professional studio. In either case, the recording is built up over time from multiple individual tracks.

The end result is similar to what you have when you multitrack a group recording—lots and lots of tracks, each representing different instruments or voices. These tracks still need to be mixed together, with the necessary EQ, processing, and effects applied. The only difference is that the artist or recording engineer probably has done some mixing along the way because the recording has been built up on a track-by-track basis.

It's likely that you will have an easier time mixing this type of project, although your skills are still necessary to ensure it all sounds good in the end.

Before You Record: Think About the Mix

As you can see, the recording engineer has a lot to do—and there's much the recording engineer can do to ensure the final recordings are as ready as possible for mixing.

What can a recording engineer do to make more mix-friendly recordings? Quite a few things, actually.

Think Through the Project Beforehand

Successful recording engineers work through all the details of a project beforehand so they're best prepared when the musicians arrive in the studio. This prerecording homework also helps create a project that is best suited for the necessary postrecording mixing.

Here's a quick checklist all recording engineers should work through before each project begins:

Prerecording Checklist

❑ What type of music are you recording?

❑ How many different instruments and voices will you be recording, and how many separate audio tracks will you need?

☐   How many musicians will be playing at the same time?

☐   Will you be recording the entire recording live, or will some parts of the recording be overdubbed later?

☐   Is the tempo constant throughout the piece, or does it vary at all?

☐   What is the destination media for this recording, and what level of recording quality will you need?

Important questions, all—and here's why. The type of music being recorded affects the entire project. As you might imagine, recording a classical string quartet is a much different job than recording a four-piece rock band—even though the same number of instruments is involved. Recording classical music requires different mic'ing strategies than does recording rock music; you might only use two mics to record the four strings, whereas the rock band might require 16 or more mics (multiple mics on the drums!) with some instruments plugged directly into the computer or mixing console via DI. In addition, you have different dynamics to worry about; classical music can vary considerably between loud and soft passages, whereas rock music is mainly loud, loud, and louder. This is why you need to know what you're recording up front, so you know what to expect and prepare for.

Obviously, knowing how many instruments you're recording determines how many tracks you need to record—and you need to set up your track arrangement before you press the Record button. Of course, the number of instruments/vocalists doesn't always translate into a like number of tracks; mic'ing a set of drums might require anywhere from four to eight mics and tracks, whereas you might have two or three background singers using a single mic on a single track. Again, plan it out ahead of time.

If you have multiple musicians playing live, you need to arrange monitoring (via headphones) for all those musicians. Recording one musician at a time is easier in this regard.

Tempo is another important consideration. If the tempo is constant throughout the piece, you probably want to record to a *click track;* on the other hand, if you have a lot of shifting tempos (or if you're playing more fluid types of music, such as classical or jazz), a click track will probably just get in the way.

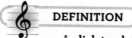

DEFINITION

A **click track** is a metronome-like click that sounds on every beat of each measure in time to the selected tempo. You use a click track to help all the musicians play to the same steady beat.

A click track is virtually mandatory if you're doing a multitrack recording in which the musicians do not play live together. The musicians need the click to play at the same tempo as the other recorded tracks. Without a click, all the tracks will get out of synch very quickly. Whichever you choose, you need to do it up front. You can't go back and add a click track after you've made a recording with a more flowing tempo.

Finally, it's important to know why you're making this recording—that is, what the destination media is. If you're making a quick-and-dirty recording for web-only downloading for a group's fan base, you don't need to record at audiophile-level quality. On the other hand, if you're aiming to release your recording professionally—via downloading, streaming, or on CD—you want to record at the highest quality-level possible.

TIP

It's probably wise to record at the highest-possible quality level, even if the end product is going to be lower quality. You can always create a lower-fidelity mix from high-fidelity elements, but you can't add sonic quality to a low-fidelity recording.

Counting the Tracks

How many tracks do you need to record? How many tracks does the mixing engineer need to create an effective mix? The answer to these questions depends, to some degree, on the type of recording you're doing.

If you're recording a large choral or instrumental ensemble, you might want to record just two tracks—right and left (for stereo). You want to capture the sound of the entire group, not of individual performers, and you won't be shifting individual performers into or out of the mix.

If you're doing a typical rock/country/pop recording, however, you'll need to record more tracks than that—a lot more, in many instances. With this type of recording, each instrument or voice matters and is treated separately during the mixing process. You want each voice or instrument to have its own track, so you can deal with it (in terms of levels, EQ, processing, and effects) individually when mixing. You may even need to replace some or all of a given instrument's performance, which you can only do if that instrument is isolated on its own track. (You can't delete a guitar solo if that solo bleeds into another instrument's track, too.)

So for the most mixing flexibility, you want each instrument or voice to be isolated on its own track, and you don't want an instrument to bleed onto other tracks. You want to be able to press the Solo button and hear only the one instrument recorded on that track and nothing else.

Some instruments may require more than one track. For example, you might want to set up two mics on a piano so the lower notes can be placed to the left of the stereo soundfield and the higher notes to the right. That requires two appropriately placed mics inside the piano, recording to the appropriate left and right tracks.

You also may set up more than one mic for an electric guitar or bass. One mic might record the direct sound from the performer's amp, and one might record reflected sounds. That's two tracks, which you can then combine into a single sound during the mixing process.

Drums definitely require multiple mics and tracks. Although some types of music (such as jazz) might suggest one or two overhead mics only, it's become standard procedure to isolate each element of the drum kit on its own track. That means one mic for the snare, one for the bass drum, one for each tom, one for the hi-hat, and two or more overhead for the cymbals. Some engineers even like to use multiple mics on the snare and bass to capture different elements of the drums' sound. In any case, you'll likely see a half-dozen or more tracks devoted just to the drum set.

 TIP

If you're recording more than one voice or instrument at the same time, you want to be sure they're acoustically isolated from one another to prevent their sounds from bleeding into the others' mics. You can do this by placing the performers in different rooms or booths in the studio or by placing acoustic baffles between them.

In many ways, recording a DI instrument is simpler than recording acoustic instruments, in that it's a single input and a single track. Same thing with MIDI instruments and any loops or clips you may incorporate in the project.

You may have to devote multiple tracks to the same performer, if that performer is recording multiple takes or passes. You don't want to (and with digital storage, don't have to) throw out anything, so record as many takes as you need and sort it all out in the mixing process.

So how many tracks should you record? As many as you need. Naturally, the more recorded tracks you have, the more work you create for the mixing engineer. But that's part and parcel of the job, especially in today's digital, unlimited-track recording environment.

Recording with or Without EQ and Effects

Here's a hot topic: should the recording engineer apply EQ when tracking, or should that be left to the mixing engineer? There is no one right answer.

Some engineers view EQ, especially on vocals, as part of the recording process. After all, if you can affect the sound of the recording by the mic you choose and where you place that mic, what difference is applying EQ at the same time?

Other engineers prefer to record everything as clean as possible and leave all the EQ (and processing and effects) for the mixing process. If the EQ is done ahead of time, you run the risk of it not being right for the final mix or of double-dipping (with an adverse effect on the final sound) by applying even more EQ during the mixing process.

Here's what I think: if the recording engineer wants to EQ while tracking, fine—but be sure the mixing engineer knows it. (Less of a problem if it's the same guy recording and mixing, of course.) This way, the mixing engineer can avoid "fixing" EQ that was intended to be there when recorded.

Same thing with EQ and processing on drums and other instruments. You may want to apply your EQ, gating, reverb, and such during recording so other musicians can hear better what the final mix will sound like when they're multitracking at a later time, and that's okay. But just be sure the mixing engineer knows this and approves. The last thing a mixing engineer wants is a pre-EQ'd track that simply can't be fixed in the mix.

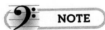 **NOTE**

> The question of who sets EQ is part of a long-running debate between who's in charge of the project, the recording engineer or the mixing engineer. (Again, if it's the same guy for both, problem solved.) If a recording engineer wants more control, he'll apply more EQ and effects while tracking. If a recording engineer is comfortable with the work of a given mixing engineer, he'll leave more of the processing for the engineer.

Setting Input Levels

One of the most important things a recording engineer can do for the mixing process is establish the proper input levels. Set the input level too high, and the recording will overload and distort; set it too low, and the audio will sound too soft, without important details.

The initial input level is set for each input on the recording console (or in the DAW) before you start recording. You do this from the program's mixer, using a given channel's fader control—the little slider that moves up and down in the input channel strip. (Note you set the recording levels using the input channel strips, not the strips for the individual tracks.)

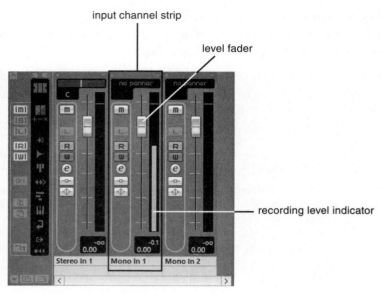

Setting input levels in the mixer.

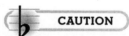

CAUTION

The input level isn't the only thing that affects the quality of the sound you record. When you're recording acoustic instruments, microphone choice and placement is at least as important as how hot you run the levels.

The way it works is simple: before you start recording, you have the musician sing or play his part, with the specific instructions to play as loud as he plans to during the actual recording. As he plays, you adjust the fader for that particular input so the green level indicator just bumps up against the 0 decibel (dB) level, which is the level you never want to exceed. In other words, you want to set the input level so the loudest sections of your recording come as close as possible to 0 dB without going over. (And you'll know when that happens; the red *clipping* indicator will light as a warning.)

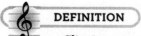

DEFINITION

Clipping occurs when an audio signal "clips" or cuts out at the maximum capacity of the amplifier or recording device. Any extra signal beyond this level is simply cut off, sometimes distorting the original signal.

You need to set input levels for every input you're recording. At this point, don't worry about the relative balance between inputs; it's okay if the rhythm guitar sounds louder than the lead guitar or if the bass drum sounds louder than the bass guitar. The final volume balance will be set during the mixing process. For now, you want to record as hot as possible (without clipping) for each and every input to get the maximum sound possible. After all, you always can make a loud instrument softer in the mixing process, but you can't turn up the volume any louder than what was originally recorded.

CAUTION

If a track is recorded too hot—that is, with the meter going into the red—you run the risk of the audio clipping or distorting, neither of which can be fixed in the mixing process.

Using a Click Track

When you're recording multiple musicians at different times or locations, you need them all playing in tempo. Even if everybody's playing all at once, you want them playing at a steady tempo, without rushing the choruses or dragging the verses.

The best way to ensure a steady tempo, especially for multitrack recordings, is to use a click track, which provides a precise click or other sound dialed in to a specific beats-per-minute rate. When the musicians play to the click, the tempo won't speed up and slow down like it might in an unregulated live performance. It also ensures that multiple tracks from multiple musicians are all recorded in synch.

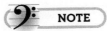

NOTE

Not all music is suited for a click track. Jazz, for an example, often has a more fluid tempo and is recorded in a single setting, making a click unnecessary. The same thing applies to classical music, where the tempo is dictated by the conductor, not a click.

Selecting the Right Audio Quality

Most DAW programs don't limit you to a single recording quality level. You can create lower-quality recordings for web distribution or higher-quality recordings for physical distribution or movie soundtracks.

You typically set the recording quality when you first begin a project. There are three settings to configure—sample rate, bit depth, and file format.

Sample Rate

The first setting to configure is the *sample rate,* which determines how many times per second the analog input is sampled into digital format. The higher the sample rate, the more samples are used to create the digital recording; the more samples used, the greater the accuracy to the original sound and the higher quality the recording. Sample rate is measured in thousands of cycles per second, or kilohertz (kHz).

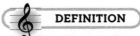 **DEFINITION**

The **sample rate** measures how many times per second an analog audio signal is sampled into digital format.

The sample rate used for compact disc audio is 44.1 kHz, so you might think that any higher rate would be overkill. This is true to a point, although some recordings targeted at the audiophile market are sampled at higher rates.

Keep in mind that the higher the sample rate you select for a recording, the larger the size of the recorded files. If your hard disk space is limited, you may need to select a lower sample rate.

Bit Depth

The next setting to consider is the *bit depth* of your recording—that is, the detail and resolution that is recorded when the analog signal is sampled to digital.

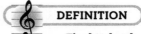 **DEFINITION**

The **bit depth** determines the detail and resolution recorded when an analog signal is sampled into digital.

A higher bit depth produces a higher-resolution, higher-quality recording. Historically, most digital recordings have been made with 16-bit resolution. However, many higher-fidelity recordings are now being made at 24- and 32-bit levels.

Not all audio interfaces support these higher bit depths, however, and you can only record at as high a bit depth as your computer's audio interface supports, so choose the bit depth appropriate for your audio interface box. For example, if you have a 16-bit audio interface and select 24-bit recording in your DAW, your recording will be made at the 16-bit level.

File Format

The final setting to configure is the *file format* used for the recorded audio files. Most DAWs can record to different file formats, but the one you almost always want to use is the WAVE (.wav) format. This is the industry standard audio format for all professional recordings. The .wav files you record are saved in your master project file and are what you use when mixing your project.

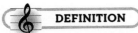

DEFINITION

The **file format** is the type of audio file used to save your recorded tracks.

The Least You Need to Know

- It's important to record the best performances possible before moving to the mixing phase; you can't fix a bad performance (or a bad recording) in the mix.
- Use as many tracks as necessary when recording; using individual tracks for each instrument gives the mixing engineer maximum flexibility.
- You can apply EQ and other processing when recording, but be sure the mixing engineer doesn't add even more when mixing.
- Use a click track when recording multitrack projects so each performer records at the same tempo.
- Select the highest sample rate and bit depth when recording, and record to .wav-format files.

Prepping the Mix

Whether you're doing your own mix or working with an outside mixing engineer, you need to prepare everything you recorded for the mixing process. It's pretty much a matter of cleaning house, straightening up the mess, and wiping off the dust before you open the doors to outsiders. Still, this is an important step because the better your prep, the faster you'll be able to dive into the mixing process proper.

In This Chapter

- Backing up your tracks
- Organizing your project for easier mixing
- Cleaning up your tracks before you mix
- Transferring your project to another DAW for mixing

Before You Begin: Making a Backup

This should go without saying, but you need to make a backup of your project before you make any changes to it. Not only do you want protection in case the project file becomes corrupted, you also want a pristine, as-recorded version you can return to if your mixing gets really off track.

Some DAW programs have a backup function, but some don't. In any case, you can simply use the Save As command in the program to create a new copy of the project. Label the backup accordingly and, if you're a belt-and-suspenders kind of guy, make a backup of the backup to store in another location (or in the cloud), just in case something happened to your entire computer system. Better safe than sorry, right?

Organizing Your Project

Backups out of the way, when it comes to prepping your project for mixing, the first thing you need to do is get everything organized. Recording can be a messy process, with tracks scattered here and there for no apparent rhyme or reason. If you can organize all those various tracks, finding specific tracks later in the mixing process will be easier.

Arranging Your Tracks

Make your life easier by arranging all similar tracks together. It doesn't do to have one background vocal track at the top of your project list and another at the end or in the middle. Take all the tracks that fit together, and move them together.

This means putting all the drum tracks together, all the guitar tracks together, in fact, all the rhythm section tracks together. Place all the vocal tracks together, all the horn tracks together, all the string tracks together, and so forth. Make it as easy as possible to find specific tracks—and to work on similar tracks—while mixing.

Tracks arranged by type, labeled, and color coded.

Labeling and Color Coding Your Tracks

If your DAW has the capability (and most do), take this opportunity to color code all tracks of the same family. You might want to make all your guitar tracks green, all your drum tracks red, and all your vocal tracks yellow. This makes it simpler to find what you need during the mix.

While you're doing this, you might as well go through and relabel any tracks as necessary. Default track names automatically created by DAW programs are typically obtuse and somewhat useless. Instead, change the labels so they're as descriptive as possible of what was recorded. For example, you can relabel the snare drum track to Snare Drum or something similar and the lead vocal track to Lead Vocal.

It doesn't have to be complicated—although it can get that way if you're dealing with a large number of tracks. What if you have three different acoustic guitar tracks? You could go with Acoustic Guitar 1, Acoustic Guitar 2, and Acoustic Guitar 3. You could even label them by performer (if it's likely the mixing engineer will know the performers), such as Acoustic Guitar Troy, Acoustic Guitar Dave, and Acoustic Guitar Chris. You can even label them more descriptively, such as Acoustic Guitar Strummed, Acoustic Guitar Picked, and Acoustic Guitar Lead.

The point is to make it easy to find individual tracks during the mixing process and be able to identify what exactly is on each track. The more descriptive you are in the labeling, the better.

TIP

It's okay to use abbreviations in your track names, as long as you and others know what the abbreviations mean. For example, when labeling drum tracks, most engineers are likely to know that SD means "snare drum," BD means "bass drum," and OH means "overhead."

Creating Track Groups

If you're going to be working on several similar tracks as a group, you can join them together into a *track group*. With tracks grouped together in this fashion, you can act on them all together, with a single action. For example, if you create a track group for all your drum tracks, you can raise or lower the levels for the entire group with a single fader.

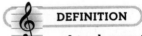

DEFINITION

A **track group** is an assemblage of related tracks that can be worked on together as a single item.

Take the time before the mix begins to create all the necessary track groups. It will save you time later, when you're mixing.

Removing Empty Tracks

As you work through the recorded project, you probably will find a few false starts—that is, tracks designated for recording that didn't get recorded on. For a cleaner project, you can delete these empty tracks. You didn't use them, so you don't need them.

Deactivating Unused Tracks

Similarly, it's likely you've recorded some tracks you won't use in the final project. Maybe it's a botched guitar solo or a half-finished bass track that got replaced by a different player later in the project. Whatever the reason, take this opportunity to deactivate these unused and unwanted tracks.

Do not, however, delete these tracks. No matter how sure you are that these tracks won't be used, you never know. Deleting a track makes it impossible to use it if you change your mind at a later date. Simply deactivating it removes it from the main mix but keeps it handy just in case you want to use it later.

Adding Selection Markers

So far we've looked at how to organize your project's tracks. You also need to organize your project in terms of the music itself—the specific sections of the song. I'm talking verses and choruses as well as bridges, solos, and important fills.

To do this, set a selection marker or memory point at the start of each major section in your project. How you do this differs from DAW to DAW, but it should be easy enough to figure out. Insert a marker at the beginning of a given measure and, if you can, label it appropriately. This makes it extremely easy to come back to specific sections while you're doing the mix.

Cleaning Up Your Tracks

Once you have your tracks organized, it's time to clean them up a little. This involves listening to each track and making any necessary changes so all tracks are suitable for mixing—little things like removing background noise, as well as big things like correcting off-pitch singers.

Removing Noise

Not all tracks you record are going to be pristine with a zero noise floor. We're living in the real world, after all, where a stray dog bark can make its way onto a recording, and where buzz and hiss never really goes away.

The first thing to do, then, is listen for unwanted noises—barks, coughs, pops, clicks, and who knows what else. When you find something that shouldn't be there, use your DAW's editing controls to either cut out that bit of the clip or lower the level at that point so the noise isn't heard. This can be a simple task or a complex one, depending on what else exists on that particular track at that point in time. If you're lucky, the unwanted noise is isolated and easy to cut out. If you're not so lucky, you may need to either live with the noise or rerecord that particular segment and drop in the new clip.

When dealing with background noise and hiss, one approach is to apply a *noise gate* to the noisy track. A noise gate is configured to mute all audio beneath a set level. In practice, this means that sections where no one is playing are silenced completely because they're below the gate level, while the areas with playing are left untouched. This doesn't remove noise from the entire clip, but it does remove noise from areas that are supposed to be quiet. Most DAWs have noise gating built in or available as a plug-in.

DEFINITION

A **noise gate** is a software plug-in or external device that reduces signals recorded below a threshold level.

If this doesn't work to your satisfaction, you'll want to use a third-party noise-reduction plug-in. You'll probably have to configure a few settings or train the plug-in as to where exactly the noise floor is, but most of these tools do a pretty good job of detecting and removing unwanted background noise.

Note, however, that too-aggressive noise reduction can adversely impact the recorded audio—so be judicious with whatever you use.

TIP

Background noise and other random noises often can be more easily heard when you're listening through headphones. It never hurts to do a headphone pass on each track, listening specifically for sounds that shouldn't be there.

Adding Fades

While we're on the topic of unwanted noises, be on the lookout for clicks or pops that sometimes result when you make a cut to an audio file. You also may find unwanted noises at the start of a recording or cut-in, like a singer smacking her lips before belting out the first note or a drummer shifting his weight and making a little squeak on his throne.

The easiest way to eliminate these startup glitches is to add short fades at the beginning and end of each audio clip, or *cross-fades* between clips. Any ghost noises accidentally recorded will be eliminated in the fade.

DEFINITION

A **cross-fade** fades out the sound on one clip as it fades in the sound on the following clip.

Fades added to the beginning and end of an audio clip.

Editing Your Tracks

Some engineers edit their tracks before the mixing process, and others do it as part of the process. I've even seen some recording engineers view this as part of the recording process.

I'm talking track editing, where you make cuts and splices to your recorded tracks to edit out unwanted bits and emphasize the good stuff. Most DAW programs have some sort of audio editing function, where you can perform anything from simple splitting and cutting to more sophisticated note-by-note changes.

This sort of editing needs to be done somewhere before the final mix, and many engineers like to get it out of the way before they start working on levels, EQ, and such. Others leave in the mistakes while they do a rough mix and then clean up the necessary tracks later in the process.

If you want really clean tracks before you start making the mix, now's the time to do it. I discuss track editing in more detail in Chapter 16, so turn there to learn more.

Correcting Pitch and Timing

For some projects, editing a track might mean correcting its pitch or timing. It's all about removing the little imperfections and making a track sound as perfect as possible.

Pitch correction, via the popular Auto-Tune or similar plug-ins, is most often necessary if a vocalist had trouble staying on pitch. You also can use it on horns if the musician missed a note or on guitars that go out of tune; it's sometimes used for effect on some pop recordings as well.

Applying pitch correction is typically as simple as identifying the note(s) that are off pitch, pointing to the correct pitch, and letting the plug-in do its thing. Pitch correction works best and most unobtrusively when a singer is just a little sharp or flat; if the singer is more than a half step off, the correction effect sounds somewhat unnatural.

Timing correction comes when not all performers play exactly on the beat. If a horn player comes in a little ahead of a cue or a drummer drags the beat a little, you can use the editing functions in your DAW to move that particular note backward or forward on the timeline. It's typically just a matter of identifying the waveform for that note and moving it with your mouse. If a performance is a little sloppy, this is the way to make it sound more in line.

Again, both pitch and timing correction are covered in Chapter 16, so turn there for more information.

Transferring Files to Another DAW for Mixing

In most small and home studios, you'll be doing your mixing on the same computer, using the same DAW program, as you used for recording. If this is the case, your prep work is all executed within that DAW, and when it's done, you're ready to start mixing.

In other instances, however, you may want to use a different DAW for mixing than you did for recording. Maybe you really like the loop-based recording of Ableton Live but need the more sophisticated mixing features of Pro Tools. In this case, you'll need to move your project files from the recording program to the one you want to use for mixing.

Depending on the project, you also may want to send your project to a different mixing studio or engineer to hopefully obtain more professional results. This happens all the time, especially with home-recorded projects. In this instance, you'll need to prep your project for transport to the other mixing studio, in whatever format they request.

On the plus side, all DAWs work in pretty much the same way, so once you get the basic files transferred over, the other program should handle them in a familiar fashion. On the downside, every DAW program uses its own proprietary file format for its project files. You can't simply import a Cubase file into Pro Tools; it won't work.

To get around this, you have to export the individual tracks from the first DAW as audio files and then import those audio files into the second DAW. This is relatively easy to do these days, although you do lose any EQ, effects, processing, and automation you've not permanently applied to the individual tracks.

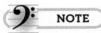

NOTE

Some DAW programs support the Open Media Framework (OMF) protocol for transferring project files from program to program. OMF sounds good on paper, in that it can theoretically transfer not just audio files but also project automation, effects, and the like. In practice, however, OMF doesn't always work that well, and it has not been widely adapted by the recording/mixing community.

Exporting Audio Tracks

For those audio tracks you've recorded, you need to consolidate and then export each track as a separate audio file.

To consolidate a track, you glue together all the individually recorded clips into one single clip. You can then use the export function in your DAW to export the track as a .wav-format audio file.

As an example, Pro Tools makes all this relatively simple with its Consolidate Regions function. Select this option, and all the clips on each audio track are merged into a single file—one for each track, that is. Other DAWs work differently. With Cubase, for example, you have to select all the clips on a track and then glue them together with the Glue tool.

Once you've consolidated all the clips on your tracks, you then select the tracks and export them as audio files. Some programs call this *bouncing,* as in you "bounce" the tracks out of your program into audio files.

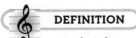

DEFINITION

In digital recording, **bouncing** a track saves it as a separate audio file. In the analog tape recording era, bouncing involved playing multiple tracks on one recorder and recording them as a single track on a second recorder.

Exporting MIDI Tracks

Consolidating and bouncing audio tracks is relatively easy these days. In older DAWs, you had to bounce each track individually; today, you can typically bounce all the tracks in a project with a single command.

In the case of MIDI tracks you have to "play" each track within your program, with the right virtual instrument connected, and then "record" that playback as an audio track. This converts or renders the MIDI track to an audio track, which is easily bounced to an audio file. Most DAWs let you render multiple MIDI tracks to multiple audio tracks in a single pass, but do so in real time.

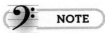

NOTE

With most DAWs, you can export as either WAV or Broadcast Wave Format (BWF) files. A BWF file includes additional metadata, in the form of time stamping, which can help you more quickly align individual files in a project. BWF files can use either the .bwf or .bwav file extensions.

The Least You Need to Know

- Before you start mixing, make a copy of your original project—just in case.
- Organize, color code, and label all the tracks within your project for easier navigation.
- Clean up all your tracks by removing noise, correcting pitch and timing, and cutting out or replacing bad notes.
- If you intend on using a different DAW program for mixing, consolidate and export all your tracks as individual audio files.

Creating the Arrangement

A great mix isn't just adjusting the faders and setting EQ levels. It's about taking the raw elements that were recorded and combining those elements in a way that creates an engaging piece of music.

When you're deciding which recorded elements to use or emphasize, you're creating an arrangement. This is the most creative part of the mixing engineer's job and one that makes the engineer an essential member of the production team.

In This Chapter

- How the mixing engineer can help arrange a song
- Deciding which tracks to use—and which not to use
- Arranging a song vertically and horizontally
- Fitting together the pieces and parts of an arrangement
- Dealing with producers and artists in the creative process

How Mixing Affects the Arrangement

Every song you hear on the radio is arranged, to one degree or another. Within the context of recording and mixing, an *arrangement* is how the individual instruments and voices are placed—as well as how the individual parts of a song are structured. The song itself is the *composition;* the arrangement takes the basic song and uses instruments and voices to best present it to the listener.

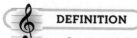

DEFINITION

A **composition** is the melody, chords, and lyrics of a song. An **arrangement** defines how instruments and voices present that composition.

In some projects, the arrangement is mostly defined ahead of time, often by a professional arranger or orchestrator. You find this a lot with larger ensembles. A big band, for example, has its music arranged on paper before the musicians ever walk into a studio.

With smaller ensembles and most popular music, however, arranging often takes place in the studio. The members of a rock band or rhythm section will hash out who plays what and where—the rhythm guitarist shifts from backbeat chords on the verses to eighth notes on the chorus, for example—and that's how they play it. The recording engineer captures the performance (live, or one part at a time) and that's what is sent to mixing.

In other instances, lots of pieces and parts are recorded. Maybe the band or producer has a sense of arrangement in mind and the parts are recorded accordingly, but there's a lot more raw material available. Maybe they recorded several versions of a guitar solo, or a few different rhythm guitar passes, or even some keyboards, just in case. Maybe there were background vocals throughout that they're now having second thoughts about.

The point is, if the arrangement isn't set in stone (which it seldom is), you have the opportunity to make some creative choices during the mixing process. Some people consider this premixing because you're still in the process of assembling all the pieces and parts, but whether it's before or during the mix, it's something the mixing engineer has a big hand in.

So what can you as the mixing engineer do to affect the song's arrangement? A lot. You can …

- Decide which instrumental or vocal tracks you keep and which tracks you mute or delete.

- Decide which versions of a part or solo you include in the final song.

- Insert new choruses or verses by duplicating existing recorded tracks.

- Delete choruses or verses by cutting them out of the project timeline.

- Emphasize particular vocal or instrumental parts by doubling or tripling them in the mix.

- Find a rhythm or riff that defines the song and copy and repeat that element throughout the entire song.

In short, you have the power—and on many projects, the responsibility—to determine what it is exactly that the listeners hear when they play the final song. Yes, the song was recorded a certain way by a certain group of musicians, but you have "editorial control" over how that original recording is used. A few clicks of your mouse here and there can transform a generic piece of music into something quite special.

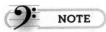 **NOTE**

For a good example of how a mixing engineer and producer can totally alter the sound of a project, listen to The Beatles' *Let It Be* album, produced by the legendary Phil Spector, and the later *Let It Be... Naked* version. The *Naked* version contains the tracks as originally recorded and envisioned by Paul McCartney and the boys; Spector substantially altered those tracks in the mixing studio for the original release of the album. The title track alone is a lesson in creative mixing, with Spector cutting and pasting entire verses and choruses and inserting duplicated guitar solos and drum parts. The *Naked* version is more straight ahead; the Spector version is longer and full of bombast. Who says mixing doesn't have an impact?

Deciding What Stays—and What Goes

The first creative decisions you get to make are which tracks stay in the mix and which don't.

Now, you might think any track that was recorded has to stay in the final mix—but that's not the case. Nothing that was recorded is so precious it can't be deleted for the sake of the final song. (Not even the lead vocal!)

Weeding Out Unnecessary Tracks

In Chapter 8, you eliminated some tracks by deleting and deactivating them. It's time to do some more editing now.

In some instances, what sounded like a good idea (and a good track) in the recording studio sounds less good when played alongside everything else that was subsequently recorded. Maybe the rhythm guitar part that sounds good in the verses doesn't sound quite as great in the choruses. Or maybe there's just too much happening, aurally, and something needs to go to make for a cleaner mix.

Editing the mix by weeding out unnecessary bits and pieces is one of the most important contributions you can make to a project. With a virtually unlimited number of digital tracks on hand, some recording engineers are tempted to record everything but the kitchen sink. What you end up with is too much happening when a cleaner sound might be better.

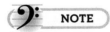

NOTE

In the predigital era, track space was limited and too valuable to record a lot of junk tracks. In today's era of virtually unlimited tracks, however, some recording engineers have fallen into the bad practice of recording *everything* and leaving it to the mixing engineer to make a song out of it. This is a sloppy practice, in my opinion, but one you're likely to run into frequently.

You can simply lower the levels of less important tracks, as you'll learn how to do in Chapter 11, but this may still result in too much aural clutter. The better approach is to dispassionately cut those tracks that simply don't work or that make the mix sound too muddy. The old adage about less being more applies surprisingly well to the recording/mixing process.

Of course, cutting a track doesn't mean you have to fully delete it. Instead, you can simply mute the track in the mixing window. This keeps the track out of the mix while still retaining the raw recording, just in case you decide to use it (or part of it) later in the mixing process.

In fact, you can use your DAW's mute function to experiment with how the mix sounds with and without specific tracks. Who knows—after making further cuts and adjusting levels, you might find you want to bring back something you cut previously. That's one of the joys of digital mixing—virtually unlimited experimentation.

Choosing the Best of Several Options

In other instances, duplicate tracks are deliberately recorded to offer a choice in the mixing process. The lead guitarist, for example, might record several different versions of a solo. The lead vocalist might record her part several times. Or the keyboard player might try a few different approaches to a pad part, not knowing which one might work best.

Your job, in this type of situation, is to determine which of several passes should be included in the final mix. That might mean choosing the best or most appropriate guitar solo, the most powerful vocal take, or the keyboard pad that fits best with the final mix.

Which takes you select definitely affect the sound of the final product. A more aggressive guitar solo might make the song sound edgier, while a more mellow solo might result in a more middle-of-the-road result. A breathy vocal has one effect; a harder-edged vocal has another. Different keyboard pads can make a song sound completely different.

The point is, when multiple takes are recorded, changes have to be made. If the producer or recording artist doesn't make them (and they may), you have to. It's a great responsibility.

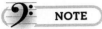

> **NOTE**
>
> Walter Becker and Donald Fagen of the band Steely Dan definitely knew how to get the most out of the multitake approach. On the track "Peg" from their classic album *Aja*, for example, they recorded a half-dozen different guitarists for the lead solo, eventually settling on the legendary solo by the equally legendary Jay Graydon. Other tracks were recorded multiple times with completely different rhythm sections to have more choices available.

Piecing Together a Single Track from Multiple Passes

Here's another way picking and choosing gets done in the mixing process. You start listening to multiple takes from the lead vocalist and realize none of them are perfect. She's a little flat in the chorus of one take and sharp in the verses of another. She forgets the words on one pass, rushes the rhythm on another, and pops her P's in the middle of a third. You might even find that the best pass you have is marred by technical problems—somebody coughed in the background, there's too much hiss, or some unknown glitch threw a pop or a click right in the middle of the big chorus.

Welcome to the exciting world of recording—where anything can happen!

It happens more often than any of us would like to admit: there's no perfect take to be found. The only way to rescue the project, short of bringing the singer or instrumentalist in to try another pass (which probably won't be any better than the others) is to piece together one perfect pass from the best bits and pieces of multiple passes.

In the old days, you did this by literally splicing together different pieces of magnetic tape, which was a bit of a challenge, as you might imagine. With today's digital recording and mixing, however, the job is a whole lot easier.

All you have to do is identify those slices of a take you want to use. It might be the first verse of take three, the chorus of take one, the second verse of take four, and so forth. You may even need to slice things further, identifying individual measures you want to use—or even individual notes within a measure.

You then use your DAW's editing tools to split a given track at the start and end points of the sections you want to use. Thus split, you can drag the selected slice to a new track. Repeat this process with the good bits from other takes, and you end up with a completely new "take" composed of individual slices from multiple tracks.

Split a track to isolate the clip you want to keep.

Once you've assembled this new track, you can glue together the individual clips into a single long clip. This lets you apply effects and processing to the entire track as a whole rather than trying to deal with all the separate clips you pasted. Just don't forget to enable this new track—and mute all the previous ones.

Piece together a new composite track from clips from other tracks.

TIP

Cutting and pasting multiple clips together sometimes results in clicks or pops at the beginning and/or end of the clip. To minimize these unwanted glitches, apply cross-fades between clips and regular fades at the beginning of the first and end of the last clip that have been stitched together.

Arranging the Song

When you're building your arrangement from all the available tracks, you need to approach the arrangement both vertically and horizontally.

A vertical arrangement looks at the song in a linear fashion, from start to finish. A horizontal arrangement looks at the song from bottom to top, in terms of the individual tracks.

Arranging Vertically

Arranging vertically requires you to think of the song in terms of its component parts—verses and choruses, intros and outros, and bridges and solos. These are building blocks you can arrange in various orders, creating different flows to the song.

The first step in arranging vertically is to identify each of these song parts. Listen to where the first verse starts, and add a selection marker at the beginning of that measure. Same with all the verses, choruses, the bridge, you name it. You also should mark the beginnings (and ends) of instrumental solos, the song's introduction, the outro, and so forth.

The building blocks of a vertical arrangement.

Thus marked, you can then use your DAW's cut and paste commands to move a given section to a new location. Obviously, you want to cut and paste all the tracks when you do this.

Some DAWs offer easier vertical arranging. Cubase, for example, lets you create an Arranger track that makes reorganization much simpler. You draw on the timeline to define specific sections and then label and color code them to your liking. You can then drag and drop sections within the Arranger Editor window to reorganize the sections of a song.

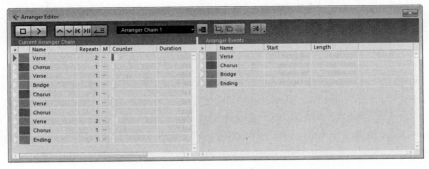

Arrange the parts of a song in Cubase's Arranger Editor window.

You can even duplicate sections. Let's say you're listening to a song and realize it would sound better if the chorus played twice at the end. Unfortunately, it was only recorded once. No problem; just copy and paste the final chorus so it repeats. Same thing if you want to repeat the first verse at the end of the song: just copy and paste the verse into the new position.

In this fashion, you can make a song longer by duplicating existing sections or shorter by cutting sections that don't work quite as well. You also can substantially alter the flow of the song by rearranging verses and choruses (and bridges and solos) as necessary.

Once you have all the sections rearranged, you can rethink other elements of the flow. For example, you might decide the first instance of the chorus needs to be softer than the second instance or the third verse would sound better if everything but the drums and vocals dropped out.

> **TIP**
>
> There are no hard-and-fast rules as to the flow of an arrangement, but choruses typically sound a little bigger than verses, and the overall volume or complexity level tends to increase over the course of a song.

Now is where you start working your mixing magic. Rearranging the flow in this fashion may be as simple as working the faders to raise or lower the overall level of a given section. Or it could be as complex as muting certain tracks in a section or adding more tracks in another.

But that's getting into horizontal arranging, up next.

Arranging Horizontally

Horizontal arrangement is all about creating the desired sound, from the bottom up. (Or from the top down—either works.) You work from track to track to build a sound for that section of the song.

When arranging horizontally, you definitely want to work on each section of the song separately. The sound you create for the verses should be different from what you create for the choruses. Each verse might have its own individual identity. The intro and outro should stand out as different, as should any instrumental solos. It's rare that a song features the exact same instrumentation, effects, and levels from start to finish.

You create different sounds for different sections by changing up the instruments and vocals you include and their levels. Add more tracks in a section, and the sound gets bigger; drop out a track or two, and you bring down the energy level.

> **TIP**
>
> Another way to make a section sound bigger is to duplicate one or more tracks within that section. If you have a rhythm guitar track, for example, you can double it, which makes it sound bigger and thicker. One long-time studio trick is to double the lead vocals for a more full sound. (You can make it sound even fuller by slightly offsetting the duplicate track.)

Now, the producer and musicians may have thought this through beforehand and arranged their own instruments differently throughout the song—or even recorded different parts in different sections. If so, great. If not, you need to use your mixing wizardry to add parts that weren't there to begin with or cut out parts that shouldn't be there.

The key is to provide contrast between the different parts of the song, via the instruments and vocals (and effects and processing) you use. You want the song to build from start to finish, and although you can do this by simply increasing the volume level, you get better results if you alter the mix of the arrangement itself.

There are actually two schools of thought on how to build a horizontal arrangement. The first builds things from the bottom up, literally. You start by muting everything but the drums and then build a solid drum track. With the drum track in place, you activate the bass track and work with that. You then move on to the rhythm guitars, keyboards, and other backing instruments. Finally, you layer the backing and lead vocals on top of everything else, and you've built your song from the bottom up.

 TIP

Many rhythm tracks are built by finding a "perfect" four-bar groove and then creating a loop from those four bars that you repeat throughout the balance of the song. This eliminates any variation in timing or groove that might have been recorded by the drummer and results in a very steady feel throughout.

The second approach recognizes that the most important track, more often than not, is the lead vocals. With this approach, you mute everything except the lead vocal track and get that sounding as good as it can get. You then start activating the other tracks around it—the background vocals, the synth pads, the keyboards, the guitars, and finally the bass and drums. You keep the vocals front and center and ensure all the other tracks support them.

Making It All Fit Together

When creating your horizontal mix, you want to ensure that everything fits together as a whole and that you're optimizing the sound of individual voices and instruments. This isn't always easy.

Setting Preliminary Levels

One of the key aspects of mixing is setting the relative levels for each and every track you're working with. I get into this in a lot more detail in Chapter 11, so turn there to learn how to do this as part of the main mixing process.

When building your arrangement, however, you can set preliminary levels for each track in each section, just to get you in the ballpark and give you an idea of how it's all going to sound.

Dealing with Aural Conflicts

You also need to think about how various instruments/tracks might conflict with one another. This typically happens when you have two or more instruments or voices in the same general frequency range. For example, the bass drum and the bass guitar often occupy the same aural space, multiple guitars sometimes get in each other's way, and guitars and keyboard sometimes overlap.

You'll deal with this more fully with EQ and other processing, but you can perform some preliminary conflict avoidance while you're building your arrangement. When you have two or more instruments that crash into each other, consider various ways to layer and separate them: raise or lower relative volume levels, pan one instrument to the left and the other to the right, or change the EQ of one or the other so they emphasize different frequency ranges. You even can use pitch correction to send one instrument up or down an octave, thus eliminating direct conflict.

The point is to be sure everything is properly layered and separated. Again, this is something you can fine-tune later in the mixing process, but you need to be aware of (and head off, if you can) potential conflicts while you're building your arrangement.

Working with Artists and Producers

Now that I've given you lots of tips and advice on how to build an arrangement while mixing, know that not all artists and producers want you to do so. Some artists and producers will be remarkably welcoming to your input; others won't want you to do anything else but "basic" mixing. It's all a matter of who wants how much control and how much the others view mixing (and the mixing engineer) as a part of the creative process.

To that end, always ask the producer and artists before you start big-footing it in the mixing room. You could just make your changes and present the result as a fait accompli, but you risk raising the ire of less-open-minded people by doing so. It's much better to suggest a change than to make it unilaterally. Ask and then act is the best approach.

TIP

It helps to have upfront discussions with both the producer and the artist about how they view your role. Before you touch a single fader, discuss how much input (and autonomy) they want you to have. Some producers and artists will encourage your suggestions; others will recoil at the thought of a mere mixing engineer involving himself in the creative process. That's the way it goes.

You'll probably find that the more experience you have under your belt—as well as the more experience you have with a particular producer or artist—the more leeway you'll have. If you're new to the business and relatively unknown to the powers involved, they'll probably want to see what you can do before trusting you to do it. You have to prove yourself, understandably.

Even after you've earned their trust and respect, you still have to realize you are just a mixing engineer—you're not the artist with his name on the label and his reputation at stake. Yes, mixing engineers have played huge roles in the production of many hit records, but few people go out and buy a record just because of the engineer. You're just someone in the background—a very valuable someone, as we all know—but still someone working behind the scenes to make the best-sounding product possible.

Remember, on every project you undertake, the artist and producer are the bosses, and your job is to make them happy. Learn to work with them in a way that uses your technical and creative talents to best effect. If you can add something creatively to the talent mix, great. If they just want you to push the sliders, then do that to the best of your ability. There will be other opportunities to get more creatively involved.

The Least You Need to Know

- The mixing engineer can creatively affect the sound of a song by arranging various elements either before or during the mixing process.
- When working with a large number of recorded tracks, you decide which tracks to use—or even build new tracks based on the best sections of multiple passes.
- You need to arrange the song vertically (organizing the sections of the song) and horizontally (fitting together all the tracks in each section).
- As you're arranging the song, you can set preliminary track levels as well as try to avoid aural conflicts between similar instruments and voices.
- Some producers and artists will welcome your creative input in creating an arrangement; others won't. Learn to live by the rules of each working situation.

Creating the Mix

Finally, it's time to start mixing. In Part 4, you explore the basic mechanics of the mixing process and learn how to make a basic mix. You also discover how to set levels and balance your tracks as well as place voices and instruments in the stereo soundfield.

Mixing Your Project

You (or another engineer) have recorded all the necessary tracks. You've organized those tracks, cleaned them up, edited them, and even done some preliminary arranging.

Now it's time to start mixing.

In This Chapter

- How mixing works
- Familiarizing yourself with the mixer window
- Creating a basic mix, step by step
- The secrets of a successful mix

Understanding the Mechanics of the Mixing Process

Up to this point in the process, you've pretty much worked with individual tracks. Things are different when you start mixing, and you now begin working with those individual tracks as a whole. You're mixing the overall recording now, not fixing individual tracks.

The mix you create will become the recording listeners hear. Yes, that mix will include individual tracks, but no individual track is of exclusive importance within the mix. What's important now is the overall sound, which the individual tracks mix together to create.

Building that sound involves finding the perfect balance between all those tracks. Some tracks need to fade into the background, while others need to take a more prominent position. Some tracks may require additional processing or equalization, while others may prove superfluous and need to be muted or deleted. That's what you do during the mixing process—adjust this track and that track to create the overall sound you want.

Most mixing operations take place, appropriately enough, in your DAW program's mixer window. It's here that you adjust the relative volume levels of individual tracks and mute any tracks you don't want to include in the final mix. You also use the mixing window to add various audio effects, as well as apply equalization.

Before we begin, though, a quick word on saving your work. After you've finished working with your individual tracks, but before you start mixing, you should save your work as a new file. You should then open this new file to begin the mixing process on it rather than your original file. When you complete your mix, you should save that as another new file. This way you can return to the unmixed tracks (the first file) if you ever want to create a different mix. Always save each new mix as a new file you can access separately if necessary.

Getting to Know the Mixer Window

Every DAW program has a mixer window, and they all look remarkably similar. That's because these software programs do their best to emulate traditional physical mixing consoles. You see a similar layout of individual track controls, faders, meters, insert and send buttons, and the like.

As an example, let's work with the mixer window in Cubase, one of the more popular DAW programs. Other DAWs, such as Pro Tools and Studio One, have similar mixer controls.

First, know that many programs offer different views of the mixer. Cubase's basic mixer, for example, displays the standard fader, meter, read/write, and send/insert controls. Click the extend button, however, and the mixer gets taller, with a new panel that can display detailed controls for sends, inserts, equalizer, and such. In general, if your screen is large enough to extend the mixer window, you should.

click to extend —

The basic mixer window in Cubase.

The mixer contains a series of *channel strips*, each representing an input, output, or recording channel or track. The channel strips in most mixers are arranged by type in four separate panes, as follows:

- The common panel, containing global settings for all channels.

- Input strips, containing controls for each individual input on your system. You use this pane to adjust the input levels when recording.

- Channel strips, with individual strips for each audio and MIDI track in your recording. These are the controls you adjust when mixing.

- Output strips, containing channel strips for your system's output and for effects processing (audition).

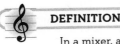 **DEFINITION**

In a mixer, a **channel strip** consolidates all mixing controls for a given channel, including volume fader, EQ, sends, and inserts.

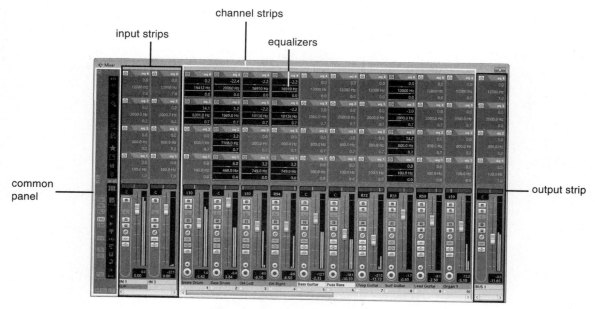

input strips

channel strips

equalizers

common panel

output strip

The expanded mixer window in Cubase.

NOTE

If you have more tracks than the mixer can display at one time, scroll bars appear below each pane. Use them to scroll left to right through the channel strips of that particular type.

Each channel strip contains a variety of controls for a specific channel or track. These controls let you adjust the track's input level, enable/disable recording and monitoring, edit channel settings, enable read and write automation, and so on.

I'll talk about these various controls as they come up in the mixing process. For now, know that the mixing window is where you're going to be doing the bulk of your work during the mixing process.

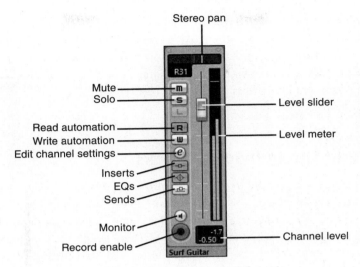

Mute
Solo
Read automation
Write automation
Edit channel settings
Inserts
EQs
Sends
Monitor
Record enable

Stereo pan
R31
Surf Guitar

Level slider
Level meter
Channel level

An audio channel strip in the Cubase mixer.

Making a Basic Mix

Now we come to the mechanics of mixing. Let's walk through the entire mixing process and then focus on what happens at each step.

Mixing 101: Step by Step

Every mixing project is different, but there are a lot of commonalities in terms of process. In general, here's what you need to do in the mixing process:

1. Organize and edit the individual tracks.

2. Arrange the tracks and sections of the song.

3. Set the initial levels for each track.

4. Set the stereo pan for each track.

5. Fine-tune the arrangement.

6. EQ each track.

7. Add processing and effects for each track.

8. Set the final levels.

Of course, the order in which you perform these steps isn't set in stone. Most engineers set levels before adding EQ and processing, but others like to get the EQ and processing out of the way before they set levels. Every engineer has his or her own approach for adding EQ, compression, reverb, and other processing, and in what order. No doubt you'll develop your own workflow over time, but the steps I present here are as good as any to start with.

Let's look at each of these steps individually.

Organize and Edit the Individual Tracks

Preparation is everything, especially in the mixing process. I discussed the basics of mixing prep in Chapter 8. As you learned there, when you first take charge of a project, you need to organize all the tracks with proper grouping, track names, color codes, and such. You also need to clean up all the tracks, removing noise, pops, and clicks. You also may need to edit some of the tracks by removing unwanted sections, correcting pitch and timing, and even cutting in replacement parts.

This is all necessary work you *don't* want to do after you start the actual mixing. When you're fussing over whether to bring up the level of the lead guitar during the bridge, you don't want your concentration interrupted by an annoying click in the middle of a splice. This is all stuff you need to get out of the way before you start adjusting levels, applying EQ, and such.

Arrange the Tracks and Sections of the Song

Mixing prep also involves arranging the parts of a song. As you learned in Chapter 9, this may involve choosing between multiple takes, piecing together a single track from multiple passes, and the like. You're not done here until you have exactly the right tracks to use in your mix.

 TIP

When you mute a track from the mix, drag it down to the bottom of the track list in the project window. This keeps your unused tracks out of the way when you're mixing.

This premixing arrangement also extends to the overall form of the song itself. You can use the editing or arranging tools in your DAW's project window to add or remove entire verses, choruses, and bridges. It's here where the entire shape of the song is decided.

In short, there's a lot of work involved before you lay your virtual hands on your DAW's mixing console. But it's worth it!

Set the Initial Levels

With the prep work done, we now come to what is arguably the most important and most involved part of the mixing process, the adjustment of each track's volume level. What's important here is not the volume of any individual track, but rather how each track relates to the other tracks and fits into the overall mix.

Setting the levels is deceptively easy, but it actually takes quite a bit of work—and a lot of listening and trial-and-error experimenting. Here's how it goes, in general terms:

1. Be sure no tracks are activated for recording, no tracks are muted (click "off" the individual Mute buttons), and no tracks are activated for solo play (click "off" the Solo buttons).

2. Rewind the project to the beginning.

3. Click the Play button on the transport panel.

4. As the project plays back, adjust the volume sliders for each channel. Move the sliders up to increase the volume levels; move the sliders down to decrease the volume levels.

5. Repeat until you're done.

I said this process is deceptively simple. That's because, although moving the volume sliders is easy enough, deciding *where* to move them requires some skill—and good ears. It's impossible for me to tell you how to mix any individual recording; what sounds good to me might not be what you're aiming for at all. A collection of tracks can be mixed together in an almost infinite number of ways, and it's always surprising to hear how different mixes create such different feels. Should the rhythm guitar be buried in the background, or should it be more up front? Should the piano and lead guitar be equal in volume, or should one take precedence? Just how prominent should the snare drum backbeat be? And is the vocal clear enough in the mix, or is it too overbearing? These are all questions that you have to address as you work through your mix—and that I cover in much more depth in Chapter 11. Turn there to learn more.

Know that at this point in the process, you don't need to be that focused on the overall volume levels. If you need to adjust the overall volume of the project, use the volume slider in the output channel strip.

 TIP

You can make the volume level of any given track change over the course of a recording. Maybe you want the lead guitar in the background during the verses but moved up in the mix during the chorus, for example. This is easy enough to do using your DAW's automation function. More on this in Chapter 16.

Set the Stereo Pan

The next part of the mixing process involves placing each instrument somewhere in the left-to-right stereo soundstage. We're long past the age of monophonic recording, and not all instruments should be *panned* hard center. You can open the mix and let the recording breathe by using the entire stereo field.

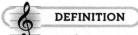

DEFINITION

When you **pan** a track, you move it from one place to another in the stereo sound-field.

Each track in your recording can be panned anywhere in the stereo field, from hard left to dead center to hard right. It's all a matter of selecting a track's channel strip and using your mouse to drag the vertical line in the pan control left or right. Some DAWs also let you enter a "Lxx" or "Rxx" number in the pan field to indicate left or right placement. By the way, you want to be subtle with your use of stereo positioning. The days of putting all the vocals in the left channel and all the instruments in the right went out with The Beatles' second album. Hard-right or hard-left positioning can be used for effect, but otherwise, it should be reserved for subsidiary instruments or background vocals. Learn more about panning in Chapter 12.

Fine-Tune the Arrangement

Track arranging isn't limited to premix prep. As you proceed through your mix, you'll sometimes find a track that sounded good in your initial prep just doesn't fit in with the final recording. No problem. Just mute the track so it doesn't appear in the mix. Problem solved.

For that matter, you may find something lacking in the mix and want to revisit tracks you previously ruled out. Everything should still be there in the project window. (And in the mixer!) Just unmute a given track to bring it back to life and decide how you want to use it in the mix.

Add Equalization

When you have your vocals and instruments where you want them and at the proper volume levels, you can think about applying equalization on a track-by-track basis. EQ shapes the tone of a signal by boosting or lowering specific frequencies. It's EQ that makes instruments and voices sound the way they do. Equalization is an important-enough topic to warrant its own chapter. Turn to Chapter 14 to learn more.

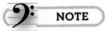

NOTE

You apply different levels of EQ to individual tracks during the mixing process. During the mastering process, you apply EQ to the mix as a whole.

Add Processing and Effects

You can add other effects and processing to the tracks in your project. Some of these effects are best applied before EQ, some after.

The first processing most engineers add is *compression,* which levels out the volume of a track over the length of the track. That is, compression makes the softest sounds louder and the louder ones softer.

Next up is reverb, which makes a dry track sound like it was recorded in a larger room. Reverb adds size to a given track and is especially important for vocals.

Speaking of vocals, adding *delay* to a vocal track is another way to make a voice sound bigger than it might in real life. Experiment with both delay and reverb on your vocals to get the effect you're looking for.

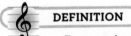

DEFINITION

Compression adjusts loud and soft passages to an average volume level. **Delay** is an acoustic effect similar to reverb, created by playing back an audio signal slightly after the original signal.

With this basic processing out of the way, you can consider adding other processing and effects. The sky's the limit here, but don't go overboard. To my ears, the best recordings are those that sound the least processed.

Learn more about processing and effects in Chapters 13 and 15.

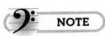

NOTE

Most DAW programs come with a variety of processing and effects built in. You can add other effects via third-party software plug-ins.

Set the Final Levels

If you've done your work right, you now have a pretty good-sounding mix. But it's not yet final because all the EQ, processing, and effects you've added have probably affected the way different voices and instruments sit in the mix. Your sweetening might cause a rhythm guitar to fade too far into the background or a bass drum to sound too aggressive.

Fear not because you still have an opportunity to adjust the relative volume levels of each track. Take a break (an hour or a day) and then come back and listen to your mix with fresh ears. Play with the faders as necessary to fine-tune all your levels, and maybe even take this opportunity to tweak EQ and other effects. This is your final pass, and you want to make it count.

When the mix is done, you're done. You can now finalize all the tracks. Good job, sport!

 **NOTE**

> Don't confuse this creation of the final mix with the mastering process that follows. Mastering (discussed in Chapter 20) fine-tunes the final mix by applying EQ and effects to the entire recording as a whole and is necessary to make the project sound as professional as possible.

Secrets of Successful Mixing

What makes one mix sound better than another? A lot of it is attention to the basics and working through the steps in a diligent manner. Of course, it always helps to have a good set of ears and to be open to suggestions from others. As I've noted, mixing is both a technical and creative process, so you need to use both sides of your brain to be successful.

All that said, here is some general advice you hopefully can use to produce better-sounding mixes.

Focus on the Vocals

It's easy to get distracted by the lesser tracks in the mix. Some engineers spend hours fussing over the proper EQ for the snare drum track and lose focus on those tracks that are more important.

So what's important? More often than not, it's the lead vocal track. If the lead vocal gets buried in the mix, you haven't done your job. Listeners want to hear the lead vocals, which means mixing them up—or sending the other tracks to the background.

Simpler Is Better

A mix can be too busy. Too much happening in the background detracts from the lead vocal—which is, I repeat, almost always the most important part of the mix. Don't get carried away by the unlimited number of tracks you have to work with. Sometimes a simpler mix is better.

Don't Fall in Love with a Track

Along the same lines, don't fall in love with subsidiary tracks. That drum groove may be happenin', but if it's too busy, you may have to simplify it. No matter how cool a track might sound to you, it's there to support the lead vocal, not to function as a solo track.

You see, it's important that you think like a producer during the mixing process, not like a musician. It's the final sound that's important, not any individual part, even if you played it yourself. Be as ruthless as you need to be to cut and fade and otherwise mold the individual tracks to achieve the most effective mix. No track (other than the lead vocal) is too important to cut.

Get Centered

Proper stereo placement is important. Seldom do you want to place important vocals or instruments hard left or hard right in the mix. Off-center placement is fine for auxiliary tracks (rhythm guitar, piano accompaniment, and so on), but for the main tracks (lead vocal, drums, bass), placement in the center of the soundfield is the least distracting way to go.

Perfect Is the Enemy of Good

As the old saying goes, "perfect is the enemy of good." It's possible to make a song sound too perfect—and that's not good. The best recordings are seldom the most flawless ones. When mixing tracks, I find that feel matters more than technical precision. Give me a take with a lot of energy and a few minor mistakes over one with zero mistakes and a machinelike soul. Most listeners will never hear the details (and flaws) you hear in the studio.

Listen Like the Audience

Remember that most people will listen to your recording in the car, on a smartphone through earbuds, or on an otherwise less-than-perfect audio system. The sound you hear on your high-priced studio monitors is almost always better than what most listeners will hear on their equipment. Consider making a "premix" you can play on various audio setups, to hear for yourself what the average listener will hear. It may sound good to you in the studio, but you're not the listener who matters.

Take a Break

Mixing can be a strenuous process. Even though you spend the whole process sitting in your comfy chair, it's still quite trying. There's a lot of listening going on and a lot of thinking.

It's important, then, to give your ears a rest from time to time. Don't mix for more than a few hours at a time without taking a break. You may even need to clear your head (and your ears) for longer periods. Sometimes taking a day off lets you come back with fresh ears and a fresh perspective.

The point is, don't work so hard that you make poor decisions. Rest your ears—and your mind—from time to time, and you'll do a better job.

The Least You Need to Know

- Mixing is all about the project as a whole, not individual tracks.
- You use the channel strips in your DAW's mixer window to perform most mixing operations.
- Mixing is most often a step-by-step process, involving organizing and editing individual tracks, arranging tracks and sections of the song, setting initial levels for each track, setting the stereo pan for each track, fine-tuning the arrangement, equalizing each track, applying processing and effects for each track, and setting final levels.
- Successful mixing engineers focus on the most important track—typically the lead vocals.
- Don't get hung up on any given track; every recorded track is subsidiary to the recording as a whole.

Setting Levels

As you learned in Chapter 10, setting the relative levels of all your recorded tracks is a huge part of the mixing process. But how do you go about this delicate task of determining where every voice and instrument sits in the mix? Read on to find out.

In This Chapter

- How to set initial monitoring volume
- How to stage gain levels
- Determining the right order for mixing your tracks
- The best ways to set individual track levels—and create an effective overall mix

Setting Monitor Levels

Before you start setting the individual track levels in your DAW program, you need to set the levels of your studio monitors. It doesn't matter what kind of monitors you're using, or even if you're monitoring via headphones; you need to set a reasonable and consistent level as your default mixing volume—and then leave it there.

What's the right monitor level? I can't give specifics because every room and system is different. In general, however, you want the volume level set quieter than you might think. Rookie engineers (and artists—always artists) are prone to cranking up the volume to ear-splitting levels, arguing they need it that loud to hear all the details or get immersed in the mix or whatever. But real people don't listen at that volume. The average listener uses music mostly as background these days, and they certainly don't turn things up enough to rattle the walls and make their ears bleed.

The best volume level for monitoring, then, is one that's loud enough for you to hear the individual tracks in the mix, yet quiet enough that you could carry on a normal conversation without the music overwhelming you. You want it just loud enough but not too loud, if you want to think of it that way.

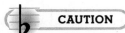

CAUTION

Changing the monitor volume while you're mixing affects how you hear your mix and, thus, affects your decision-making. If you think you have a decent mix going but then accidentally tweak the volume level up or down, you'll suddenly rethink your previous decisions and starting changing levels in a detrimental fashion.

While you're setting the overall volume level, you also need to ensure your DAW controls are properly set up for mixing. That means doing the following:

- Turn off the master EQ.
- Turn off the master sends and inserts.
- Mute all channels not in use.
- Set all unused channel sends and inserts to zero.
- Route to the left/right channels only.

In other words, be sure there's nothing "on" that could add unnecessary noise to the mix or cause confusion later in the mixing process.

Setting the Initial Gain

Next, you need to set the appropriate initial gain of each of your recorded tracks—what the pros call *gain staging*. This is kind of like a premixing or configuring each track so they all have the same relative volume level.

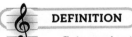

DEFINITION

Gain staging is the process of setting the initial gain or levels in each stage of the project workflow to optimal levels to prevent noise and distortion.

Understanding Gain Staging

It's possible some tracks were recorded "hotter" than others. If you have unequal volume levels across the tracks you're mixing, you're not setting out with a level playing field. It makes sense to work through each track so it hits the same relative volume level as each of the other recorded tracks. You want all the track levels to be as identical as possible before you start mixing.

Gain staging also helps give you adequate headroom when you're mixing. If all the tracks run a little hot (which they tend to do), then you don't have enough room to mix any of them higher in the mix. It's better to bring down the gain of all the tracks so you have plenty of headroom to do your mixing.

NOTE

Gain staging before you adjust track levels has to do with signal flow. When you're playing your recorded tracks for mixing, the audio passes through the gain control first, then through the EQ, panning, inserts and sends, and channel fader. So when you set the gain control, you're setting levels before you add EQ, processing, and other effects.

Where should you set the gain levels? To provide enough headroom for subsequent mixing and processing, you want to aim somewhere in the −10 to −15 *dB* range. Now, this may seem low—especially if you look at meters and don't see a lot of action—but setting initial gain in this range gives you a good amount of headroom for mixing the track up or down in the mix while still placing you above the noise floor for any background noise or hiss in your recording.

Starting with all the tracks at this level also helps you avoid overloading the overall output as you work through the process. (This is not a hard-and-fast rule, however; just be sure you have enough room left over for everything else you need to do in the mixing process.)

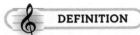

DEFINITION

dB stands for *decibel*, which is a measurement of sound levels. The decibel scale is not linear; raising the level by 1 dB increases volume by 10 percent, while raising the level by 6 dB results in a 200 percent increase. (It doubles the volume.)

Setting the Gain

You set the gain by soloing each track, one at a time. You adjust the gain with the gain control knob, typically located somewhere near the top of each channel strip in your DAW program. (You may have to extend the mixing window to make the gain controls visible.)

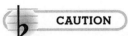

CAUTION

You do *not* set the gain with the channel fader. Use of the fader is reserved for the real-time mixing process itself.

Here's how to set the gain:

1. Set all the volume faders to 0 dB.

2. Move to the first track in your project.

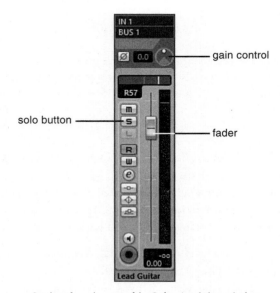

Setting the gain control in Cubase's mixing window.

3. Click to engage the solo button.

4. Start playback.

5. Watch the level meters as the track plays and then tweak the gain control for that track so the majority of the track hits in the −10 to −15 dB range.

6. Click to disengage the solo button.

Repeat steps 2 through 6 for all the tracks in your project.

After you've worked through each track, solo multiple tracks together. If one track is sticking out from the rest as too loud or too soft, tweak that track's gain control to bring it in line.

TIP

If a track sounds too soft—quieter than you remember it being recorded, or reflected by the level meter—it's possible it's out of phase. (This sometimes happens if an instrument or voice is picked up by two or more microphones when recording, and the tracks essentially cancel each other out.) Look for and click the INV button next to the gain control to invert the phase and bring the track back to normal.

Determining Mixing Order

When you're ready to mix, you start, of course, with silence—that is, with all tracks turned completely down. Then you bring up each track, one at a time, to build your mix. But which track do you start with?

The order of tracks is, to some degree, a personal preference, but there are some practical considerations, as well. First and foremost is the fact that each new track you bring up has the potential to obscure other tracks in the mix. This happens in terms of overall volume level, of course, but also in terms of frequency response. This is why you always want to mix your most important tracks—those you deem most significant—first. You'll be sure to have those essential tracks mixed properly before you add other tracks that may obscure them.

Which tracks are the most important? For most recordings, the lead vocal is the most significant track. Beyond that, you can determine track priorities based on the type or genre of song recorded, what the listener expects to hear, what makes the song "pop" off the radio or online, or even what the artist and producer prefer.

Let's look at a few different approaches.

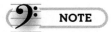

NOTE

Mixing in priority order recognizes the reality of limited resources. You focus on the most essential tracks first, while you have plenty of time and energy (and money). Then, if time or money gets tight later and you need to rush to finish, you've got the important stuff done already.

Vocals, Rhythm, and Backing

For most songs that include vocals, the vocals are the most important tracks. You want to hear what the singer is singing and not have the vocals overpowered by one or more backing instruments.

Now, this priority might change somewhat during instrumental passages or solo breaks (yeah, the lead guitar is most important during the guitar solo), but overall, the lead vocal track becomes the top priority.

TIP

Instrumentals, jazz recordings, and the like obviously don't have lead vocals. Instead, focus on the lead instrument or instruments at any given point in time, and prioritize the solo instruments or sections throughout the song.

Because the lead vocal is your top priority, set the levels for that track first and then set everything else relative to it. The key is to make the vocal track sound as good as it can before you move to the other tracks. You don't want the vocals to be so loud it's overpowering, nor so soft you can't clearly hear it. Listen to the entire track to determine the softest and loudest sections and then work to get them into the best overall volume range. You want the loudest sections to sound powerful but not screaming and the softest sections to sound intimate but not passive.

It's obvious that vocals (and solo instruments) are the highest priority in your mix. What comes next? This particular approach works with the drums and bass tracks next, followed by other backing voices and instruments.

The overall mixing order looks like this:

1. Lead vocals and solo instruments

2. Drums

3. Bass

4. Rhythm guitars, keyboards, and other background instruments

5. Background vocals

6. Backing percussion (tambourine, shakers, congas, etc.)

7. Pads, strings, and other ambience

This mixing order makes a lot of sense for most types of recordings. You want the vocals to always be front and center but then you need the pulse of the rhythm section to drive the song. After that, you add all the appropriate backing instruments and pads in the background, and you're set.

 TIP

To make mixing easier, organize the tracks in your DAW into similar groups so like instruments/sections are next to each other.

Top to Bottom

Another approach is to work from top to bottom in terms of vocal/instrument range. You still start with the lead track (typically vocals) but then move down to the backing vocals, then the lead guitar, then the rhythm guitar and keyboards, then the pads, then the bass, and finally the drums.

Here's the mixing order:

1. Lead vocals and solo instruments

2. Background vocals

3. Rhythm guitars, keyboards, and other background instruments

4. Pads, strings, and other ambience

5. Bass

6. Drums

7. Backing percussion (tambourine, shakers, congas, etc.)

This approach lets you focus on the more melodic tracks first, before you move to the rhythmic backing. You can get a good mix between lead vocals, background vocals, and accompanying instruments before cluttering the mix with all the rhythm tracks. This places drums and bass subsidiary to the other instruments, but that's the way it is in some types of recordings.

Bottom to Top

The mirror image to the top-to-bottom approach is to mix your tracks from the bottom up. That is, you start with the drum tracks and get a good groove established, move to the bass, and build the backing tracks up from there. Many engineers working on dance, hip-hop, and other groove-based music prefer this approach. The focus here is creating the best groove, from the bottom up, and then adding everything else on top of that.

Here's the mixing order:

1. Drums

2. Backing percussion (tambourine, shakers, congas, etc.)

3. Bass

4. Rhythm guitars, keyboards, and other background instruments

5. Lead vocals and solo instruments

6. Background vocals

7. Pads, strings, and other ambience

With this approach, getting a good drum sound and mix is essential. Start with the bass drum track and get the best, most punchy sound you can. Then bring up the other drum tracks, and then the other backing percussion, to create the overall drum mix. The bass drum is the anchor, and the other drums slide in accordingly volume-wise.

When you have the drum tracks mixed together, start adding the other instruments—bass, rhythm guitar, keyboards, and so forth. Then, when the backing tracks are happening, layer in the lead and then background vocals. Finally, sweeten the entire deal by adding any pads or string tracks.

Setting Individual Track Levels

Whichever order you choose, setting the volume levels for each recorded track is the most important step in the mixing process. This is when you determine where each track sits in the mix—which tracks sound louder and which ones fit more in the background.

Your goal is to set the optimal volume level for each track to create a pleasant-sounding mix where the most important tracks are appropriately prominent. You need to set the levels so each track sounds great on its own and in relation to the other tracks you're working with.

To do this, you work with each track individually, one at a time. Start with the most important track given your preferred approach—lead vocals, drums, whatever. When you get the levels set for that first track, move to the second track, the third, the fourth, and so on.

To set the levels, move the project timeline to the start of the recording, initiate playback, and adjust the fader control for the current track. It's really as simple as sliding the fader up and down until you get the levels you want.

Well, not quite *that* simple. Let's look at a few tips you can use to set the right levels for your mix.

Work Clean

This should go without saying, but I'll say it again: you need to set track levels *before* you apply EQ, compression, reverb, and other processing and effects. You want to hear the raw sound and then you can sweeten any or all tracks as necessary. So turn off any effects and processing you might have applied previously, and work with as clean a sound as you can.

Use the Faders, Not the Gain

When you're in the mixing phase of your project, you use the volume faders (sliders), *not* the gain control knob.

Remember, you set the gain controls up front. When they're set, leave them alone. Use the faders to adjust the mix volume levels.

Different Tracks, Different Levels

Some rookie engineers might think every track should be set at the same level so all the channel meters peak or average at the same dB number. This is not a good approach.

The reality is that every track needs to be set at its own unique level. If every instrument and vocal is at the same volume, you get a muddy, unlistenable mix. Some tracks need to be more prominent than others, and some need to be in the background rather than in the forefront.

You need to set *relative* levels to achieve a pleasing mix, not optimal levels (in terms of being loud but not distorting) for each track.

Bring Them Up, Gradually

When you have the level set for the first track in the mix, move to the second track, then the third, then the fourth, and so on. Adding a new track to the previous one(s) is a challenging business.

You might think you know the approximate range for a given track and immediately move the slider to that position. It'll get you in the ballpark, you might think.

Your thinking, however, would be wrong. Never start with an assumed volume level. Instead, move up the slider for the new track gradually, letting it ease into the mix you're creating. Use your ears, not any preset level markings, to tell you when you've reached the right level.

The key to adding a new track is to move up the volume *gradually,* pushing up the slider in small increments. Make small moves until the level is where it needs to be. If you go too loud, back it down a smidge. Just don't jump ahead with a large volume increase. That sort of mistake is difficult to recover from, short of moving back down to zero and starting over.

One Track at a Time (with Exceptions)

In general, you want to bring up the faders on each track individually. You want to hear how that single track adds to the mix you've established with the previous tracks. If you add more than one track at a time, you run the risk of overwhelming your ears so you don't know which tracks did what. When you add a single track, you can tell immediately its impact on the mix.

One possible exception to the one-track-at-a-time rule concerns the drum tracks. Because most drums are recorded on multiple tracks for multiple components (snare, bass, toms, cymbals, etc.), your drum mix isn't a single-track thing. Think of the drum kit as a single instrument, even though it's recorded across multiple tracks.

The solution here is to work on the drum tracks alone (use your DAW's solo controls) to achieve the best mix for the combined kit. Set the bass drum in relation to the snare, fit in the hats and cymbals, and get some punchy tom sounds. Then combine the drum tracks into a single group, and add that group as a single element into your mix. That way, if the drums are too loud, you don't have to worry about changing the sound by adjusting multiple tracks individually. Instead, you slide down a single fader to control the drums as a whole.

You might want to work with other instrument sections in a similar fashion. If you have multiple tracks for background singers, you can group them into a single background vocal group. Same thing, perhaps, with horn section tracks or multiple strings.

CAUTION

Use this grouping approach sparingly and only when a group of tracks effectively becomes a single element in the mix. You wouldn't group the lead guitar and bass, for example, because they serve distinctly different functions. Grouping a handful of horn tracks, however, might make sense. Use your best judgment, but allow yourself the opportunity to adjust individual tracks separately if need be.

Vary the Levels Throughout

When you're first setting a track's level, try for an average level that works throughout the entire song. Know, however, that that track doesn't have to sit at the same level from start to finish. You can—and often should—vary the level of a track from section to section.

For example, you might want to bring up the lead guitar during solo passages or at the end of a chorus but keep it back in the mix during the rest of the song. Or maybe there's a spot where the background vocals need to move into the foreground, or where a rhythm guitar or synth pad needs to be dialed back. In recordings, just as in live performances, there's a give and take, volume-wise, between all the instruments and voices.

 TIP

When it comes to varying volume levels throughout the recording, you can "ride the faders" and adjust levels manually in real time. This becomes problematic when you're working with dozens of different tracks that all need to be worked simultaneously though. Instead, use your DAW's automation function to "record" the changes as you make them. (Read more about automation in Chapter 16.)

Make Important Tracks Louder

If you're working with a lead vocal or instrumental track, be sure that track is mixed a little louder than the backing instruments. Listeners need to hear the melody—and, in the case of vocals, the singer's words—and that's difficult if the lead track is too low in the mix. Make the lead track more prominent, and fit everything else in below it.

This is why it's important not to set all the tracks at the same level. The tracks that are most important need to be louder in the mix, and the less-important tracks need to be quieter. The exact hierarchy differs from song to song and from genre to genre, but in general, you use different levels to distinguish different voices and instruments in the mix.

For example, if the lead vocal is most important (and it generally is), the drums and bass are second most important, and the other tracks follow accordingly, you might end up with a relative volume mix that looks something like the following:

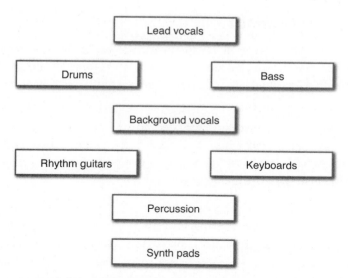

Relative volume levels in a typical vocal-heavy band mix.

On the other hand, if you're mixing a pop or cabaret-type song, the drums and bass may take on a subsidiary role, while the accompanying piano rises in level of importance. Mix the levels accordingly, and you get something like this:

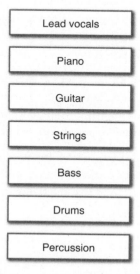

Relative volume levels in a mix that relies more on piano accompaniment.

You see how it works. The most important tracks need to be up in the mix and the other tracks softer. Listeners will hear the louder, more important tracks first—and that's the way it should be.

No Track Is Sacred

You may have several dozen different vocal and instrumental tracks to work with, and the temptation is to make every track as prominent as possible.

That's a nice thought, but not every track is created equal. The rhythm guitar track, no matter how cool it is, just isn't as important as the lead vocals. You don't want it up so far in the mix that listeners hear the guitar instead of the vocalist.

Really, the only person who truly wants to hear every squeak and slide of an individual instrument is the person who played that instrument. (And maybe his mother.) It doesn't matter if a given guitarist or keyboardist or drummer is playing something really out there; that track exists solely to serve the whole.

As such, you need to feel that you can turn down—or turn *off*—any individual track. If it makes for a better-sounding mix, slide down the fader. No track is so important you can't get rid of it. It's the final mix that matters, not the individual tracks.

Keep the Levels Down

I feel a good mix can—and possibly should—be achieved without looking at any of the level meters. You need to use your ears to determine where each track sits. If it sounds right, it is right.

That said, you do need to pay some attention to the meters as you mix. In particular, you want to ensure that none of your tracks goes so hot that it induces *clipping* and distortion.

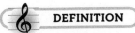

DEFINITION

Clipping occurs when an audio signal becomes louder than the maximum level that can be reproduced; the sound becomes distorted. In most DAW programs, clipping can occur when levels exceed 0 dB.

How loud is too loud? Keeping each track out of the red is imperative. If the level meter goes into the red, you need to back it down, *now*.

That said, if you wait for the levels to go into the red, you've waited too long to bring down the volume. You want to keep the levels for each individual track below 0 dB. If a track goes above 0 dB, it will start to clip and distort, and that's not a good thing. Keep the level a few decibels below 0 dB, so you have room to move it up a little if necessary later in the mix.

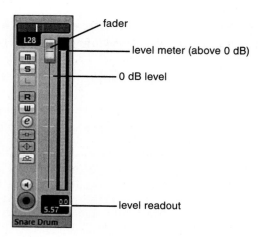

A track mixed too loud—above the 0 dB level.

Take Them Down, Not Up

What do you do if you need to bring up the level of a given track but doing so puts you above 0 dB? Instead of making that track distort, you need to pull down the levels for all the other tracks.

That's right, if you max out the meters for the lead guitar during the guitar solo, back down that track to 0 dB and then move down all the other tracks accordingly. It's quite common to start a mix off too hot and then not have any room to go louder when you start stacking later tracks. If this happens to you, just back everything down so the loudest tracks and passages stay within acceptable levels.

TIP

If you need to lower the levels for all your tracks, link them together in your DAW so pulling down a single fader affects all the tracks.

Stay in the Overall Range

Similarly, you need to pay attention to the overall mix and be sure the master stereo output level stays in the acceptable range as well. This range needs to be just a little lower than what you apply to individual tracks. Keep the master volume no higher than −6 dB to provide necessary headroom during mastering.

The master output channel controls the overall volume level of your final mix, which means you *could* just adjust that master fader to bring down the overall levels. But now we're messing with what is technically the mastering process, and we don't want to do that just yet. Instead, adjust the individual channel faders (individually or collectively) to bring the overall mix levels into range.

Mix, Mix, and Mix Again

As you start bringing up the faders on individual tracks, the quality of your mix changes, often making previously mixed tracks sound different. For this reason, you might need to go back and readjust one or more of the earlier tracks as you move through the mix.

This constant fine-tuning is a necessary part of the mixing process. Remember, even though you're working with one track at a time, everything has to work together. It really is a process that mixes together individual tracks to create a unique new whole.

So if adding a synth pad obscures the backing vocals, you either need to back off on the synth or go back and slide up the fader for the vocals. Each new track you add affects how you hear the previous tracks. No single track exists in a vacuum; every track has to mix together with the others.

 TIP

Be sure your mix starts a second or so before the first note and ends a second or so after the last fade out. This gives the mastering engineer enough space to add a short fade-in at the start and end so the final sound doesn't sound unnaturally cut off.

Avoiding Common Balance Mistakes

When working with levels, many inexperienced mixing engineers fall into some common traps. Here are a few of the things you want to try to avoid when working the faders.

Noise in the Mix

If you didn't do your premix prep, you might end up with unwanted noise throughout the mix. I'm talking hiss, hum, clicks, lip-smacks, and even count-offs from the musicians, all caught on the recording and not cut beforehand. This is why you need to solo each track before you start adjusting levels and cut out all the extraneous noises that make a recording sound amateurish.

Inconsistent Levels

Yes, you can change the levels of a given instrument or voice to reflect different parts of the song. But the lead vocal needs to be the same volume at the end of the song as it is at the start, and you don't want the drums and bass getting louder and softer without reason. Your levels need to be consistent throughout the mix.

No Point of Interest

When the lead vocalist is singing, that should be the main point of interest. But when the vocalist takes a break, what fills the interest gap? You need to bring up something in the mix to hold the listener's attention. If not, attention wanders—and that's not a good thing.

The Song Doesn't Go Anywhere

Some musical genres, such as electronic dance music (EDM) and New Age, don't have a lot of peaks and valleys. But most songs need to start low and peak high. It's important to have contrasting sections and elements throughout a song. Some of this contrast is provided by the song's structure and arrangement, but a lot of that relies on how it's mixed. If everything is static from start to finish, you have a boring song.

It Sounds Flat

Look, a good recording has a little punch and air. If the instruments and vocals don't pop, you haven't done all you can do. Flat-sounding recordings are boring recordings; add a little punch to liven things up.

Not Focusing on the Mix as a Whole

This is the biggest mistake you can make when setting levels. Rookie engineers tend to direct so much attention to getting everything just right on individual tracks (levels, panning, EQ, you name it) that they forget to listen to how all the tracks fit together in the overall mix.

It's the entire song that matters, not individual tracks, and that's the balance you need to achieve. Having a hot-sounding drum track might make you feel really good about your work, but if that hot drum track doesn't fit well in the overall balance, you haven't done your job.

The Least You Need to Know

- Before you start mixing, set the volume on your monitors to an appropriate listening level.
- Set the gain controls for each track so levels average in the –10 to –15 dB range.
- Determine the track order for mixing based on what's important in that particular recording. (More often than not, the lead vocal is the most important track.)
- Use the channel faders in your DAW to bring up the levels for each track, one at a time.
- Try to keep the peak levels for each track below 0 dB and the overall output level below –6 dB.

Utilizing Separation in the Soundfield

When you mixed your tracks' levels, as discussed in the previous chapter, you placed each track *vertically* in the mix, from the loudest (at the top) to the softest (at the bottom). You used relative volume levels to make some tracks more audible than others and, thus, tell listeners what they should be listening to.

If all you do is place tracks vertically by level, however, you're not taking advantage of all the tools at your disposal. Plus, you end up mushing together everything—all the voices and instruments—in the same crowded center space of the stereo soundfield. We have two ears, and we hear in stereo, so why not use the entire stereo soundstage?

This brings us to the topic of panning and placing elements spatially from left to right. By using the entire stereo sound-stage, you can better separate individual instruments and voices in the mix—and create a more pleasing soundfield for the listener.

In This Chapter

- Discovering how stereo placement affects your mix
- How to work your DAW's panning controls
- The best practices for stereo panning
- Arranging instruments and voices on the stereo soundstage
- Understanding mono and surround-sound mixing

Understanding Stereo Placement

Most recordings today are released in stereo. That wasn't always the case, however; mono ruled until the mid-1960s or so. But stereo is the norm today, and for good reason. We hear in stereo; we have two ears, one on the left and the other on the right, and they enable us to hear an enveloping soundfield that matches our stereoscopic vision.

When we listen to anything and everything in the real world, our ears let us precisely identify the position of any particular sound source. Look out your front door, and you might hear a bird tweeting on your left, a neighbor's lawnmower on the right, and kids playing directly in front of you. You don't need to open your eyes to hear all this and know where the sounds are coming from. Your ears hear where the sounds are, and your brain pulls together all the positioning information.

Because we hear in stereo, it makes sense to produce recordings in stereo as well. When you record a live performance, you use the stereo soundstage to reproduce the position of the instruments on the physical stage. And when you reconstruct the elements of a studio recording, you naturally want to place all the various instruments and vocals in appropriate places in the stereo soundfield. You want to hear the performers spread out on a stage in front of you, not grouped together in a single position in the middle of the stage.

In the recording/mixing world, stereo placement is accomplished via *panning.* The panning controls in your DAW program let you place each track in a specific position, left to right, in the soundfield. You can pan a track all the way to the left, all the way to the right, dead center, or anywhere in between those positions.

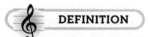

DEFINITION

Panning enables the placement of audio elements along the width of the stereo soundstage.

The capability to place different tracks in different places, left to right, enables you add breadth to your recording. It really expands the mix, moving everything from dead center to surround the listener with music from all sides. This makes the recording sound more natural, effectively reproducing a physical stage.

In addition, by moving some tracks to the left and some to the right, you can further separate the sounds of different instruments. This lets you include more tracks without obscuring or interfering with the others. Yes, setting different volume levels also does this to some degree, but physically moving instruments away from each other in the soundfield is even more effective. In essence, you're creating horizontal separation in addition to your previous vertical separation.

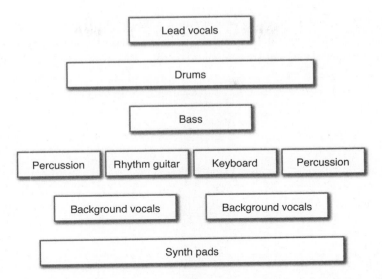

With vertical and horizontal separation in the mix, levels go top to bottom and panning goes left to right.

In short, panning is important in attempting to re-create a physical soundstage and in providing separation between instruments in the mix. Effective panning makes a recording sound "bigger" while enabling the listener to better distinguish between all the instruments involved.

   **NOTE**

Stereo placement in a mix doesn't have to mimic natural placement. In the case of live performances, most listeners in the real world are far enough away that they effectively hear the sound in mono, coming from a space dead center on the stage. Panning during the mixing process creates a more idealized soundstage, one in which listeners are hearing acoustic instruments in close quarters and, therefore, are better able to determine their physical positioning.

Working the Panning Controls

On a physical mixing board, the panning control is a little knob you can turn left and right. Turn this knob, sometimes called a *panpot*, to the left to move the track to the left in the soundfield; turn it to the right to move the track to the right.

In most DAW programs, that physical panning knob is replaced either by a virtual onscreen knob or, more often, by a horizontal slider control. Each channel has one panning control, typically located near the top of the channel strip, above the fader.

panning slider

The panning slider in Cubase's mixing window.

To position a track left or right in the soundfield, use your mouse or mixing controller to move the panning slider to the left or right. Some DAWs also let you input a number for a specific amount of pan, such as L32 or R24.

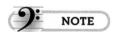 **NOTE**

When entering a specific panning number, 0 is dead center. The larger the number to the left or right, the farther to the side the sound is positioned.

As with level mixing, you want to attack track panning one track at a time. Work through your tracks in order of importance, placing each element across the width of the soundstage. As you add more tracks, figure out where they fit in the soundfield. If there's no open space for that instrument, you may need to go back and re-pan one or more previous tracks.

Best Practices for Stereo Panning

When it comes to panning your tracks, you have a lot of issues to consider. Every engineer, producer, and artist has his or her own opinions of where each element needs to sit, and those opinions inevitably change from project to project. There is, however, some common wisdom as to how you should approach the panning portion of the mixing process, which I discuss next.

Plan Your Panning in Advance

You can charge through the panning process, playing it "by ear" as you experiment with different positioning, but more experienced mixing engineers like to plan things out a little first. You may find it useful to sketch out a crude diagram of the desired stereo soundstage, with marks for where you want to place each instrument. This initial guideline helps you get started and lets you roughly position each track before you start fine-tuning the soundstage.

Pan First, Then EQ—or Vice Versa

Many, but not all, mixing engineers recommend panning after you set levels but before you apply EQ and other processing. This enables you to position each track before you start working on the final sound.

Other engineers say you should apply EQ before panning. (But still apply other effects after, of course.) The thinking behind this approach is that the EQ'd sound of each track affects the panning. You might think, for example, that you need to separate two similar guitar tracks spatially, but if one guitar is EQ'd high and the other low, spatial separation may not be necessary. Better to work with the EQ'd sounds, then, say adherents of this approach.

I tend to go with the pan-first, EQ-second approach myself, but I understand the merits of the other method. As you become more experienced in the mixing world, you'll develop your own preferences in this matter as well.

Start with Mono

However you decide to approach things, when you get to the panning phase of the process, begin with every channel panned dead center. This essentially starts you off with a mono mix, which you can then turn into a stereo mix via panning.

Listen to how everything sounds centered, and readjust levels for clarity if necessary. Then, and only then, are you ready to start panning.

Choose Your Perspective

As you configure the placement of instruments within the stereo soundstage, you need to give some thought as to where you imagine the listener sitting. For example, if you're mixing an orchestra, the audience sees and hears the violins on the left and the cellos and basses on the right. Orchestra members (except for the conductor, of course), hear things just the opposite: facing the audience, they hear the cellos and basses on the left and the violins on the right. The question, then, is whether you want the listener to hear things from the perspective of the audience or the orchestra.

You face a similar issue when panning drums. Assuming it's a right-handed drummer, the drum kit, from the drummer's perspective, has the hi-hat and snare drum on the left and the floor tom and ride cymbal on the right. The audience, however, sees and hears the ride cymbal and floor tom on the left and the snare drum and hi-hat on the right. (The bass drum is dead center, whichever perspective.) Do you want to mix your drums as the drummer hears things or as the audience does?

> **NOTE**
>
> Keyboard instruments—piano, organ, and even mallet percussion such as vibes and xylophone—present a similar but different challenge. The player sees the keyboard with the low notes to the left and the high notes to the right. The audience may sometimes see and hear the opposite of this but more often than not hears the keyboard in mono. So should you present the instrument in mono or stereo, and if in stereo, from which perspective?

This is definitely a personal preference, and talented engineers argue strongly for either side. Myself, I'm a drummer, so I prefer to hear mixes as the drummer hears them. Same thing with keyboards; if the piano or organ or whatever is recorded and mixed in stereo, I want to hear those low notes coming from my left speaker, not the right one. On the other hand, for orchestral and choir work, my preference is to take the audience's perspective. It would be odd to hear basses and cellos on the left side of the mix. Like I said, it's a personal preference—but one you'll have to decide eventually.

Pan Like It Was Recorded

When you're dealing with instruments and voices recorded separately, as with most rock and pop music, you have total control over where each element is positioned on the stereo soundstage. However, if you're dealing with a simpler live recording of an orchestra, choir, jazz big band, or even a smaller jazz ensemble, it's likely that the entire group was recorded with just two or three mics in front. In this instance, you don't have to do anything fancy in the panning process, just duplicate the positioning of the microphones. You can widen or narrow the stereo image a bit if you like, but basically you want to recreate what the audience experienced during that live performance.

Not Everything Needs to Be Panned

Here's something to keep in mind before you start twisting the panpot: not every track in your mix needs to be panned. It's okay to leave some tracks in the center—and in fact, some tracks sound better placed in the middle of the mix.

It's easy—too easy—to start panning tracks and trying to fit everything together across the width of the stereo soundstage. Every track has its place and must be placed at a specific position, left to right, or so the thinking goes.

But it doesn't have to be that way. Some instruments and vocals need to be placed dead center because that's where your ears expect them to be. Other elements simply have more impact when centered and lose impact if they're moved off-center.

In short, you don't have to pan every track. Place each track where it makes more sense and has the most impact. If that's in the center of the mix, so be it.

Separate Like-Sounding Elements ...

One of the benefits of using a wide stereo soundstage is that you get more space to keep instruments from bumping into each other, sound-wise. Use the full soundstage to separate like-sounding elements to help the listener distinguish between them on playback.

For example, acoustic piano and organ have a similar *timbre* and frequency response range, which means they can obscure each other if they're coming from the same general place in the soundfield. The same thing occurs, believe it or not, with the cello and the human tenor voice because they sound very, very similar.

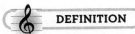

DEFINITION

Timbre is the character or quality of a given voice or instrument, separate from the pitch and frequency range.

Separate these instruments and voices, however—pan the piano or voice a little to the left and the organ or cello a little to the right, for example—and all of a sudden, each element stands on its own in the mix.

If you're having trouble distinguishing similar-sounding elements in the mix, pan them in different directions. Separate them a little spatially, and listeners will be better able to hear each individually.

... or Combine Like-Sounding Instruments

That said, sometimes you *don't* want to separate elements in the mix. When you have like-sounding instruments playing the same parts, you might want listeners to hear those multiple instruments as a single instrument.

For example, you might have the tenor sax and viola playing the same notes, or the organ and a synth pad, or the baritone sax and trombone. In these instances, you might not want to separate the instruments spatially. Instead, pan both instruments to the same spot on the stereo soundstage so the listener hears them sounding together. That creates the new "instrument" you're aiming for, with its own unique timbre and tonality.

> **NOTE**
>
> Brian Wilson of The Beach Boys is famous for combining two or more instruments to create innovative new sounds. He did it during the recording process, by having both musicians play into a single microphone, and controlled the blend by having them move closer or farther away as necessary.

Center Lead Voices and Instruments

With all this talk about panning instruments and voices to one side or the other, let's not forget those elements that need to be heard in the center. For most recordings, the center is where you want to place the lead vocals—and any solo instruments that pop up throughout the song. Placing the vocals in the middle gives them a presence and power the listener can easily notice.

Put another way, you don't want to shuffle your most important tracks to the fringes. If it's important—as lead vocals almost always are—it needs to be front and center. Don't bury it level-wise or by panning it to the edges of the soundstage.

> **TIP**
>
> Subsidiary voices and instruments don't have to be positioned off-center. You can achieve the sound of center placement by duplicating a track and panning the two tracks on opposite sides in the mix, either closer in or farther out. When your ears hear the same signal coming equidistant from both sides, your brain imagines a virtual center channel—sometimes called the *phantom center*—that effectively places the instrument or voice in the center of the soundstage, even though the sounds are actually coming from the sides. The true center isn't cluttered by this additional track, but the listeners think the track is there. It's a neat aural trick.

Center Low-Frequency Sounds

Anything with strong bass notes—electric bass, acoustic bass, synth bass, bass drums, and the like—also belongs in the center of your soundfield. There are a few reasons for this.

First, low-frequency sounds are fairly nondirectional. Go ahead and pan the bass guitar to the right, but listeners will still hear it in the middle of things. (This is why you can place a subwoofer anywhere in your room; it's not directional.)

Second, low-frequency instruments, such as electric bass and bass drum, contain a lot of energy in the mix—and require a lot of headroom. Pan them to the center, and both speakers will share the load of reproducing those frequencies.

Pan Brighter Instruments Left or Right

Low-frequency sounds are nondirectional, but high-frequency sounds are very directional. A flute, triangle, or tambourine is going to cut through the mix wherever it's placed and clearly announce where it is.

For this reason, you don't want to throw these brighter-sounding instruments in with other strong elements of your mix. The higher-frequency elements will draw too much attention to themselves and overpower the more important elements. Instead, pan brighter instruments to the left or right. The brighter the instrument, the farther out to the sides it should be.

Balance the Channels—or Not

Some engineers like to have their mixes sound relatively balanced—that is, have the same number of instruments or relative volume levels pretty much equal between the left and right channels. Symmetry, after all, sounds pleasing to the ear.

If you want a balanced mix, be sure to pan similar numbers of like-sounding elements to either side of the soundstage. If you pan too many high-energy or high-frequency instruments to one side, you end up with an off-balance mix that just won't set right with some listeners. Don't throw all your shaky percussion or rhythm guitars to one side either. Balance those like-sounding instruments between the left and right channels.

That said, don't be afraid to be somewhat asymmetrical in your mix. It's okay to focus attention for certain types of elements to one side or the other, as long as the center is firmly anchored by the lead and bass parts.

Move Things Around If Necessary

Instruments don't have to stay anchored in one place throughout the entire song. It's okay to have the rhythm guitars panned to the far left during verses but closer in during choruses, or to have backing vocals spread left and right during some parts of the song and centered during others. You need to position each element so it best serves the final recording. Don't limit yourself or the recording to a static, left-right placement.

NOTE

If you change the panning of a track mid-song, use your DAW's automation controls to "record" the changes. See Chapter 16 for more on track automation.

Pan for Effect

You can create even more dramatic effects by panning instruments in real time, creating a kind of ping-pong effect. My favorite example of this is on Spirit's *Twelve Dreams of Dr. Sardonicus* album, which is best listened to with headphones. (It's kind of a '60s psychedelic thing.)

You want to park your pans by default, but moving elements around the stereo soundstage can sound really cool. Just be sure to use this effect sparsely—too much ping-ponging definitely sounds gimmicky.

Fine-Tune Levels After Panning

After you've panned all your tracks, go back and listen to your mix-in-process. With various instruments separated spatially, you might find that you need to readjust some volume levels. That's cool; every single change you make affects everything else in the mix. Some tracks might need to be a little louder now while others might not need to be as loud as you thought to stand out. Listen to the mix as a whole, and fine-tune your levels to best complement your stereo placement.

Placing Instruments and Voices on the Stereo Soundstage

Now let's look at where specific instruments and voices should be placed on the stereo sound-stage. As you've no doubt gathered, there's no right or wrong when it comes to stereo placement. But some common settings have been used on thousands of different recordings and, thus, feel "right" to the listening audience.

The following illustration shows what some might consider the default panning positions for the elements in a typical pop or rock recording, relative to the listener. Now, these positions are just suggestions, or maybe even a good place to start. You'll need to fine-tune your own spatial positioning because every recording is different.

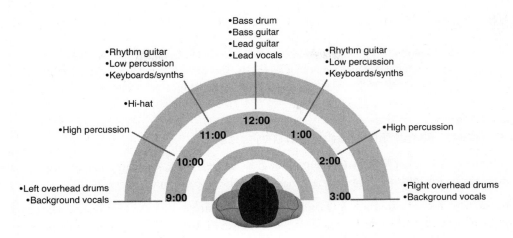

Suggested default positions for a typical recording.

Lead Vocals

This one's simple: lead vocals are almost always panned dead center in the mix. That's where listeners expect the singer to be, so that's where you need to put him or her.

Backing Vocals

Backing vocals need to be separate from the lead vocal track. That means moving them to the side. However, having them come from only one side sounds a little strange. You want the backup vocals to surround the lead vocals, so either record them in stereo or, if they're on a mono track, duplicate that track so you have two tracks to work with.

Once duplicated, pan one track all the way to the left and the other all the way to the right. This will provide the separation you need while still making them sound somewhat centered, as your left and right ears will hear the two tracks at the same time and your brain will interpret them as coming from the middle.

By the way, if panning the backing vocals hard left and right sounds too separated to you, move both sides in a bit, maybe to the 10:00 and 2:00 positions instead. Remember, these aren't hard-and-fast rules, but rather suggestions to help you get started before you start your own fine-tuning.

TIP

Some mixing engineers like to record or duplicate a third backing vocal track and position it dead center with the lead vocals. This provides a bit more depth to the backup vocals while still giving them space in the stereo soundstage.

Lead Guitars (and Similar Instruments)

Lead guitars and other lead instruments should be treated the same way you treat lead vocals—pan them dead center for prominence. There are a few exceptions, however.

First, if the center channel is too cluttered, you might want to pan the lead instruments just slightly off-center. Either side is fine; just move it away from everything else in the middle.

Second, centering the lead instrument applies primarily during solos and instrumental passages. If the lead guitarist or saxophonist is wailing away behind the singer during a song's verse or chorus, you might want to position the instrument somewhat to the left or right so it doesn't interfere with the lead vocals. Use your ears to determine what works best.

Rhythm Guitars

The lead guitar track is typically centered, so you want to place rhythm guitars slightly off-center, either left or right at the 11:00 or 1:00 positions. Which side you choose doesn't matter, but be sure to balance things by placing the keyboards and other backing instruments on the other side.

By the way, if you're using more than one rhythm guitar, you can either place them on the same side so they sound together or put them on opposite sides to create a nice stereo effect. If you choose the dual-sided approach, you might want to spread them apart a little farther, to the 10:00 and 2:00 positions.

Piano and Keyboards

Rhythmic keyboard tracks, such as piano or organ tracks, should be panned the opposite side of your rhythm guitar tracks. You also want them slightly off-center, so if you have your rhythm guitar to the left at 11:00, pan your piano track to the right at 1:00. As with so many other setups, there are exceptions to this, too.

If you're mixing a jazz trio or quartet, you could still pan the piano off to one side, or it might be better to pan it more toward the center because it's more central to the overall sound. You want to give each instrument its own place on the soundstage, and with so few instruments to deal with, you don't have to bother with always placing the lead instrument dead center. If you do pan the piano off to one side, make it slightly so.

If you're mixing a pop/cabaret sort of thing where it's all about the vocals with piano accompaniment, either record the piano in stereo and pan it accordingly, or duplicate a mono piano part and pan them hard to either side. Your goal is to surround the vocals with the piano accompaniment without having them stacked directly on top of each other.

Bass

Moving down to the bottom of the mix, remember that low-frequency sounds tend to be non-directional and are best placed in the center of the mix. That's exactly where you want to place your electric and acoustic basses—dead center in the middle of everything. Bass tracks anchor your entire recording, so put the anchor where it does the most good.

 TIP

> If you want a more spacious bass sound, duplicate the bass track and pan one far left and one far right. This is also a good way to separate the bass and bass drum tracks in the mix. (Assuming you leave the bass drum in the middle, that is.)

Drums

Drums are the one instrument that benefits from the extra space afforded by a stereo soundfield. You certainly can combine all the drum tracks and pan them to the dead center, but the drums will sound more spacious and natural when they're spread out across the soundfield—much as they sound in real life.

The general theory here is to duplicate the spatial presence of an actual drum set. Assuming you have a right-handed drummer, here's where you want to pan the individual drum tracks:

- Snare drum: Center

- Bass drum: Center

- Hi-hat: Off-center to the left, at about the 10:30 position

- Tom 1 (typically the small riding tom): To the left at the 11:00 position

- Tom 2 (either the second riding tom or first floor tom; if the drummer only has two toms, ignore this one): Center

- Tom 3 (typically the large floor tom): To the right at the 1:00 position

- Left overhead: Hard left at the 9:00 position

- Right overhead: Hard right at the 3:00 position

This positioning assumes you want to mimic the sound of the kit from the drummer's perspective, which is my preference. If you'd rather have things sound from the audience's perspective (a valid if less-used approach), just do the mirror image of this setup.

If the drummer has more toms, start panning the first one farther left and end the panning for the largest one farther right. If the cymbals are mic'd individually rather than with dual overheads, place those cymbals in the appropriate positions left to right, starting at the far left and ending at the far right. You want to achieve a natural stereo spread for the entire drum kit. With this approach, listeners will hear each drum and cymbal separately in the mix, which really opens the drum sound.

If, on the other hand, you want the listener to hear the entire kit as a single instrument, pan everything dead center. This will create a lot of clutter in the middle, as you might expect.

Panning all the drum tracks like this only works if you recorded each drum on its own individual track and used two overheads to record the cymbals and general ambience in stereo. This is the way most drums are recorded these days, but it wasn't and isn't always the case.

Some recording engineers prefer a simpler, four-mic approach for the drums, with one mic on the snare, one on the bass, one centered over the kit, and the fourth off to the side over the floor tom. This is the way legendary engineer Geoff Emerick recorded Ringo Starr and John Bonham on many Beatles and Led Zeppelin tracks, and it works surprisingly well. Many jazz gigs are still recorded with just two mics in front of the kit and nothing else.

If you're dealing with fewer mics like this, be sure you center the snare and bass (if you have them) and spread out the remaining tracks hard left and right. Otherwise, do your best to position each element of the kit as naturally as possible across the stereo soundstage.

Auxiliary Percussion

Many recordings feature a virtual armory of auxiliary percussion instruments, from congas and djembes to tambourines and shakers. Where do you place all these wonderful pieces in your mix?

In general, you want to pan auxiliary percussion instruments off-center so they don't interfere with the snare drum, bass drum, bass, and lead vocal tracks. How far left or right you pan depends on the instrument.

Percussion instruments that lay in the lower-frequency ranges—typically hand drums such as congas, bongos, cajóns, djembes, and the like—should be panned just barely off-center, at either the 11:00 or 1:00 positions. Those instruments with higher-frequency characteristics—like tambourines, shakers, triangles, etc.—should be panned farther out, at the 10:00 or 2:00 positions.

If you have a lot of percussion instruments, pan them all at slightly different positions so they don't run into each other.

 TIP

If you only have a single shaker or tambourine, position it exactly opposite the hi-hat. So if you have the hi-hat panned left at the 10:30 position, pan the shaker or tambourine right to the 1:30 position so they balance each other.

Synthesizers

No matter the genre, today's music features a lot of synthesizers. Synths are commonly used as background pads, but they also can be used rhythmically and for lead lines.

With that in mind, here are suggested approaches:

- Lead synths can be panned center during solo or instrumental passages or slightly to one side when they serve more of a backing role. Some engineers even like to play with the panning of synth leads, ping-ponging them left and right throughout the song.

- Rhythmic synths should be treated like auxiliary percussion instruments and panned either left or right. The brighter the patch, the farther it should be placed to the sides.

- Synth pads need to envelope the listener and should be placed both left and right. If the pad is in stereo, just mix it accordingly. If it's a mono track, duplicate it and pan the two tracks hard left and hard right. The goal is to put the pads in both ears of the listener and leave the middle free for the lead vocals or instruments.

Strings

Strings are a bit like synth pads. You probably want to record them in stereo and place the two tracks hard left and right. If you're dealing with a lead string line, move it toward the middle. When working with strings, space is your friend. Use the entire stereo soundstage to envelope the listener in that wonderful sound.

Of course, you always can go with the traditional stage placement for various string ensembles:

- For an orchestra or chamber orchestra, pan the violins left, the violas center, and the cellos and basses to the right. Pop recordings are a little different; you might want to move the basses to the center with the other lower-frequency instruments.

- For string quartets, pan the violins left and left-center, the viola right-center, and the cello right.

Your goal, however you choose to go, should be to use the full width of the soundfield to give the strings natural space and presence.

Horns

The days of Chicago and Blood, Sweat and Tears jazz rock are long gone, but plenty of horn parts can be found in music today. How they're used determines where you should place them.

If your horns are used more for stings and accents, as with a lot of classic soul music, you probably want to pan all the horns to the same position—off-center left or right. The point here is to make the listener hear the entire section as a single instrument, so separating them doesn't make sense.

If the horns do more than just bark out the accents—that is, if there are more melodic lines or the different instruments have different rhythmic parts—you definitely want to spread them out on the soundstage. Put some of the horns mid-left and some mid-right to let the listener better hear what they're doing. How you group the horns depends somewhat on the arrangement. You probably want to put contrasting lines opposite each other.

Of course, if the horns were recorded live as a group, use the recorded tracks accordingly. In these instances, you probably have stereo tracks to work with (left and right mics positioned in front of the ensemble), so spread them out left and right in the mix until you get the desired blend.

Stereo Instruments

Many synths and virtual instruments are recorded in stereo. That's good, and it gives you a nice head start in the panning process.

Depending on the instrument or sound, you can pan the stereo signal either wide or narrow. A wide pan is best for pads and other tracks with longer notes to fill in the background. A narrow pan is better for more rhythmically active parts so the instruments have more of a physical presence on the soundstage.

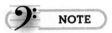 NOTE

Stereo tracks sometimes have balance controls rather than panning controls. Use the balance control to position the instrument left, center, or right in the mix.

Creating Nonstereo Mixes

So far in this chapter, I've addressed panning in terms of the stereo soundstage. But what if you're not mixing in stereo?

Mixing for Mono

Half a century ago, you didn't find a whole lot of stereo mixing going on, as most records were pressed in mono. (AM radio was mono back then as well.) You didn't have to worry about panning left or right, either. Everything sat together dead center in a single speaker.

Not many mono recordings are produced today. Sure, the occasional artist wants to replicate that vintage sound, but almost everybody else records and releases in stereo.

That doesn't mean mono isn't important. You might not deliberately create a mono mix, but you still might want to check your mix in mono. Listening to a stereo mix in mono helps you avoid phase issues with stereo sources or duplicated tracks.

Here's something else: sometimes engineers overuse stereo separation to avoid having instruments in similar frequency ranges run into each other. That's well and good, but just separating tracks spatially doesn't make frequency collisions go away. It's always better to use EQ to avoid these frequency collisions, even if you still separate the tracks in the soundfield.

Listening to your mix in mono, without that spatial separation, will tell you how well you're doing in avoiding frequency collisions. If your mix sounds clean and detailed in mono, it will sound great in stereo, too.

Creating a Surround-Sound Mix

Then there's the issue of mixing in surround sound. Not a lot of surround-sound audio recordings are made these days (save for a small but hungry audiophile market), but you'll run into surround sound a lot if you're mixing the audio for video projects. Movies, TV shows, even video games incorporate surround-sound audio, so if this is what you're mixing for, you'll have to learn how it works.

Most higher-end DAW programs incorporate surround-sound functionality. Obviously, you'll also need to equip your mixing room with the appropriate number of surround-sound speakers as well as one or more subwoofers. You'll be panning tracks to all five, seven, or nine of those channels, so you'll need to know how it sounds.

How many channels do you need to work with? Several different surround-sound standards are in use today, but the most common for home use are 5.1- and 7.1-channel systems. With 5.1-channel surround, you have front left, front center, front right, side left, and side right channels, plus a subwoofer channel. (The subwoofer is the ".1.") With 7.1-channel surround, you add a rear left and rear right channel.

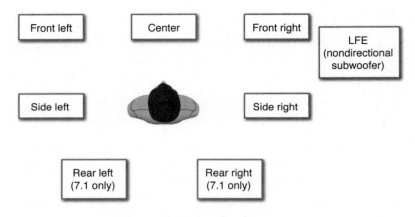

Surround-sound speaker placement.

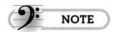 **NOTE**

The subwoofer channel is technically called the low-frequency effect (LFE) channel. Some newer surround formats incorporate two LFE channels.

If you're mixing for movies, you need to deal with the pro formats used in Hollywood. Some of these formats utilize up to 64 individual channels, with speakers placed all throughout the movie theater—even on the ceiling! That's a lot to deal with, and probably nothing you'll see when you're first starting out or in a small studio.

This book doesn't focus on surround-sound mixing, so I'll leave you to find additional resources if this is your gig. Know, however, that traditional panning techniques apply equally well in the surround-sound field: place the most important stuff in the center channel, pan individual elements or effects left or right as appropriate, and try to avoid in-your-face use of active panning and side/rear channel effects. The side and rear channels should be used to envelope the listener or help place elements in the 360-degree soundfield.

The Least You Need to Know

- Use panning to place individual instruments and voices left to right on the stereo soundstage—and to give each element appropriate breathing room in the mix.
- Use your DAW's panning controls to place each track in a specific left-to-right position.
- Pan the most important elements, such as lead vocals, dead center. You also should put all low-frequency instruments in the center of the mix.
- Position subsidiary and higher-frequency elements farther to the sides, and take care to arrange elements so your mix feels balanced.
- Spread out pads, strings, and other background elements to surround the lead tracks in the mix.

Enhancing the Mix

Mixing is more than just setting levels. In Part 5, you learn how to "sweeten" your mix with EQ, reverb, delay, compression, and other processing and effects. You'll be surprised how much better your mixes will sound!

Applying Dynamic Effects

During the mixing process, you can apply all manner of effects and processing to fine-tune the final sound of your recording. Applying dynamic compression, reverb, equalization, and the like can alter the recorded parts in very distinctive ways.

In this chapter, I address those effects typically applied first in the mixing process. These dynamic effects let you change the volume levels of your recorded tracks in both significant and subtle ways.

In This Chapter

- How audio effects work—and how to apply them
- Using a compressor to even out volume levels
- Applying a limiter to avoid peak levels
- Using a noise gate to remove unwanted noise
- Applying a de-esser on vocal tracks

Understanding Audio Effects

Audio effects have traditionally been added to recordings via *plug-ins*. In tape-based recording, these were outboard boxes that literally plugged into the recording console; with computer-based recording, the plug-ins can be either outboard boxes or software programs or utilities that perform similar functions.

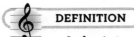

> **DEFINITION**
>
> A **plug-in** is an external box or add-on software program that provides different effects.

Most DAW programs offer a variety of effect plug-ins as part of the overall package. More-expensive DAWs tend to offer more plug-ins than do less-expensive ones.

Adding Plug-In Effects

Each plug-in effect you select is inserted into the audio signal path at a given point and affects the audio signal from that point onward. The effect is applied in real time, which means the audio processing requires a fair amount of computing horsepower. Because the processing is in real time, and is applied after the original audio signal enters the system, the original audio is not altered by the effect—only the resulting sound is changed.

When you choose to apply a plug-in effect, you also have to choose when in the recording/mixing/mastering process to apply it. You can apply plug-in effects at five different points in the process:

Input insert effects These are added to the input bus as the recording is being made so the recorded track includes the effect processing. Input insert effects are best used for adding real-time compression when recording lead vocals. Once added, you can't remove them.

Offline processing These are added directly to the recorded audio event—*not* to the entire track. Once added, offline processing effects cannot be removed from the recorded event. Offline processing is typically applied after recording but before the mixing process as part of the pre-mixing preparation.

Insert effects These are inserted into the signal path just after the original channel input and before equalization and volume are applied. Insert effects are applied to an entire track during the mixing process. They're most often used to affect the dynamics of a track, via use of EQ, compression, limiting, gating, and the like. Insert effects typically are applied one track at a time, not to multiple tracks.

Send effects   These are added to the end of the signal path as separate effects tracks; the final audio is routed to the effects track as the final step in the process. Send effects are applied to an entire track during the mixing process. They typically change the spatial nature of a track and include reverb, delay, and chorus effects. A single send effect can be applied to multiple tracks.

Master insert effects   These are inserted into the master output bus during the mastering process, after the individual tracks have been mixed to a stereo signal. Master insert effects are applied to the entire mix, not individual channels. These effects are part and parcel of the mastering process, not part of mixing.

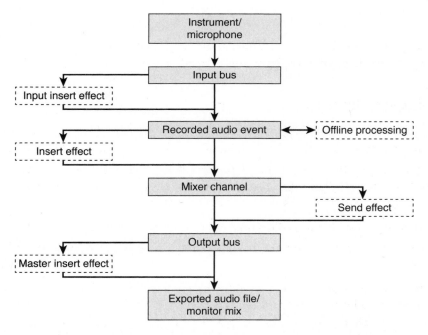

The different points in the recording and mixing process when effects can be added.

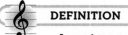 **DEFINITION**

Input insert effects are added during the recording process. **Offline processing** is applied to recorded events before mixing. **Insert effects** are added to the input of the mixer. **Send effects** are sent from the mixer to the output bus. **Master insert effects** are applied to the entire mix during the mastering process.

Applying Inserts and Sends

The two types of effects typically applied during the mixing process are insert and send effects. They don't work exactly the same and are typically used for different types of effects. You typically use inserts for compression and other dynamic effects and sends for reverb and other spatial effects. Send effects can be applied to multiple tracks, while insert effects are for just one track at a time.

For the rest of this chapter, we focus on some of the more commonly used effects that change the volume level of the tracks in your recording. We look at equalization, which affects both dynamics and the timbre of a sound, in Chapter 14, and we turn our attention to those effects that change the spatial positioning of tracks in Chapter 15.

Using Compression

Dynamic effects deal with a track's dynamics—the volume levels of the track—and enable you to make soft passages louder and loud passages softer. You even can mute sounds beneath a set volume level, which is useful for getting rid of unwanted background noise. (And for shaping that punchy tom sound on your drum tracks!)

These dynamic effects are typically used as insert effects during the mixing process. As such, you apply them on a track-by-track basis rather than send multiple tracks to the plug-in.

The most-used dynamic effect is compression. A *compressor* does exactly what the name implies—it compresses the volume levels of an audio track. You'll find compressor plug-ins included with most DAW programs, and plenty of third-party compressors are available.

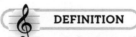
DEFINITION

A **dynamic effect** is a plug-in that affects a track's dynamics, or volume levels. A **compressor** is an audio effect that compresses the high and low volume levels of a track into a narrow range.

What Compression Does

In basic terms, when the volume level of a track gets too loud, the compressor kicks in and reduces the volume. When the volume level gets too soft, the compressor raises the volume. The result is a track that is neither too loud nor too soft and sits within a comfortable volume range for easier listening.

Why—and when—is compression useful? Here are just a few of its common uses:

- Compression helps maintain a consistent volume level when a vocalist moves into and away from the mic. (In fact, compression is most used in this way as an insert input effect during recording—although you can add further compression during mixing.)

- Compression also keeps a steady groove in the rhythm section, especially the bass and bass drum, by maintaining a constant volume level for the underlying pulse.

- It evens out notes on instruments where some notes inherently sound louder than others.

- Compression reduces transients and clipping by bringing down the peak levels on a track.

- Finally, compression makes weak attacks more pronounced by bringing up softer levels.

In short, compression is useful whenever you want to reduce the dynamic range of a track or the entire recording. When you don't want to overwhelm listeners with sudden loud passages or make them listen too hard to hear extremely soft passages, compression is your go-to effect. You end up with a more consistent sound so listeners don't have to constantly twiddle with their volume controls.

Consistent volume levels also make it easier for you to work with a given track during the mixing process. With a compressed track, you can bring up the levels of that track without worrying about it distorting or sticking out in the mix.

Compression is also popular during the mastering process, where it's used to bring up the low levels and create a louder, punchier mix. Remember that: mastering engineers use compression to make louder recordings. Compression is seldom used to make things softer. In practice, then, compression is all about bringing up the lows to the levels of the highs.

Steinberg's Compressor plug-in, included with Cubase.

Understanding Compressor Settings

Whatever compressor plug-in you're using, you can use several common settings to tailor the compression effect:

Threshold   This determines how loud a signal has to be before the compression is applied. For example, if you set the threshold at −5 dB, any signal louder than this level will be subject to compression; anything below it is left uncompressed. Adjust the threshold until the peaks on the signal are just pushing over the threshold and triggering the compressor. (The exception here is if you want to heavily compress the entire track, in which case, adjust the compressor so even the lowest levels are above the threshold.)

Ratio   This specifies how much compression is applied, in terms of the ratio of the input signal level to the resulting output level, for signals that exceed the threshold level. For example, a compression level of 4:1 says that for every 4 dB above the threshold, the output level is actually 1 dB. Using this same example, if you set the threshold at 10 dB, a 14 dB signal on a track would be compressed to 11 dB. The higher the ratio you set, the more compressed the sound will be.

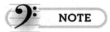   NOTE

The threshold and ratio controls work in tandem. Changing one affects the other.

Attack   This defines how long, measured in milliseconds (ms), it takes for the compressor to reach its maximum level.

Release   This defines how long (also measured in ms) it takes for the compressor to stop after the signal dips below the threshold level.

Knee   Some compressor plug-ins have a setting labeled "Knee." This controls how gradually the compression is applied. A hard knee (low number) kicks in the compression immediately when the threshold is reached. A soft knee (high number) applies the compression more gradually after the threshold. Use a soft knee for more subtle compression on vocals and other melodic tracks and a hard knee on more rhythmic instruments, such as drums and bass.

Gain/output   Sometimes labeled "Make Up," this control sets the overall output level of the compressor. You use the Gain control to bring up the volume of the softest signals. The higher the gain, the louder the soft passages will be.

Tips, Tricks, and Traps for Effective Compression

Mastering engineers apply compression to the entire mix during the mastering process. That's not what I'm talking about here. When it comes to applying compression to individual tracks during the mixing process, here are some things to keep in mind:

Compress before you equalize   You want to apply compression (and all other dynamic effects) before you EQ your tracks. If you try to EQ before you compress, any compression you apply defeats any EQ settings you've previously set. Do the compression and other insert effects first and then work on equalization. (Learn more about equalization in the following chapter.)

De-ess before you compress   Vocal sibilants become more prominent if you compress before you de-ess. For that reason, apply the de-esser before you apply the compressor. (More about de-essing later in this chapter.)

Gate before you compress   Here's the thing with compressors. When they bring up the level of softer passages, they also bring up any low-level noise you might have on a track. I'm talking hiss, hum, rumbles, and even ambient room noise. If it's on the track, a compressor will make it more noticeable. For that reason, you might want to employ a noise gate (discussed later in this chapter) before compressing to remove any unwanted noise.

Not every track needs to be compressed   Yes, you'll probably compress the vocals (especially if they weren't compressed during recording), snare and bass drums, and bass guitar, but you might not need to apply much if any compression to your other tracks. For example, many engineers shy away from compressing acoustic piano and acoustic guitar to capture their full dynamic range. Let each individual project and instrument dictate where and when you should compress.

Keep it subtle   Overcompression can suck all the life out of a track. (Unless you're looking for that specific effect, of course.) It's better to use a more gentle compression, with a low ratio (2:1 or under) and a low threshold. The low threshold keeps the compressor working for most of the track, but not working much.

Little changes add up   Another reason to take it easy on the compression front is that all those little changes you make on individual tracks soon add up to very noticeable changes in the overall mix. Apply small changes, and keep listening to how the overall mix is affected as you build things up.

Turn up the gain   You need to turn up the gain control to make the softer passages louder; otherwise, all you're doing is bringing down the loud levels without compensating the lower-level increases. Most engineers set the compressor's gain to the same decibel level as the plug-in is compressing.

Use the Auto button   If your compressor has an Auto button or setting, use it—especially when you're just starting out, or if you're not sure what settings to use. In most instances, the Auto setting gets you in the ballpark, and you can fine-tune things from there.

Watch the meters   Many compressor plug-ins have a graphic meter that shows how much the audio is being compressed. If the meter doesn't frequently return to normal (which happens when the compressor disengages), your threshold is set too low.

Play with the release time The release time makes a big difference in the sound of the compression and doesn't have to be the same throughout the course of a song. You might want to change the release time for the chorus or bridge to suit changes in instrumentation, dynamics, and the like. In general, the faster the release time, the louder the track will sound, and vice versa. Too fast a release time can create unnatural-sounding pumping or breathing effects.

Don't go too low Unless you want a specific effect, avoid low attack and release times. Speaking of which …

Accentuate the attack To create a bigger attack of a given instrument, set a slower attack time on the compressor.

Add some punch To add punch and thump to a track, set a high ratio (4:1 and up) and a high threshold.

Warm it up To warm up or thicken the sound, use a lower ratio (2:1 or so) and a lower threshold.

Don't be too hard Set a high ratio with a low threshold, and you get a very hard compression effect, which sounds too squashed and lifeless.

Turn your compressor into a limiter If you turn the compression ratio to its maximum setting—20:1 or so—you effectively create a limiter. (More on limiters later in this chapter.)

Lower ratios for higher-frequency instruments When compressing instruments in the mid- and high-frequency ranges, use a lower compression ratio—something in the 2:1 to 4:1 range.

Compress the bass and bass drum together The bass guitar and bass drum are typically the most heavily compressed instruments in a mix. As such, experiment with compressing them together rather than with separate settings. In many cases, this will create a rock-solid rhythmic bass for your song.

Compressing bass drum tracks Set the threshold around −15 dB. Use a 6:1 or so ratio for harder rock music and something in the 3:1 to 4:1 range for softer songs. Use a fast attack and medium-to-fast release, and set a hard knee. To get more punch on the bass drum, set the attack to 15 to 20 ms range.

Compressing snare drum tracks Use a ratio in the 3:1 to 4:1 range for rock and something in the 2:1 to 3:1 range for softer music. Use a fast attack and medium-to-fast release. To get a snappier sound, set a slower attack time that allows the entire transient to pass. Use a hard knee regardless.

Compressing other drum tracks Set a ratio in the 3:1 to 4:1 range for the toms and in the 2:1 to 3:1 range for the overheads. Set a fast attack and medium-to-fast release—faster on the toms than the overheads. Use a hard knee.

Compressing bass tracks   For the bass guitar, set the threshold between −20 and −2 dB, set the ratio between 4:1 and 10:1, and set fast attack and medium release. For synth bass, set the threshold between −8 and −4 dB, use a 4:1 ratio, and keep the fast attack and release. Use a hard knee for both.

Compressing electric guitar   For lead and rhythm electrics, set the threshold in the −14 to −10 dB range, and set the ratio between 2:1 and 5:1—even higher if you want more sustain for a lead guitar. Set a fast attack and medium release, and use a hard knee.

Compressing acoustic guitar   Not everybody compresses acoustic guitar tracks, but if you do, set a threshold in the −14 to −10 dB range, use a 2:1 to 5:1 ratio, and use a fast attack and medium release. Knee can be either hard or soft, depending on the sound you want.

Compressing acoustic piano   Same thing here; not every engineer compresses the piano. If you do, set a ratio in the 2:1 to 4:1 range, and use a fast attack and a slow release to capture all of the instrument's lingering harmonics.

Compressing horn tracks   For saxes and brass, set the threshold between −14 and −10 dB, use a threshold in the 2:1 to 8:1 range, and set fast attack and release.

Compressing string tracks   Whether you're talking solo or ensemble strings, set the ratio between 2:1 and 4:1.

Compressing vocal tracks   Set a threshold in the −8 to −3 dB range and a ratio in the 2:1 to 6:1 range. You'll want a fast attack, a medium release, and a soft knee. (Use a little faster release and a slightly higher ratio—in the 4:1 to 10:1 range—for harder rock vocals.)

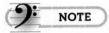 **NOTE**

In regards to attack and release times, fast = 25 to 50 milliseconds, medium = 100 to 500 milliseconds, and slow = 1 or 2 seconds.

Of course, these are all just suggestions. For the best results, you'll need to use your own ears. Know what you want each track and the overall mix to sound like, and use compression to achieve those sounds.

Using Limiting

Limiting is another popular effect that affects the dynamics of a recorded track. In essence, a *limiter* is just a simpler and more effective compressor. If you take a compressor and set both the threshold and ratio to the highest levels possible, you have a limiter.

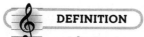

DEFINITION

A **limiter** is an effect that restricts the loudest volume level of a track to a preset level.

How Limiters Work

What a limiter does, pure and simple, is limit the volume level of a track. It shaves off the loudest levels—everything above the threshold level. Limiting doesn't affect softer levels, only the loudest ones.

Steinberg's Limiter plug-in, included with Cubase.

The result is a track that never exceeds the specified volume level or begins to clip. The track can sound more than a little harsh, unlike the smoother results from a compressor. Everything below hard ceiling sounds normal but then there's a drastic and unnatural attenuation of levels above that level.

You typically find the following controls on a limiter plug-in:

Input   Turning up this control boosts the signal going into the limiter. Some engineers boost the input to increase the volume level of the limited track.

Output   Set this control to the loudest level you don't want this track to exceed.

Release   This determines how quickly the signal returns to its original level.

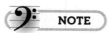

NOTE

Some more sophisticated limiters set the higher-level limit via a Threshold control.

Should You Limit?

Some mixing engineers use limiters to ensure a track never exceeds a preset level, but a lot don't. You can achieve similar but more natural-sounding effects with the more versatile compressor plug-in.

Limiting is more useful postproduction, when radio or television stations (or even streaming services) process the audio to not exceed set levels. If you do use a limiter, set the threshold to only the top 2 or 3 dB of signal peaks.

Using Gating

What do you do if you have some low-level noise on a track? Maybe you can hear the vocalist breathing between phrases, or perhaps there's a little hiss or hum in the background. Or maybe there's even some ambient room noise the microphone picked up.

When there's noise on a track you don't want to hear, it's time to bring out the *noise gate*. This is a plug-in that removes any noise from a track below a preset level. When the volume gets low enough, the noise gate makes it completely silent. (The assumption here is that you only need to remove noise during otherwise-silent passages; any hiss or noise is more or less hidden when the instrument or vocalist is playing or singing and only audible during the nonplaying bits.)

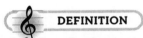

DEFINITION

A **noise gate** is an effect that removes sounds from a track when the original signal drops below a specified threshold.

Understanding Noise Gate Settings

How does a noise gate work? It's simple, really. You set a threshold level for the gate to kick in. When the volume on a track falls below that level, the gate kicks in and silences the audio. When the recorded audio exceeds the threshold level, the gate opens to let the signal through. On for silence below the threshold; off for the full signal above that level.

TIP

Always gate tracks before adding reverb, if you can. It's too easy for a noise gate to chop off the tail end of a long reverb. Plus, adding reverb after a gate can hide any artifacts when the gate goes to silence.

Here are the settings you can adjust on most noise gate plug-ins:

Threshold This is the specified decibel level at which the gate opens and closes. The higher the threshold, the louder the signal must be to open the gate. The lower the threshold, the more sound that passes through when the gate is open. Set the threshold too low, and some background noise may pass through. Set the threshold too high, and you may cut off some actual notes from the performance—or the decay at the end of a note.

Attack This determines how fast the gate opens after a period of silence. Too short an attack time may sound unnaturally harsh—even clicky. If you hear a click when the gate engages, dial in a longer attack time.

Hold This is the minimum time the gate stays open. If the gate is constantly opening and closing, you get what's called "chatter." Set a longer hold time to eliminate this unwanted effect.

Release This determines how fast the gate closes after the sound drops off. To capture a natural decay, you need a longer release time. Use a shorter release time to achieve a nonringy drum sound.

Steinberg's Gate plug-in, included with Cubase.

Range This determines how much the gated signal is reduced. Not all gates have a Range control; if there's no Range control, the gated signal is dropped all the way to silence.

To employ a noise gate to eliminate unwanted noise while still sounding natural, set a lower threshold and longer attack and release times. To capture only the full part of an instrument's sound, without prehits and natural decay, set a higher threshold and shorter attack and release times.

Gating Drum Tracks

Noise gating is useful for removing unwanted noise, of course. It's also useful for achieving specific drum effects, particularly on snare drum and tom tracks. Intelligent employment of a noise gate will cut off the ringing sound after the drum has been played, resulting in a punchy, full-yet-dry modern drum sound.

Of course, gating your drum tracks also deals with the spillover you're likely to get from other drum mics. Tom mics, for example, are likely to capture sounds from the bass drum, snare drum, and nearby cymbals. Employing a noise gate ensures that these spillover sounds are minimized.

Gating on drums works best, of course, when the drums are close mic'd. You want the gate to affect the sound of a single drum, not the overall kit sound.

Whether you're dealing with snare, bass, or toms, you need to set a high threshold level so other drums or cymbals don't accidentally trigger the gate. You also want to set a short attack time to match the short natural attack of these percussion instruments.

It's the release time that really shapes the drum sound. You want the release short but not too short. The goal is to capture the natural resonance of the drum without the after-ring. For the classic punchy tom sound, you want to go shorter rather than longer; if you want to capture more of the natural ring, go longer.

 TIP

You don't always want to set your gate to 0 when the gate is closed. It might sound more natural if a low level of background sound is still audible between the main sounds. This is particularly so when gating drum tracks because dead silence after a snare or tom hit just doesn't sound right. In addition, the gate opens faster if the range control is set to around 12 dB rather than the maximum.

Using a De-Esser

Our final dynamic effect helps reduce the strong sibilants produced when some vocalists say their S's and T's. The plug-in is called a *de-esser*, and it's a kind of compressor that works primarily in the frequency band that contains these hard, explosive vocal sounds. (For males, it's the 3 to 6 kHz range; for females, it's between 5 and 8 kHz.) When a sibilant is sung, it's compressed down so it doesn't stand out in the mix.

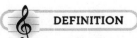 **DEFINITION**

A **de-esser** removes unwanted sibilants from vocal tracks.

Most de-esser plug-ins have just two controls:

Threshold This determines the volume level where the de-esser kicks in. Dial down the threshold until the sibilants are attenuated; dial it back up if the de-esser is kicking in where there aren't any sibilants.

Reduction/Range This sets how much sibilants are attenuated. Too large a reduction might sound unnatural.

Some de-essers also let you adjust the frequency range. If you don't have a Frequency control, the plug-in uses a preset range. You also may find a Release control that affects the smoothness of the effect.

Steinberg's DeEsser plug-in, included with Cubase.

Use your de-esser moderately. Some sibilance is normal and helps define the individual sound of a vocalist. It's better if you can avoid recording all those pops and hisses by using a pop filter on the vocalist's microphone. Still, if the S's and T's are really annoying, dial in the de-esser as necessary.

The Least You Need to Know

- Audio effects can be added during the mixing process as inserts (before the level controls) or sends (after the level controls).
- Dynamic effects let you alter the relative volume levels of each track and are typically applied as insert effects.
- Compression evens out the high and low volume levels of a track, making louder sounds softer and softer ones louder. Compression is typically used to increase the overall volume level of a track or mix.

- A limiter is like a very harsh compressor that keeps the top volume level beneath the desired threshold.
- Noise gates cut all sound beneath a threshold level and are useful for both eliminating unwanted background sound and achieving specific effects—particularly on drums.
- Use a de-esser to de-emphasize unwanted sibilants on vocal tracks.

Applying Equalization

The sound of an instrument or vocal stretches across a large band of frequencies. Even if a singer sings just one specific pitch at a specific frequency, that pitch is colored by harmonics and resonant sounds that exist at other frequencies. And of course, few recordings consist of a musician singing or playing just one pitch.

When an instrument or vocal doesn't sound quite right to your ears, or it doesn't cut through in the mix, it's time to start thinking about adjusting the volume level of specific frequencies reproduced by that instrument or vocalist. A subtle boost or decrease of a given frequency can make a vocal sound warmer, give a snare drum more "crack," clean up a muddy bass guitar, or make a lead guitar cut through the backing instruments.

In This Chapter

- How EQ effects your recordings
- Ways to apply EQ when mixing
- The most useful equalization settings for various instruments and voices
- Carving EQ holes
- Effective EQ tips—and common mistakes to avoid

This adjustment of specific frequencies on a recorded track is called equalization. Applying equalization is a key component of the mixing process and can make or break the sound of a recording.

How EQ Works

Equalization (or *EQ* for short) is an important tool for mixing engineers. By adjusting the shape of an instrument or voice's EQ curve, you change the color or timbre of that item. You can make a voice sound warmer, a bass drum sound punchier, a lead guitar sound brighter, and more. In addition, you can "separate" like-sounding instruments in your mix by using EQ to make them sound slightly different—boosting a specific frequency for one while cutting the same frequency for the other. It's a lot of fine adjustments that make both subtle and significant changes to the sound of your recording.

Equalization shapes the tone of a signal by boosting or cutting selected frequency ranges. It's kind of like a more complex version of the simple bass and treble controls you have on your home or car audio system. When you turn up the bass, you boost the low frequencies; when you turn up the treble, you boost the high frequencies.

An equalizer lets you do much the same thing for your recorded tracks, but with much finer detail. Instead of boosting all bass frequencies, for example, you can boost only selected frequencies. This lets you really fine-tune how a given voice or instruments sounds.

Each track in your mixer can be equalized separately; most DAW programs include one or more *parametric equalizers* that let you adjust different frequency ranges. You can EQ individual tracks (which is what you do in the mixing process) or your final mix as a whole (which you do during the mastering process). You also can EQ tracks while you're recording, although it's better to record "flat" and apply EQ during mixing.

 DEFINITION

Equalization, or **EQ,** is the process of adjusting the balance between the different frequency components of an audio signal. A **parametric equalizer** is a type of equalizer in which the range of frequencies affected by level boosts or cuts is adjustable.

Most equalizers provide three settings you can adjust:

- The frequency you want to boost or cut
- The amount you want to boost or cut that frequency
- The "Q" level

Let me explain.

Frequency

The first setting, frequency, is fairly simple. Of the entire 20 to 20,000 hertz (Hz) frequency range, you can pick any given frequency to boost or cut. We get into what effects result from fiddling with certain frequencies later, but for now, it's enough to know that you can choose to boost the volume of the 500 Hz frequency or cut the one at 8,000 Hz—or both.

That's right—you can boost or cut multiple frequencies for any single track. That means you can boost the bass while cutting the treble, or vice versa. This is how you shape the sound for any given instrument or voice.

Boost/Cut

Next, you specify how much you want to boost or cut that frequency. Volume level is measured in decibels (dB), and that's how you specify the boost/cut level. Most equalizers let you boost or cut the frequency up to 24 dB—that's a +/–24 dB range for each frequency you equalize.

Q

Finally, we come to the mysterious Q setting. Well, it's not that mysterious—it's just an odd name. The Q level specifies the width of the frequency range that is affected by the boost or cut. With a very high Q level, your boost/cut is applied narrowly, pretty much to the selected frequency, without overly affecting adjacent frequencies. A very low Q level widens the range of frequencies affected by the EQ.

Without getting too technical, the Q level corresponds to a set number of octaves that are affected by the EQ boost/cut. For example, a Q of 0.7 affects a bandwidth of two octaves, a Q of 1.4 affects one octave, and a Q of 2.8 affects one half octave. That's why a lower Q number affects a wider frequency range.

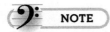

NOTE

Many engineers believe the "magic Q" setting is 1.0, which corresponds to a one and a third octave range. This happens to be the bandwidth that best matches how different instruments cover the different frequency ranges. For more melodic instruments, you can broaden the frequency range covered by using a lower Q number; for less melodic instruments, such as drums, you can use a higher Q number to narrow the EQ effect.

For example, the following figures both show equalization graphs for a 10 dB boost at 1,000 Hz. The first figure has a high (12.0) Q level, which dictates a narrow EQ range; the second figure has a low (1.0) Q level, which dictates a much wider EQ range. As you can see, the high Q level in the first figure results in a very fast ramp up to the 10 dB boost, while the low Q level in the second figure has a much longer and more gradual ramp up to the 10 dB boost. With the low Q level, a much wider range of frequencies is affected by the equalization.

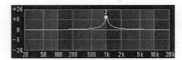

Boosting 1,000 Hz by 10 dB with high (12.0) Q.

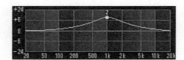

Boosting 1,000 Hz by 10 dB with low (1.0) Q—a much gentler curve.

NOTE

EQ can be either additive or subtractive. Additive EQ boosts (raises) a given frequency, while subtractive EQ cuts (lowers) the frequency. You can apply both additive and subtractive EQ to the same track, although many engineers believe the subtractive more naturally shapes the resulting sound.

Applying EQ

How you apply EQ depends on the DAW program you're using. Most DAWs have at least one equalizer built in, although this may be a simple three- or four-band equalizer. (When you're using an equalizer plug-in, it's typically applied as an insert effect.)

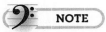

> **NOTE**
>
> The number of bands in an equalizer indicates how many frequencies you can adjust. A three-band equalizer lets you adjust three frequencies; a four-band equalizer lets you adjust four frequencies.

With this type of equalizer, you may only be able to apply rough boosts/cuts. For example, the Studio One DAW has a built-in three-band equalizer that lets you cut rough Bass, Mid, and High frequencies—without any Q adjustment.

The simple three-band equalizer in Studio One.

Higher-end DAWs, such as Pro Tools and Cubase, have more functional equalizers built in. For example, Cubase's includes a four-band equalizer that lets you adjust the boost/cut amount, frequency value, and Q value. That's a lot more versatile.

Cubase's more versatile four-band equalizer, complete with visual frequency curve.

If you want even more control over your EQ, you can use a third-party equalizer plug-in. For example, the Q10 Equalizer from Waves is a 10-band parametric equalizer that lets you adjust not only level, frequency, and Q, but also the shape of the curve for each frequency adjusted. Other equalizers offer similar and even more advanced functionality. Prices range from free up to several hundred dollars.

The 10-band Q10 Equalizer plug-in (waves.com).

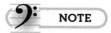

NOTE

Many equalizers include presets for various instruments and voices. You can try these presets (some sound okay), and they may be good starting points for basic equalization, but you're probably better off making your own manual adjustments for your specific project.

Common Equalization Settings

With all this talk of boosting and cutting frequencies, I've neglected one important discussion—which frequencies should you boost and cut? This leads us to the whole topic of which instruments and voices utilize which frequency ranges. Of course, examining this topic fully would require a book or two and maybe even a degree in acoustical physics, so I'll try to focus on the important points in as practical a fashion as possible—which means providing some guidance for applying EQ for specific types of tracks.

Before I start, however, know that there are no golden rules when it comes to EQ. What works in one situation might sound horrible in another. That's because so many factors are involved—the individual instrument (or vocalist), the microphone used, how the instrument was recorded, the room in which the recording was made—you name it. And that's not even considering personal taste. So you should take the following advice with a grain of salt and let your own ears tell you what what's right and what's wrong.

Vocal Tracks

In general, you want to apply as little EQ as possible to your vocal tracks. When working with vocals, EQ should be used only if the voice has some specific defects you need to fix, if you're trying to achieve a particular effect, or if the vocals are getting buried in the mix. To this end, you should try to work with as narrow (high) a Q setting as possible to avoid distorting the overall sound of the vocalist.

 TIP

> In addition to applying EQ, the other important effect to apply to a vocal track is de-essing, which reduces sibilance—those hard, spitty S's, Z's, and CH's. When you use a de-esser, you can add back upper mids and highs in the EQ process, which helps push the vocals above the other tracks in the mix. (Learn more about de-essing in Chapter 13.)

That said, here are some tips on how to use EQ for best effect on your vocal tracks:

- Reduce audible low-frequency noise in the vocal track (include mic handling noises) by cutting all frequencies below 100 Hz.

- If the vocalist has a soft, wispy sound, try cutting by about 7 dB at 100 Hz.

- To add warmth and fullness to a vocal track, try a gentle boost in the 100 to 200 Hz band.

- To reduce nasality, try cutting in the 1,000 to 2,000 Hz range.

- To reduce harshness, cut the 2,500 to 4,000 Hz range.

- To improve projection and help the vocal cut through the mix, add a slight boost around 2,500 to 3,000 Hz (for men) or 3,000 to 3,500 Hz (for women). Also, try boosting around 500 Hz (men) or 1,000 Hz (women).

- To add presence to a vocal and also help it cut through the mix, try a slight boost around 5,000 Hz.

- To make the vocal sound a little brighter, apply a slight boost above 6,000 Hz.

- To reduce sibilance, try cutting in the 4,000 to 8,000 Hz range.

- To add some "air" to the vocal, add a wide (low Q) boost between 14,000 and 16,000 Hz.

> **TIP**
>
> Backing vocals sit better in the mix if you slightly roll off the bass frequencies.

Acoustic Piano Tracks

A well-recorded acoustic piano shouldn't require much equalization. That said, here are a few tips to create a more prominent piano sound:

- To add a fuller bottom, boost the 60 to 120 Hz range.

- To add a little warmth, boost the 100 to 200 Hz range.

- To improve clarity, add a slight boost at 2,500 Hz.

- To add airiness, boost the 8,000 to 15,000 Hz range.

Acoustic Guitar Tracks

As with acoustic pianos, a well-recorded acoustic guitar should stand pretty much on its own with little additional EQ necessary. Still, if you find your acoustic guitar fading back into the mix, consider these changes:

- To reduce string squeaks, roll off all frequencies below 60 Hz.

- To reduce muddiness and boominess, cut the 80 to 150 Hz range.

- To reduce harshness, apply a cut between 1,000 and 3,000 Hz.

- To add a little warmth and body during solo passages, apply a slight boost in the 120 to 200 Hz range.

- Add some definition to the sound by boosting around 2,000 Hz. Be careful, however; too much boost here makes the instrument sound harsh.

- To add a little sparkle to the sound, use a boost between 5,000 and 10,000 Hz.

Electric Guitar Tracks

You can apply many types of equalization to electric guitar tracks, depending on the type of sound you want to achieve:

- Remove that muddy low-frequency rumble by rolling off all frequencies below 100 Hz.

- Improve the sound of direct-injected rhythm guitars by trying a large boost between 3,000 and 6,000 Hz.

- Reduce a boomy sound by cutting between 100 and 250 Hz.

- Fatten up a thin sound by boosting between 100 and 250 Hz.

- Create a fuller sound by boosting in the 150 to 400 Hz range.

- Reduce a boxy sound by cutting in the 250 to 500 Hz range.

- Improve clarity by boosting in the 900 to 3,500 Hz range.

- Add bite to a lead guitar by boosting between 2,000 and 6,000 Hz.

- Remove high-frequency hiss by rolling off all frequencies above 4,000 Hz.

 TIP

To separate two rhythm guitars in your mix, boost one at 3,000 Hz and the other at 4,000 Hz, which should give them slightly different tonal textures.

Bass Guitar Tracks

Bass tracks are often problematic. If your bass sounds too muddy or indistinct, try some of these EQ tricks:

- Remove rumble by rolling off all frequencies in the 40 to 80 Hz range.

- If the bass is too boomy, apply a cut around 180 to 200 Hz.

- If the bass isn't cutting through in the mix, boost the instrument's upper harmonics in the 200 to 600 Hz range.

- Improve articulation and add a little fret noise by boosting in the 1,000 to 2,000 Hz range.

- If the bass is too prominent in the mix, roll off the overtones between 7,000 and 12,000 Hz.

- Create a warmer sound by cutting in the 12,000 to 18,000 Hz range.

- For ballads, try boosting both the 100 and 500 Hz frequencies and cutting at 300 and 12,000 Hz.

- For a more aggressive sound, boost the 1,000 to 2,000 Hz range and apply a cut at 200 Hz.

- For an early Beatles-like bass sound, add a slight boost around 100 Hz.

- For a "twangy" country and western sound, apply a slight boost at 100 and 1,000 Hz and a larger cut between 200 and 250 Hz.

- For the James Jamerson Motown sound, apply a slight boost at 100 and 200 Hz and a larger cut at 5,000 Hz.

Drum Tracks

Some engineers spend all day trying to get the "perfect" drum sound. The key is to equalize each of the drum mics separately because each type of drum and cymbal has different sonic characteristics and EQ needs. Here are some tips:

- For the bass drum (sometimes called the "kick"), apply a slight boost between 80 and 100 Hz, cut aggressively between 200 and 500 Hz, and apply a slight boost at 2,500 Hz. The more you boost the 80 to 100 Hz range, the punchier the kick will be.

- If you want to hear more of the beater attack on the bass drum, apply a boost in the 2,000 to 4,000 Hz range.

- If the bass drum is sounding too ringy or muddy, apply a cut in the 200 to 2,000 Hz range.

- For dance-oriented music, add an additional boost to the bass drum at 4,000 Hz.

- For death metal and similar styles, create a clickier bass drum sound by adding a large boost at 10,000 Hz.

- For the snare drum, add slight boosts between 100 and 300 Hz, 1,000 and 3,000 Hz, 5,000 and 8,000 Hz, and 9,000 and 15,000 Hz.

- For an even fatter snare drum sound, boost even more in the 100 to 200 Hz range.

- To get rid of unwanted snare drum ring, apply a cut in the 400 to 800 Hz range. Note, however, if you cut this range too much, the snare will lose a little presence and start to sound dead.

- For the toms, add a slight boost between 80 and 100 Hz, a cut between 300 and 500 Hz, and boosts between 5,000 and 8,000 Hz and between 9,000 and 12,500 Hz.

- For a boomier tom sound, boost somewhere in the 100 to 300 Hz range, depending on the tom.

- For the hi-hat cymbals, apply a big cut between 60 and 120 Hz and a slight boost between 7,000 and 10,000 Hz.

- For a louder hi-hat "chink" sound, apply a slight boost around 200 to 300 Hz.

- If the hi-hats are too bright, apply a cut at 9,000 Hz.

- To add some life and air to ride and crash cymbals, apply selected boost above 6,000 Hz.

TIP

In general, when you want an instrument to blend into the mix, roll off the top frequencies a little. When you want an instrument to stick out, roll off the bottom.

Carving EQ Holes

There are two main reasons to apply EQ—to adjust the timbre of the sound, as I've been discussing, and to make room for certain instruments (or vocals) in the mix. This second approach is called *EQ carving* because you use equalization to "carve out" a hole a specific instrument can sit in.

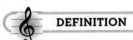

DEFINITION

EQ carving is the process of cutting a specific frequency range from one instrument or voice to make room for another instrument or voice in that same frequency range.

The most common use of EQ carving is to make vocal tracks stand out. Because vocal intelligibility relies on frequencies in the 1,000 to 4,000 Hz range, if you cut this range in other instruments, such as guitars and keyboards, you reduce the overlap with the vocals. This pretty much gives this range to the vocals alone, which makes them easier to hear and understand in the mix.

Another use of EQ carving is to reduce competition among similar instruments. A good example of this is the bass guitar and bass drum, which both compete in the lower frequency ranges. To make the bass guitar a little more prominent and the bass drum a little kickier, try cutting the bass guitar at 60 Hz and boosting it at 100 Hz and then boosting the bass drum at 60 Hz and cutting it at 100 Hz. This reduces the competition between the two instruments and makes the bottom of your mix a little less muddy.

Tips, Tricks, and Traps for Effective EQ

Now let's look at a few tips and tricks you can use to enhance your equalization—and some common traps you need to avoid.

First, know that many rookie engineers make the mistake of applying EQ solely while listening to a track solo. Although this is a good way to get started, it ignores the fact that the sound of any instrument on a recording is dependent on the sound of *all* instruments in the mix. Start EQ'ing solo but then listen to how that track sounds with all the other tracks activated.

In addition, any changes you make to one instrument in the mix affects how the other instruments sound. Boosting the bass guitar, for example, has a big effect on the clarity of the bass drum. This is another good reason not to make EQ changes without considering the rest of the mix—and to consider carving EQ holes when necessary.

Next, you should try to boost less and cut more. (That's subtractive EQ, remember?) This approach is best because the ear is used to hearing a reduction in musical energy due to the way sound-absorbing objects and material interact with the sound. In general, a 6 dB boost sounds about the same as a 9 dB reduction. That means it's better to reduce unwanted frequencies than it is to boost desired ones.

Similarly, you can make a desired frequency stand out by cutting frequencies on either side of it. Instead of applying a boost at 1000 Hz, for example, try cutting at 900 and 1,100 Hz.

 TIP

One quick and easy way to fix a muddy mix is to apply a *high-pass filter*, which rolls off all frequencies below 100 Hz or so. This eliminates rumble and noise that don't affect the instrument's sound. (Except for bass drum and bass guitar, that is, which should *never* have high-pass filtering!)

It's also important to know that it's easy to be too subtle with your EQ. Not many people can hear changes of just 2 or 3 dB. That said, lots of subtle changes can be very effective in shaping the overall mix, even if the average listener can't hear the individual changes.

Listeners can hear big changes, of course—which is why you also shouldn't be overly aggressive in applying EQ. Boosts or cuts of 9 dB or more should be avoided when at all possible.

Here's another general rule that may be useful: when you're boosting a frequency, use a wide Q; when you're cutting a frequency, use a narrow Q. You want your cuts to be more specific and your boosts to have a broader effect.

Finally, know that all the EQ in the world can't cover up a bad recording. If the recording was made with good levels using a quality well-tuned instrument in a good-sounding room, you won't need much EQ. On the other hand, if the recording was made with too little gain using an out-of-tune instrument in a room full of unwanted reflections, you can spend all day working on the EQ and not be able to save it.

Start with a great recording, and the rest of your work will be a lot easier.

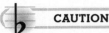

> **CAUTION**
>
> The mixing engineer should always ask if EQ has been applied during the recording process. The last thing you want to do is "double EQ" a track—further boost or cut frequencies that have already been boosted or cut or undo an existing boost or cut by going in the opposite direction during mixing. It's always best to record flat and EQ during mixing, but if the recording engineer has already EQ'd the tracks, you need to tread gingerly when applying even more EQ in the mixing process.

The Least You Need to Know

- Equalization works by boosting or cutting the volume level of specific frequencies or frequency ranges.
- You can adjust three EQ settings—frequency, amount of boost or cut, and Q level (how wide a range is affected).
- Most DAWs include simple three- or four-band equalizers built in. For more control, you can use third-party equalizer plug-ins.
- Always factor the effect of EQ on the entire recording; EQ'ing one track makes all the other tracks sound a little different, too.
- EQ is a great tool, but it's not a magic bullet; it can't make a horrible recording sound like a great one.

Applying Spatial and Modulation Effects

You've used compression and other dynamic effects to adjust the volume levels of your tracks and equalization to shape each track's sound. Now it's time to talk about spatial effects—ways to make each voice or instrument sound bigger and reside in a physical space.

In This Chapter

- Using reverb to add space to your tracks
- Fattening up thin-sounding tracks with delay
- Applying modulation effects to create unique sounds

Adding Reverb

Almost every recording today features some amount of reverberation. Reverberation, or *reverb* for short, makes your recording sound bigger by adding reflective sounds and echoes to the original signal—just the way performances sound in the real world.

Reverb can be recorded naturally, by nonclose mic'ing in a big, "live" room during the recording process. If that's your plan, you don't need to read this section.

It also can be added via audio processing during the mixing process, which you need to do if your recording is too dry sounding.

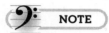 **NOTE**

A track with little or no reverb is referred to as *dry*. A track with full reverb is *wet*. Most reverb plug-ins let you adjust the wet/dry mix for any given track.

What Reverb Is and How It Works

You're used to natural reverberation, whether you realize it or not. Stand in an empty stairwell, and start singing—that echoey fullness you hear is reverberation, from your voice bouncing off all those hard surfaces. You also hear natural reverb when you listen to an orchestra performing in a large concert hall or a choir singing in an old church. Reverb is essentially a plethora of reflected echoes, all hitting your ears at slightly different times.

Reverb adds life to vocals and instruments by giving them a sense of space. You can add all different types and amounts of reverb to one or more tracks in your mix or to your entire mix as a whole during the mastering process. Reverb can help create the illusion of realism in a recording or make a track sound unnaturally boomy and echoey. Done right, reverb can turn a dry and lifeless mix into something that sounds bigger and more natural.

Most DAW programs come with reverb either built in or as part of the package's available plug-ins. Because reverb is so essential to today's recordings, don't compromise with a lower-quality plug-in; this is one area where you might want to spend money on a third-party plug-in to get the best-sounding reverb available.

 **CAUTION**

In addition to creating the illusion of a natural space, reverb also can smear the localization of the original sound source. If precise placement on the stereo soundstage is important, tone down the reverb or use a mono reverb panned to the same position as the source.

Applying Reverb to Your Mix

As noted, you can apply reverb to your mix as a whole, but that's something typically done during the mastering process. During mixing, you get to apply reverb to individual tracks to make each track sound as good as possible—and to best fit within the overall mix.

This means you can apply different types and amounts of reverb to different tracks. The reverb you add to the snare drum track will be different from what you apply to the lead vocals, for example. Each instrument or voice needs its own specific reverb, so you'll need to work on a track-by-track basis.

Here's where you might—or might not—apply reverb:

Vocals   The most common and most important use of reverb is on vocal tracks, both lead and backing. Reverb is essential for filling out a vocal track and also making it sit better in the overall mix. (Remember how much better your singing sounds in a stairwell or shower; that's reverb at work.) Too much reverb, however, can actually push the vocals back in the mix, so you need to work to apply just the right amount.

Piano   Reverb is also widely used on acoustic piano tracks, especially where the piano is in the forefront or there aren't a lot of other instruments in the mix. In these situations, use reverb to make the piano sound as if it's in a large room, which gives you a nice, full sound. On the other hand, if the piano is just one instrument in a large mix, dial back the reverb to make the instrument a little more distinct and push it back in the mix.

Of course, if an acoustic piano is recorded with both instrument and room mics, you have your reverb already recorded and don't have to add much of any in the mixing stage.

Guitar   Acoustic guitars, like acoustic pianos, can benefit from room reverb, either captured during recording or added during mixing. Electric guitars need more subtle reverb and can get a little muddy if you overdo things. In addition, because guitarists like to add their own effects, don't let the reverb you add conflict with whatever reverb pedal or processor the guitarist added during recording.

Bass guitar   Many engineers don't apply any reverb to the bass. Adding long reverb to the bass tends to muddy the low end of your mix, so you're probably better off leaving the bass track dry. If you want to apply reverb to the bass track, use a very short *decay*.

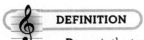 **DEFINITION**

Decay is the trailing section of a waveform, the last sounding part of a note.

Drums   As with the bass guitar, you probably don't want to add much, if any, reverb to the bass drum. Reverb can help fatten the snare drum sound, however, and many engineers like a fair amount of reverb on the toms. It doesn't hurt to add a little reverb to the overheads as well, to introduce a little air into the kit.

Synth pads   Most virtual instruments sound pretty good on their own and don't need additional reverb. This is particularly true with synth pads. They need to sit in the background, and adding reverb brings them forward too much. This is one track you leave the reverb off of.

The point is that you need to work with each instrument and voice individually when applying reverb. It's not a one-size-fits-all effect—although, if several tracks need a similar reverb effect, you can group those tracks and use common reverb settings.

Choosing the Right Type of Reverb

Not only can you dial in different amounts of reverb; you also can apply several different types of reverb effects:

Hall   This type of reverb attempts to replicate the acoustics of a concert hall. Hall reverb is full bodied, with decay in the 1.2- to 3-second range. This is the most common type of reverb, as it adds dimensionality to your recording.

Chamber   This is like a hall reverb, but in a smaller space. Chamber reverb results in more clarity than hall reverb, yet still provides the necessary sound dispersion. Decay is typically shorter, in the 0.4- to 1.2-second range.

Room   This type of reverb emulates the characteristics of a smaller room, with a shorter decay time (in the 0.2- to 1-second range). Room reverb is good for adding realism to instruments that were close-mic'd or recorded with direct injection in the studio.

Plate   This is an artificial reverb that emulates a metal plate that vibrates when soundwaves strike its surface. Plate reverb produces minimal initial reflections but a full-bodied reverb sound. This type of reverb is often used to make vocals and snare drums sound bigger.

Spring   A spring reverb is similar to a plate reverb, but it emulates the reverberation of metal springs, like the kind found in guitar amplifiers. As such, spring reverb is great for electric guitars and similar instruments; it's also a good alternative to plate reverb for vocals.

TIP

It's important to choose the right kind of reverb for specific instruments, for all voices, and for individual projects. The natural hall, chamber, and room reverbs are great for string instruments and classical and jazz recordings; the artificial plate and spring reverbs are better for vocals, drums, and guitars.

Configuring Reverb Settings

Many reverb plug-ins have presets for different types of reverb—large hall, small hall, medium room, and so forth. These presets work fine in many settings, but you still might want to fine-tune the settings for your particular recording.

All reverb plug-ins work a little differently, but most feature some variation of the following controls:

Mix   Sometimes labeled Direct/Reflect or something similar, this control sets the mix between dry (direct) and wet (reflected) sounds. You can go from 100 percent dry (no reverb) to 100 percent wet, or anywhere in between. The wetter the mix, the more distant the original source will sound in the mix.

Predelay   This control specifies the amount of time between the start of the direct sound and the start of the first reflection, typically in milliseconds (ms). Predelay is useful for creating the size of the soundstage and for placing an instrument in the front or back of the mix. A shorter predelay moves the source back in the mix; a longer predelay moves the source closer to the listener.

Decay   Sometimes labeled Reverb Time, this control specifies how long the reverb itself lasts after the direct sound has ended. Too much decay time—if the reverb runs into the next sound from that instrument—and the source starts to sound muddy and less defined.

Steinberg's Roomworks reverb plug-in, included with Cubase.

Some reverb plug-ins also offer the following additional settings:

Size   This controls the size of the simulated room or hall.

Width   This controls the size of the stereo reverb image.

Early Reflections   This controls the sound of the first reflections of a sound before the main reverberation arrives.

Diffusion   This control lets you determine how evenly sound is distributed throughout the simulated space.

Dampening   High- and low-frequency dampening let you shorten the reverb decay at high- and low-frequency extremes. Low-frequency dampening simulates solid, sizeable spaces; high-frequency dampening simulates warmer, smaller rooms.

Stereo Versus Mono Reverb

Most digital reverbs are in stereo, which places even mono tracks in the three-dimensional soundfield. This is how you hear sound in the real world, so stereo reverb sounds natural to your ears. You typically can select how wide a stereo effect you want on any reverb track; the wider the reverb, the more natural the sound.

Some reverb plug-ins let you use mono reverb, which might be better for filling out specific tracks, such as individual drums in a kit. If you use a mono reverb, be sure it's panned to the same position as the original sound. In this situation, you want to anchor the reverb to the sound, not have it coming from another direction.

Tips for Best Results

Now that you know how important reverb is to your mix, let's look at a few tips that will make for better-sounding results:

Remember a little reverb goes a long way   It's always a good idea to err on the side of using too little rather than too much reverb. Go whole hog, and a track will sound muddy or even gimmicky. Add too little, and you can always add more if necessary. You don't want the reverb to draw attention to itself.

Go for realism   In the case of vocals and acoustic instruments, picture the performer in an acoustic space, real or imagined, and use reverb to try to re-create that space around him. That's how you get natural-sounding reverb.

Use short decay to make a track sound bigger   I'm talking reverb decays shorter than 1 second. Shorter decays make for a bigger, fuller sound without muddying things up.

Time the reverb to the tempo   You get a smoother-sounding and less-noticeable reverb when it's timed to the tempo of the song. You can do this by triggering the reverb off the snare drum backbeat and then adjusting the decay so it dies just before the next snare hit. This makes the decay "breathe" with the pulse of the track.

Pan reverbs for depth   Add more depth to a track by panning the source hard to one side and then send it to a mono reverb track panned hard to the other side. EQ each track a little differently, and you've added depth to the soundfield.

Adding Delay

Many engineers and musicians prefer to fatten their recordings with *delay* effects instead of reverb because reverb isn't very clean. You can have multiple reflections from multiple surfaces with reverb. In contrast, delay creates a single copy of the original sound, placed precisely after the original, which results in a much cleaner and more focused sound.

> **DEFINITION**
>
> **Delay** is an effect that creates a single copy of the original sound, positioned slightly after the original.

What Delay Is and How It Works

Delay is similar to but considerably simpler than reverb. It takes the original sound, copies it, delays it slightly, and adds the copy back to the original. This fattens the original sound without muddying it.

Yes, delay deals with reflected sound, like reverb, but with only a single reflection. Reverb, in emulating natural reverberation, contains multiple reflections from multiple directions. Reverb better positions a sound in the overall soundfield, while delay, when used properly, does a better job beefing up the sound while maintaining the original clarity.

Because of this simplicity, many engineers prefer using delay on some individual tracks, especially vocals. (You'll never hear delay used during the mastering process, however.) Delay is easy to control and won't balloon into the echoey effect you sometimes get with reverb. It's especially useful for adding some fullness into otherwise dry-sounding musical styles because it's a much cleaner effect than reverb, without the inherent muddiness introduced by reverb's multiple reflections.

Like reverb, delay can be either mono or stereo. Mono is probably more common when working with individual instruments or voices, although stereo delays can blend more subtly into the mix.

Applying Delay to Your Mix

Delay is typically added as a send effect to an individual track. Most DAWs provide their own delay plug-ins, and plenty of third-party plug-ins are available, too.

Steinberg's StereoDelay plug-in.

Here are the most common settings you can fiddle with in delay plug-ins:

Delay   This sets the timing of the delayed signal. A shorter delay positions the echo very close to the original signal; use longer delays for a more pronounced effect.

Feedback   This setting routes a proportion of the delay signal back through the delay line, creating a distinctive "regenerating" effect of delay after delay. If the delay is up in the mix, keep feedback relatively low. Set a higher feedback level if you want a spacier sound.

Mix   This configures the wet/dry mix of the effect.

Pan   For stereo delays, the pan setting helps you spatially position the delay channel in the soundfield.

In addition, many delay plug-ins offer one or more filters (typically high and low) to boost or cut the effect at given frequencies.

Tips for Best Results

How do you best use a delay plug-in? Here are some tips:

Use a mono delay to add depth to a track   In particular, apply a mono delay with a longer delay time to add ambience to a track.

Long delays push tracks back   Use delays longer than 100 ms to push a sound farther away in the mix.

Time the delay to the tempo   When you time the delay to the tempo of the track, you add depth without sticking out. This makes the delay pulse in time with the music and seem to disappear in the mix. If you *don't* time the delay to the tempo, it's too noticeable to the listener.

Fatten the sound by doubling   If you want to really fatten the sound of a voice or instrument, use delay to effectively double the track. Add a delay of between 60 and 120 ms, turn the feedback control to minimum, and raise the level of the doubled track to the same as the original source.

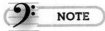

NOTE

Producer George Martin achieved a stronger vocal sound for The Beatles by having them actually sing their vocal lines twice. (That's manual doubling!) The slight inconsistencies in timing and pitch between the two performances made otherwise thin vocals sound that much thicker. Abbey Road engineer Ken Townsend automated this process with what he dubbed artificial double-tracking (ADT), which John Lennon nicknamed the "flanger"—and later led to the development of the similar flanging effect, discussed later in this chapter.

Adding Modulation Effects

Related to spatial effects are *modulation effects,* which modulate aspects of the original audio signal to create unique sounds. Modulation plug-ins use a low-frequency oscillator (LFO) to sweep a series of frequency notches throughout the frequency bandwidth. This creates a pulsing effect, as you hear the unnotched frequencies as peaks in the signal.

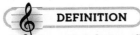

DEFINITION

Modulation effects modulate low-frequency notches on copies of the original track.

The most common modulation effects are choruses, flangers, and phasers (phase shifters). A phaser creates a small number of notches spread evenly across the frequency spectrum; flangers and choruses create a larger number of notches spaced harmonically in the spectrum.

Key for all modulation effects is the delay time. Phasers have the shortest delay, of only a few milliseconds. Flangers have a slightly longer delay time, in the 5- to 15-ms range. A chorus plug-in has a very long delay time, around 30 to 35 ms—close to what you find on a normal delay effect.

Chorus

Let's look at the *chorus* effect first because it's closest to the delay effect discussed previously. Use a chorus plug-in to simulate the sound of multiple instruments or voices playing or singing the same notes, complete with all the fluctuation in pitch and timing real musicians might produce.

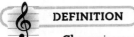

DEFINITION

Chorus is used to simulate the sound of multiple instruments or voices by modulating and delaying copies of the original.

The chorus effect works by mixing the original sound with one or more phase-shifted copies of that signal. The relatively long delay between the original sound and the copies is what makes it sound similar to the delay effect.

Use of a chorus really thickens the sound of a given track. It's very lush sounding and even can widen a track if you use it in stereo. Chorus is more commonly used on instrumental tracks (especially lead instruments, such as electric guitar or sax), but you also can use it on lead and background vocals to fatten the sound.

Steinberg's Chorus plug-in.

 TIP

If a vocal track is *slightly* out of tune, you can use the chorus effect to bring it back into the proper range. It's a subtler and more natural-sounding adjustment than applying autotuning.

Flanger

The *flanger* is much like the chorus effect but with significantly shorter delays. The original signal is copied, delayed slightly (typically less than 10 ms), modulated, and then added back to the original. The result is one you're no doubt familiar with, a kind of whooshing effect as the modulated peaks and valleys sweep by.

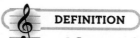 **DEFINITION**

A **flanger** modulates and delays a copy of the original sound to create a unique whooshing effect.

Whereas choruses help fatten a sound, flangers create a dramatically different sound that really stands out in the mix. Because of this, a little flanging goes a long way. Most flangers include a feedback control that lets you feed the sound back onto itself, creating more phase cancellations. You can use flanging on both instrumental and vocal tracks.

Steinberg's Flanger plug-in.

Phaser

A *phaser* (also called a *phase shifter*) is similar to a flanger in that it modulates a copy of the original sound and then feeds that copy back to the source. The big difference is that the phaser doesn't modulate the copy much if at all, so you end up with a less-dramatic but still distinctive whooshing effect. A phased sound seems to rise and fall as the modulation sweeps by.

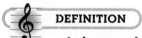

DEFINITION

A **phaser** or **phase shifter** modulates a copy of the original sound with little or no delay.

Steinberg's Phaser plug-in.

Tips, Tricks, and Traps for Effective Effects

As you've learned, the most used and most useful spatial effects are reverb and delay; modulation effects, although also useful, have more specialized use.

With that in mind, here are a handful of tips for improving your use of these and other effects—along with a few pitfalls to avoid.

Don't overprocess   Too many effects can ruin an otherwise okay track. It's about the performance, not the effects—no matter how much fun you might be having with them.

You can't save a poor performance with effects   It may be tempting to try to cover over a particularly poor track with layers and layers of distracting effects, but all you're doing is putting perfume on a pig. Yes, you can fatten up a thin performance with reverbs and delays, or even hide an out-of-tune performance with choruses or autotuning. But you can't fix really bad performances in the mix, no matter how hard you try. You just end up with an overprocessed mess of a track you're better off replacing or deleting.

Use delay instead of reverb for vocals   For many projects, delay may be a better choice than reverb to fatten up thin-sounding vocals (and instruments). It's a simpler effect that doesn't affect the spatial nature of the source. You also can try fattening up a lead vocal with delay and then applying a little reverb to add the necessary presence.

Stereo treatments can mess up your mono mix   It's fun and useful to apply various stereo effects such as reverb, but they may adversely impact how your song sounds in mono. Yes, I know you're mixing for stereo, not mono, but the song is still likely to be heard on some mono sources, such as AM radio or tinny television speakers. Always monitor your mix in mono at some point to be sure it still sounds good through a single speaker.

The Least You Need to Know

- Reverb is typically used to add space and presence to a track, making it sound as if the performer is in a larger room or concert hall filled with echoes and reflections.

- Delay is similar to reverb but with only a single echo; it's used to fatten up thin-sounding tracks.

- Modulation effects, such as choruses, flangers, and phasers, are applied more for effect—they can fill up the sound a little but also create their own unique modulated sounds.

Creating Better Mixes

How do the pros do it? Anybody can make professional-sounding mixes, if you know the secrets. In Part 6, you discover mixing techniques for vocals, acoustic and electric instruments, and drums. You also learn advanced techniques for better mixes and read about how mixing leads into the mastering process.

Applying Advanced Techniques

With the basics behind us, now let's look at some of the more advanced techniques you can employ to improve your mixing. I'm talking pitch correction, timing correction, automation, and much, much more.

Some of these techniques, such as pitch and timing correction, fall more into the premixing stage of the process. Others, like automation, are definitely part of mixing proper. In any case, these are advanced techniques that can result in better-sounding mixes.

In This Chapter

- Correcting pitch and timing
- How to automate complex operations
- Useful tips for a more successful mix
- Avoiding common mixing mistakes

Correcting Pitch

Auto-Tune. You've heard it. It's a plug-in that enables you to correct off-pitch vocals. It's used on a lot of the top songs of the past decade or two, whether you know it or not. Used subtly (and for only slightly off-key vocalists), you don't even know it's there. Used more aggressively, it creates distorted, slightly robotic-sounding vocals.

What Pitch Correction Does

Auto-Tune is a *pitch correction* plug-in. You can use it on vocal or instrumental tracks, although you hear it most used on lead vocals. (And truth be told, vocalists need it most.)

> **DEFINITION**
>
> **Auto-Tune** is a leading pitch correction plug-in. **Pitch correction** does exactly what its name implies—it automatically corrects the pitch of lead vocal or instrumental tracks.

When do you need pitch correction? It's useful when a singer can't stay on pitch. If the vocals go a little flat here or a little sharp there, or if the vocalist really misses a note, pitch correction can bring the flats and sharps more in line. Even though Auto-Tune and similar plug-ins require a lot of computer processing power, it's a lot easier than rerecording the vocalist—who might make even more mistakes the second time around.

You'd be surprised how often Auto-Tune is employed in modern recordings. I'm not sure if it's because today's singers are not quite as good as their historical predecessors (quite possible), or because as listeners we're less tolerant of little mistakes. All this computerized postprocessing has led us to expect perfection, and that's seldom found in the real world—even if we can artificially produce perfection with our computerized DAW programs and plug-ins.

That said, I feel Auto-Tune is too widely used. Hey, vocalists don't always sing perfectly on pitch. They just don't. An A isn't always sung at 440 Hz; sometimes a singer pitches it up to 441 or down to 439. Big deal. It's those slight variations from the norm that give great singers their distinctive voices. So Sinatra slid his notes; that's part of his sound. Apply Auto-Tune to the great singers of old, and they wouldn't sound quite like themselves, or near as great.

But that's just my opinion. Today's singers (and producers—especially producers) want everything to be pitch perfect. So they Auto-Tune the hell out of every vocal track and many lead instrumental tracks, too. It may not be natural, but it's what people expect.

Remember, as well, that Auto-Tune can create that distinctly robotic sound that's also way too common in today's music. When you crank up the various parameters to their illogical extremes, you get something like a vocoder effect, a not-so-subtle electronic, overprocessed, and definitely manipulated sound. Some people like it, and it's big in certain genres.

You also can use a pitch correction plug-in to create artificial harmony vocal parts. Just set the plug-in to correct the pitch to a harmony note instead of (actually, in addition to) the original note, and you have instant vocal harmony. Some pitch correctors can even add vibrato to the newly created part.

NOTE

Auto-Tune, from Antares Audio Technologies (antarestech.com), is just one of several pitch-correction plug-ins. It's the most popular, to be sure, but you can achieve similar effects with the Waves Tune (waves.com), Melodyne (celemony.com), or Mu Voice (mu-technologies.com) plug-ins. Steinberg even includes the PitchCorrect plug-in free with the Cubase DAW. All these pitch correction plug-ins do pretty much what Auto-Tune does, in pretty much the same way.

Using Auto-Tune

How do you use pitch correction? Although each plug-in is unique, all work in pretty much the same fashion.

AutoTune in action.

Auto-Tune has both an automatic and a graphical mode. The former is the easiest to use; the latter lets you fine-tune pitches visually, looking at the actual sine waves. At least when you're first starting out, go with the automatic mode, and follow these steps:

1. In the Input Type section, select the type of voice—soprano, alto, tenor, or bass.

2. In the Scale section, set the key of the song.

3. In the Pitch Correction Control section, set the Retune Speed. For a more natural sound, set this between 50 to 80 ms. For a more robotic sound, set it lower—all the way to 0 for most obvious effect.

4. Set other effects, such as Correction Style, Humanize, and Natural Vibrato, to taste.

Activate the plug-in, and your vocal track will be corrected, automatically.

Fixing Timing Issues

If you can alter the vertical position (pitch) of a note, why not the horizontal position (timing)? Well, you can, even though that requires a lot more work in your DAW.

Timing correction may be necessary if you have a drummer who doesn't always play on the beat—some of his snare hits might be a tad behind the beat or ahead of it. Or both. Or maybe the lead guitarist took a few too many liberties with the rhythm, and his line just doesn't sound right. Or maybe the entire horn section got a little off on a big accent. All these things happen.

Fortunately, most DAWs let you edit the individual audio samples that comprise each track in your mix. In Cubase, for example, this is done by double-clicking on a sample to open the sample editor. From there, you can define the underlying beat and then cut and paste pieces of the sample to line up with the beats.

A better approach is to "warp" sections of the sample to better fit the underlying beat. Pro Tools calls this Elastic Audio; Cubase calls it Time Warp. Whichever DAW you use, you apply warp markers or tabs to the important transients. On a drum track, these typically represent the bass drum and snare drum hits, often on quarter notes or eighth notes. You then use your mouse to click and grab the markers to move them into better positions on the grid. This provides a more natural repositioning of the beats than simple cutting and pasting and is a little easier to do, too.

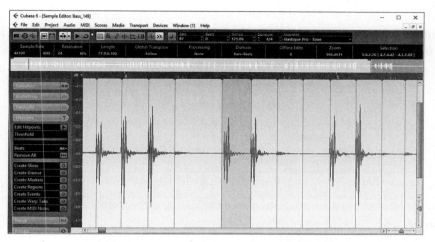

Working with warp markers in the Cubase sample editor.

Timing correction of this sort can be used on any track in your mix. It's most often used on drum tracks to help the bass drum and snare drum hits line up more precisely with the underlying beat, thus establishing a steadier groove that doesn't speed up or slow down from measure to measure.

 TIP

Another way to create a "perfect" drum part is to find one perfect measure, where every note is in exactly the right place, and then copy that measure to fill out the entire song.

Using Automation

Mixing is complicated enough when all the settings stay constant throughout the entire length of a recording. But what do you do when the settings need to change halfway through—when you need to change a track's volume level, or temporarily apply a specific effect?

In the old days, the final mixdown took place in real time. The final mix was recorded direct to tape, which meant the engineer had to twiddle the knobs, slide the sliders, and punch the buttons as the tape rolled. If he missed an operation, he had to rewind the tape and try it again. This made mixing a somewhat stressful process.

Today, fortunately, the process is less stressful. Thanks to computerization, all the mid-project adjustments you make are recorded along with the audio tracks in a special *automation* track. When you play back the mix, the automation track is played back as well, with the adjustments you recorded earlier automatically applied. And when you master your mix to the final stereo file, all the automated changes take place, just as if you were twiddling the knobs yourself.

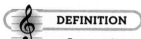

DEFINITION

Automation enables you to program control changes into your recording, so that on playback, these changes happen automatically.

Automating changes to your mix is as easy as following these steps:

1. Click the "write automation" button for a given track or tracks within your DAW.

2. Start playback.

3. Make your changes in real time as the track plays. This can be any type of change, from inserting an effect to sliding the faders or panning controls. Any changes you make are recorded to the automation track.

Play back the automation by pressing the "read automation" button to enable the automation track during playback and mixdown.

By the way, once you create an automation track, most DAWs let you edit it. For example, to edit volume changes, use your mouse to move the volume level up or down on the automation track.

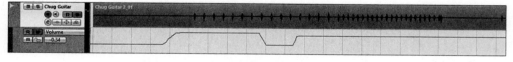

An audio track and its accompanying automation track in Cubase.

Tips for a Better Mix

Now let's look at some tips you can employ to make your mixes more solid. There's a lot of good stuff here, in no particular order.

Know What the Artist Expects

Your job is a lot easier if you know what the artist and producer expect from you. To that end, it helps if they provide you some examples of what they like and what they're looking for. When you get these reference tracks, *listen to them*—and figure out how a particular sound was achieved.

Listen Before You Mix

You should start every new session by listening to the raw tracks recorded by the recording engineer. (Even if you made the recordings, you should still listen to them.) Most recording engineers do a little premixing while they're recording, so you'll know kind of what they had in mind. In any case, this initial mix is a good place to start.

Take a Break

As a mixing engineer, your ears are your instrument—and you can overwork them. Force yourself to take a 5- or 10-minute break every hour or so to give your ears a rest. When you come back to the mixing console or computer keyboards, your ears will be refreshed, and so will you.

Start Over If You're Stuck

It happens. You're hip-deep in a project, and all of sudden everything goes south. Nothing sounds right, and you can't fiddle enough with the faders to bring it back into range. The more you fiddle, the worse it sounds.

When you've blocked yourself into a corner like this, the best thing to do is to start over. Bring down all the faders, and start fresh. Yeah, you'll lose a little work, but you had already lost your way anyway.

Mix for Depth

I've talked a lot about positioning elements left to right in the stereo soundfield and higher or lower in terms of volume level. But you also need to think in terms of depth—whether specific voices and instruments are pulled forward or pushed back in the mix. Levels affect depth, of course, but so do effects such as reverb, delay, and chorus.

The more effects you pile onto a track, the farther back it fades. Drier tracks sound more up front.

Utilize depth not only to emphasize key elements such as vocals, but also to separate tracks in the mix. You want to create a three-dimensional mix that adds some depth to the recording.

Make It Wider

Most instruments are recorded and mixed in mono. That's fine, but sometimes you want to create a wider soundstage for a given track.

You can do this by duplicating the mono track so you have two identical tracks. Pan one to the left and one an equal distance to the right. This creates a phantom center channel while creating a wider image for the track. Make one side louder than the other to position the phantom image off-center.

 TIP

You can beef up the phantom center effect even more by creating a third copy of the original track and positioning it dead center.

Another option here is to use a mono-to-stereo plug-in. This type of plug-in uses a comb filter to separate the source into two channels, with the phase of one side the inverse of the other. Played back, they sum back together to create a phantom mono center track.

Double-Track the Vocals

Here's a trick that dates all the way back to the early days of The Beatles: you can make a thin lead vocal track sound thicker by double-tracking it.

The crudest way to double-track vocals is to have the vocalist sing his or her part twice. Mix the two tracks together in a pleasing way, and you have automatic vocal thickening.

Another approach is to copy a single vocal track. In your DAW program, grab the copy and nudge it slightly left or right, ahead of or behind the original. This adds a delay to the vocal, which fattens up the sound.

How far apart should the two tracks be? If the delay is too short, the two signals cancel each other out and actually make the sound thinner. If the delay is too long, you get an echo effect, which you probably don't want. Use your ears to determine the optimal delay time.

TIP

Double-tracking isn't limited to just lead vocal tracks. You can double-track any instrument or vocal part, including both lead guitars and backing vocals.

Sync Effects in Tempo

When dealing with time-based effects such as delays and choruses, be sure the effect is sync'd to the tempo of the song. This way the listener hears the result of the effect without the effect itself sticking out. The pulse of the effect is masked by the pulse of the song.

Mute the Vocals

Now, a noise gate will achieve the same affect, but you also can mute vocal tracks any time you have a silence of more than a 1 or 2 seconds. Vocalists tend to do a lot of throat clearing and coughing and harrumphing and such (the animals!), so mute 'em when they're not singing.

Less Is More

When it comes to EQ and effects, a little goes a long way. Inexperienced engineers apply effects a little too liberally; engineers with more experience (and skill) know they need to add the minimum amount of processing to their tracks.

When in doubt, dial down the effects and minimize the equalization. You can always add more if it isn't enough.

Mix for the Medium

It's important to know that every listener listens differently—and on different devices. You're listening to your mix on expensive studio monitor speakers, which few if any listeners have. Some people listen through big audiophile speakers in their living rooms; some listen through smaller bookshelf speakers; some listen through tiny, tinny surround-sound cubes or sound bars; some listen through the small speakers in their laptop computers; some listen through the speakers built into their car audio systems; and some listen through earbuds on their phones or iPods.

You need to take all these listening experiences into account and be sure your mix sounds good on every popular device. That means adding different types of speakers in your mixing room, as well as creating MP3 files of your mix and streaming them to a laptop computer or downloading them to a smartphone. A mix might sound perfect in the mixing room but not have the right stuff for listeners jogging with headphones.

Avoiding Common Mixing Mistakes

Now that you've learned some tricks that will punch up your mixes, let's take a look at some traps you want to avoid.

The Low End Is Too Loud

Yes, a solid bottom is important. But too much bass can overpower the more important lead parts—as well as eat up too much headroom and make it more difficult to get a sufficiently loud master.

This often comes from an improperly set up mixing environment. If you aren't getting good lows in your mixing room, the tendency is to boost the bass to compensate until it sounds good, too. However, if your monitor speakers aren't putting out the bass, or if your room is absorbing too much bass, what you're really doing is overcompensating. When the bass-boosted tracks are played back on a better system or in a room with better acoustics, the low end will be way too loud.

So work on the acoustics of your mixing room, and add a subwoofer if your main monitors don't have enough oomph. And don't let yourself pull up the sliders too far on the bass and bass drum. You want the low end of your mix to be punchy but not overpowering.

The Mix Is Too Harsh

Just as cranking up the bass is often an irresistible temptation, so is going too bright—typically by boosting frequencies between 2 and 5 kHz for various tracks. This adds energy to the mix, no denying it, but too much of a good thing turns the whole mix harsh.

The solution is to use subtractive instead of additive EQ. Instead of boosting a track in the magic range to make it stand out, cut that range in surrounding tracks. You still achieve the intended result of making a given track or tracks stand out, but you do so without harshening the entire mix.

The Mix Is Muddy

The mix gets muddy when there's too much happening in the low end and you have multiple low-frequency tracks (or even brighter tracks with low-frequency noise) competing with each other. To fix this, start by applying high filters on any tracks that don't play in the low end. This will eliminate the unwanted noise. Then work on carving EQ holes for the bass, bass drum, and other low-end tracks so they fit better together. It's kind of like fitting together a giant jigsaw puzzle, but you'll clean up that muddy mix.

Too Much in the Middle

Remember that time I said you want to pan important tracks to the middle? Or that other time I said the same thing? Or the 32 other times I repeated that advice?

Well, I'm glad you took that advice to heart, but you can overdo it. If every track is so important that you pan them all to the center of the soundstage, you have a very muddled middle. You need to reassess your priorities and move some of those tracks off to the side. If every track is the most important, none of them are important. Be sure the lead vocals (and bass and bass drum) are in the middle, and pan everything else somewhere else.

The Details Are Buried

When you have a lot happening in the mix, it's easy for some of the important details to get lost. You need to direct the listener toward the most important elements from moment to moment. That means leveling up individual tracks for a measure or beat or two and then bringing them back down so something else gets a chance to shine. You need to know what's important and when and then use your mixing magic to bring it forward at the right time.

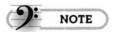 **NOTE**

Don't let important stuff get buried in the mix; if it really can be buried, maybe it shouldn't be there in the first place.

Constancy Isn't Always Best

It's tempting to get a great sound for a particular instrument or voice and then lean back and use that sound over the entire length of the song. That might be a good idea, or it might not be.

Sometimes the same instrument or voice needs to sound different in different sections of the song. A solo piano intro on a ballad requires one set of EQ and effects, but that same piano needs to sound different when it's providing rhythmic backing in a later section. Be prepared to re-EQ and re-effect any track in different sections of the song, either via automation or by splitting the track in places and applying different EQ and effects as necessary.

Not Listening

It's easy to apply the advice given here and in other places and just automatically dial in specific EQ settings or effects. That kind of by-the-book mixing gets you in the ballpark, but it won't let you hit any home runs. Any recommended settings you run across are just starting points; you need to then fine-tune the settings for your particular project and situation.

Bottom line: use your ears and let them tell you when it sounds right. All the numbers in all the books in the world are not as good as your ears telling you that you need a different EQ or effect.

Not Listening Through Different Speakers

This is another point I've tried to make throughout the book, but remember that not every person out there will listen to your music through the same set of speakers. Be sure you preview your mix through a variety of speakers, from high-end audiophile floor-standing units to cheapie little Bluetooth speakers you use to listen in the shower. Listen in stereo and mono, and through speakers, headphones, and earbuds. Only sign off on the mix when you know it sounds great under the most common listening conditions.

 TIP

Remember to save your work regularly (every 10 to 15 minutes or so) and always—*always*—back up your work at the end of the day. You don't want to lose a day's work, or more, if your computer crashes. Better safe than sorry.

Hoping It Can Be Fixed in Mastering

Maybe you're not perfectly satisfied with a given mix. Maybe you think it outright sucks. But you're tired of fighting it and need to move on. No problem, right? The mastering engineer can fix it up.

Except he probably can't. Just as you can't fix a bad recording in the mix, you can't fix a bad mix in the mastering. Mastering is time for polishing and fine-tuning, not for enacting massive changes. If it doesn't sound right, the mastering engineer won't be able to fix it.

A bad mix is your responsibility. If it ain't right, fix it before passing it on.

The Least You Need to Know

- Pitch correction, in the form of Auto-Tune and similar plug-ins, lets you correct off-key singers—and create that robotic vocal effect common in today's music.
- If a drummer or other musician is playing off the beat, use your DAW's editing or warp features to drag the part back where it should be.
- Most DAWs let you automate complex mixing operations so you can change levels, EQ, and effects in the middle of a song.
- There are lots of things you can do to improve your mix—and avoid mistakes—but the best thing you can do is trust your ears. If it doesn't sound right, fix it!

Mixing Vocals

In the next few chapters, we look at how to mix specific instruments and vocals—starting, in this chapter, with vocals. What do you need to do to create powerful-sounding vocal tracks? Read on to find out.

In This Chapter

- The best ways to record vocals for mixing
- The most effective settings for panning, EQ, compression, reverb, and more
- How mixing backing vocals differs from mixing lead vocals

Recording Vocals

A great vocal mix starts in the recording studio. Recording vocals isn't quite the same as recording most acoustic instruments.

Finding the Right Space

The first thing you need to consider when recording vocals is where exactly you'll be doing the recording. Now, this isn't an issue when you're in a big professional recording studio, but it can be problematic if you're recording in your own home.

First, you probably don't want to record your vocals out in the middle of everything else. Most vocalists prefer a little privacy when they're singing, which you can achieve by sectioning off your main recording space with baffles or by putting the singer in a separate room or vocal booth.

Some engineers prefer a vocal space to have some degree of reverberation. To this way of thinking, it's better to record vocals with a little natural reverb than to lay down totally dry tracks; the sound of a "live" room adds presence to the vocals, filling them out. (This is why you like the sound of your voice singing in a shower stall or stairwell; a full voice sounds better than a thin one.)

If you're going for a sound with natural reverb, don't rule out recording your vocals in a stairwell, garage, or bathroom. (Don't laugh; many professional studios use some variation of this technique.) These areas have a very "live" sound with lots of reflections and reverberation from all the hard surfaces. You want some of that reverberation to make its way back to the microphone to mix with the vocalist's natural singing voice.

Other engineers prefer to minimize the effect of the room on the vocal tracks. This means recording in a relatively dry room, without any natural reverberation or reflections. Reverb and other effects can then be added later in the mixing process.

To record this type of neutral vocal track, position the microphone in the middle of the room, away from any reflecting walls or surfaces. You also may need to use some acoustical foam, screens, or room dividers to soak up any stray reflections.

Choosing a Vocal Mic

Garbage in, garbage out—that old adage applies particularly to recording vocals. A recording made with a low-quality microphone is going to sound mediocre, no matter how much post-recording processing you apply during mixing. Start with a recording from a high-quality mic, however, and your mixing job gets a whole lot easier.

In other words, to create a high-quality recording, you have to start with a high-quality mic.

Three primary types of microphones are used for recording today:

- *Dynamic mics* record via electromagnetic induction, with a small diaphragm inside the mic vibrating under sound pressure.

- *Condenser mics* also utilize a vibrating diaphragm inside the mic; these mics are powered by an outboard power source (sometimes called *phantom power*) and are more sensitive than dynamic mics.

- *Ribbon mics* are even more sensitive than condenser mics, with a smoother sound. They're also the most expensive mics out there.

Of these three types, condenser mics are most suitable for recording vocals. (They are not well suited to recording loud instruments—they're too sensitive for that.) Yeah, these are pricey mics, but vocal tracks are your most important tracks, and the vocal mic is your most important mic.

If you're using a condenser mic, you'll probably need a preamplifier to generate a strong-enough signal for recording. Many different models are available, but look for one with tube emulation that gives a little added warmth to the vocals.

To record lead vocals without any room reverberation, use a mic with a slightly directional *cardioid* pattern. To add natural room reverb, or to record a group of vocalists, use a mic with an *omnidirectional* pattern.

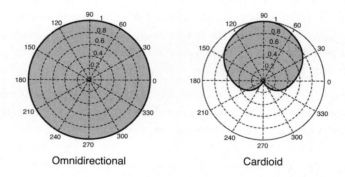

Ominidirectional and cardioid pickup patterns.

DEFINITION

Dynamic mics record via electromagnetic induction and require no external power. **Condenser mics** are more sensitive and require an outboard power source. **Ribbon mics** also need outboard power and are even more sensitive than condensers. **Phantom power** is the outboard power source used to power condenser mics. **Omnidirectional** mics pick up equally well from all directions. **Cardioid** mics pick up sound in a heart-shaped pattern in front and to the sides of the mic.

If you're recording a group of singers (either backing vocalists or a choir), you probably want to use two microphones. When you set up two mics, you give yourself the option during mixing to pan the vocals across the entire stereo soundfield.

Making the Recording

Whatever type of sound you're going for, you need to place the mic in front of the vocalist on a sturdy stand. You definitely don't want the singer to hold the microphone when recording; you also don't want to tempt the singer to grab the mic stand as she would during a live performance. (Any movement of the mic or the stand will be heard on the recording—not ideal.) The best approach is to use a tall boom stand that lets you hang the mic down in front of the singer. And always use a windscreen or pop filter to reduce sibilance.

That brings us to the recording process itself. Vocalists can sometimes be maddeningly inconsistent, not only in their pitch and vocal inflections but also in how they approach the microphone. Don't be surprised to see the vocalist backing up and leaning forward throughout the recording, which plays havoc with your input levels. If she's too close to the mic, the meters go into the red; if she's too far away, the meters might not move at all. Short of nailing the vocalist in place precisely 6 inches away from the mic (a near-perfect distance), how do you cope with this?

One solution, of course, is to work the sliders mercilessly throughout the entire recording. This requires a lot of skill and no little amount of effort, but good engineers can make it work. A better solution, however, might be to invest in an outboard compressor unit, which is inserted into the chain between the mic (or mic preamp) and the mixing board/input box. Just like the compressor plug-ins you use during the mixing process, the outboard compressor automatically lowers the volume when the input exceeds a certain threshold, thus guarding against level peaks when the vocalist leans too far forward or turns up the volume. The compressor also can be set to boost low volume levels, thus evening out any dynamic flux. You'll probably still want to add a little more compression during mixing, but compressing during recording is de rigueur for recording vocals.

Mixing Lead Vocals

I've talked a lot about recording vocals throughout this book, but let's centralize and elaborate on that information here. I'll start with the lead vocal track—the most important part of the mix.

Setting Levels and Panning

Because the lead vocal is the most important track, you want to be certain it's mixed up front in the mix. That means ensuring it's louder than the backing tracks and dead center in the stereo soundfield. It's probably the first track you want to mix, so make it as prominent as you can.

Applying EQ

As noted in Chapter 14, vocal tracks benefit from minimal equalization. Use EQ only if you're working with a weak voice or one that has peculiar vocal characteristics you want to minimize, or if you're having trouble with vocals getting buried in a busy mix.

I won't go into all the EQ tips discussed in Chapter 14, but know that cutting or boosting in specific frequency bands can dramatically impact the color of the vocal sound, in effect correcting a singer's unique limitations. Note the following bands and how they affect vocal characteristics:

100 to 200 Hz: Warmth

1,000 to 2,000 Hz: Nasality

2,500 to 4,000 Hz: Harshness

5,000 Hz: Presence

6,000 Hz: Brightness/dullness

 TIP

If the vocals are having trouble cutting through a busy mix, add a slight boost around 2,500 to 3,000 Hz (for men) or 3,000 to 3,500 Hz (for women). Don't boost too much, however, or the vocals will get harsh.

There's one more EQ tip you may want to apply to the lead vocal track: as discussed in Chapter 14, you can carve holes in the EQ of other tracks to help the vocal tracks stand out. Because vocal intelligibility relies on frequencies in the 1,000 to 4,000 Hz range, if you cut this range in other instruments, such as guitars and keyboards, you reduce the overlap with the vocals. This pretty much gives this range to the vocals alone, which makes them easier to hear and understand in the mix.

Applying Reverb, Compression, and Other Effects

Vocal tracks benefit from applying a variety of insert and send effects. In particular, you need to consider noise gating, compression, reverb, and de-essing.

Let's start with the noise gate, which removes low-level noise from a track. This is particularly important for vocal tracks because a gate can get rid of unwanted lip smacking, page turning, and breathing noises recorded by the vocal mic. It's essential, so set a medium threshold to cut off the noise without losing any intimate notes.

Next is the compressor. Now, the vocals were probably compressed to a degree during recording, but you still may need to apply a little more compression during the mixing process. A good place to start is to set a threshold in the −8 to −3 dB range, along with a corresponding gain. Experiment with a 2:1 to 6:1 ratio, and be sure you set a fast attack, medium release, and soft knee. If you're dealing with loud vocals in a loud hard rock mix, you can set a little faster release and a slightly higher ratio—in the 4:1 to 10:1 range.

Another important effect you can apply to a vocal track is de-essing, which reduces sibilance—those hard, spitty S's, Z's, and CH's. When you use a de-esser, you can add back upper mids and highs in the EQ process, which helps push the vocals above the other tracks in the mix.

Now we come to reverb and delay, both of which are important for fattening up your vocal tracks. Delay especially makes a vocal track sound fuller, and many engineers apply delay almost as a matter of course. Time the delay to the tempo of the track, either in eighth or quarter notes. Some engineers like to a use a stereo delay with different timings on either channel—quarter note on one side and dotted eighth note or eighth note triplet on the other. Other engineers like a shorter slapback delay. It's your choice.

TIP

Many engineers like to use a long delay, in effect doubling the vocal track. Doubling the track fattens out the sound, which is nice if you have thin vocals. (You also can use the chorus effect for this.)

After you've added delay, if the vocal track still sounds too thin or dry, you can apply a little reverb. Don't go overboard here; you don't want a rock singer to sound like an opera singer in a big concert hall. Too much vocal reverb is the sign of an inexperienced engineer. You want to apply reverb subtly and only if necessary. For this reason, a plate reverb might be a better choice than a hall or room reverb. Whatever type of reverb you use, dial up a longer initial delay time with fewer early reflections and more later reverb to make the vocal sit farther forward in the mix.

NOTE

Learn more about gating, compression, and de-essing in Chapter 13. Turn to Chapter 15 for more on reverb and delay.

Mixing Backing Vocals

Just about everything noted about lead vocals also applies to backing vocals. It's better if you have two tracks to work with, of course (from recording with two mics) so you can pan the vocals away from the center. You want the backing vocals to be panned hard left and hard right. If you don't have two tracks available, copy the single track and pan them to either side, as noted.

You want the backing vocals to sit behind the lead vocal, so that means sliding down the faders a tad. You also can use EQ to make the backing vocals sound a little less aggressive. Roll off the bass frequencies to make them sit a little better in the mix.

Reverb is also a good effect to apply to backing vocals. You want more reverb on the backing vocals than you do on the lead. Dial up the predelay and early reflections to push the backing vocals farther back in the mix.

You want the backing vocals to sound good but sit in the background. They should support the lead vocal, not compete with it.

The Least You Need to Know

- To make mixing easier, record vocals with a quality microphone with a pop filter and add compression during recording.
- Use EQ sparingly, if at all, to correct thin or otherwise imperfect vocals.
- Gate the vocals to remove unwanted noise, and use a de-esser to reduce sibilants.
- Apply additional compression if necessary during mixing.
- Add delay to fatten the sound, and throw in a little reverb if it still sounds too dry.
- Apply these same techniques to backing vocals, but be sure they're mixed lower and panned hard left and right in the mix.

Mixing Instruments

I covered mixing vocals in the previous chapter; as you learned, you can employ a number of tricks to enhance recorded vocal tracks during the mixing process. But unless you're recording an a cappella choir, you also have to deal with one or more instruments in the mix.

Whether you're dealing with a solo piano, a string quartet, or a rock or country band, you need to know how to mix all those various instruments together. That's what I explain in this chapter.

In This Chapter

- Recording acoustic and electric instruments
- The best ways to mix electric and acoustic guitars
- Ways to mix bass guitars
- Ways to mix pianos and keyboards
- Ways to mix horns and strings

Recording Instruments

As you've learned, a great mix starts with a great recording. You can fix some things in the mix, but your work will be a lot easier if you have great-sounding tracks to begin with. That means you or your recording engineer has to work with each instrument being played to produce the best possible recording.

Not surprisingly, you approach each instrument differently in the recording studio. How you record a horn section differs from how you record a lead guitar or electric piano, from the types of mics you use to how many tracks you employ.

In addition, the type of music you're working with affects your recording strategy. As you might imagine, recording a classical string quartet is a much different job than recording a four-piece rock band—even though the same number of instruments is involved. Recording classical music requires different mic'ing strategies than recording rock and other types of popular music does. You might only use two mics to record the four strings, while the rock band might require 16 or more mics (multiple mics on the drums!) with some instruments plugged directly into the computer or mixing console. What's more, you have different dynamics to worry about. Classical music can vary considerably between loud and soft passages, whereas rock music is mainly loud.

This is why you need to know what you're recording up front, so you know what to expect and prepare for.

Recording Acoustic Instruments

Let's start with how you approach recording acoustic instruments—acoustic piano and guitar, horns, and strings. (Drums are trickier and get a chapter of their own—Chapter 19.)

First, you need to choose the right type of microphone. For most acoustic instruments, dynamic mics are best because they can better handle a wider dynamic range and louder volume levels. They're especially suited for louder instruments, such as brass and woodwinds.

The only exceptions to this are some softer acoustic instruments, such as strings, that can be mic'd with more sensitive condenser mics. Know, however, that condensers are not the best choice for louder instruments.

When you're mic'ing together a group of instruments, such as with a string or horn section, choose a mic with an omnidirectional or cardioid pattern. (This type of mic is also good for recording solo instruments when you want to capture some of the natural room reverberation.) Use a directional mic if you want to record a solo instrument really dry with no reverb.

TIP

If you're on a budget, a good all-around microphone is the Shure SM57, priced about $100. This dynamic mic (with a cardioid pattern) is a longtime standard for both live and recording purposes and can be used to record just about any kind of instrument, from acoustic guitars to drums. In a pinch, you also can use the SM57 to record vocals.

Now let's examine how you want to record specific instruments:

Acoustic piano   Most rock, pop, and jazz recordings feature close-mic'd pianos. You can use a single mic, but you'll probably opt for placing two mics inside the piano—one toward the lower strings and the other toward the upper. For the most direct sound, position the mics just a few inches from the strings; for a more open sound, pull the mics back a bit (up to 1 foot, max). For a more classical sound, position the mics a few feet in front of the piano. Whichever approach you use, the dual mics give you two tracks you can use to create a strong stereo effect during mixing.

Acoustic guitar   Given its softer acoustic nature, you can get good results by using condenser mics on this instrument, although a good dynamic mic will work in a pinch. Use a single mic, facing the area between the soundhole and the top of the fretboard, for a mono track. If you want to record in stereo, you have a variety of options. You can position two mics on top of each other (head to head, next to each other, facing slightly apart) or with one mic near the soundhole and the other farther up the neck. Position the mics closer to the instrument for a warmer sound.

Solo horns   You want to use a dynamic mic to record both brass and woodwinds (except flutes, which benefit from a more sensitive condenser mic). Position the mic 3 to 6 feet from the instrument and about 6 inches below the line of sight of the bell or horn. Move the mic in for more warmth or back to capture more of the room sound.

Horn sections   You have lots of choices when mic'ing a horn section. How you do it kind of depends on if you want the section to sound like a single instrument or if you want to hear each instrument separately. For the former, use a set of stereo mics positioned together in a V shape in front of the section. For the latter, use one mic per player, 1 or 2 feet in front of each instrument. Or you can bridge the two approaches by employing one mic per every two (or so) players.

Solo strings   For violins and violas, position the mic 2 to 4 feet above the instrument, aimed at one of the f-holes. For cellos and basses, position the mic 1 or 2 feet in front of the instrument, aimed directly at the bridge. Move in a little closer if you want more warmth. Use a condenser or ribbon microphone.

String sections   Use two mics to record a string section, positioned in front of the strings at about head height. Place the two mics about 1 foot apart—the approximate distance between your ears. You can then experiment with pointing the mics directly forward or slightly outward in a V shape. Use condenser mics.

Recording Electric Instruments

Electric instruments, such as electric guitars and basses, can be recorded via microphone (aimed at the instrument's amplifier) or via direct injection (DI), where the instrument is plugged directly into the computer or mixing console. There are avid proponents of each approach.

Many guitarists prefer to set up their entire sound using a combination of pedals and amplifier settings. (Obviously, the instrument matters, too.) In this situation, you want to position a dynamic microphone directly in front of (almost touching) the front grill of the amp.

Many engineers prefer to direct inject electric instruments. This approach puts more control in the hands of the engineer and often results in cleaner recordings (no room noise and less opportunity for hum and hiss). Use a quality *DI box* to connect the instrument directly to the computer or mixing unit. With this approach, effects can be added later to achieve different types of sound.

DEFINITION

A **DI box** is a unit that converts an instrument's mic-level balanced signal into a line-level unbalanced signal.

Some engineers like to mix the sound recorded via direct injection with that recorded by placing a microphone in front of the instrument's amplifier, getting the best of both worlds.

Behringer's DI600P DI box (behringer.com).

Mixing Guitars

You can employ lots of mixing techniques when including acoustic and electric guitars in your recordings. Which you use depends a lot on the role of the specific instrument.

Levels and Panning

The lead guitar needs to come up in the mix when it's soloing and push back when it's noodling around behind the vocals or other instruments. It's typically panned in the center of the sound-stage unless the center is really cluttered, in which case you'd pan it slightly off-center.

Rhythm guitars need to stay back in the mix. Pan them to either the 11:00 (left of center) or 1:00 (right of center) positions, on the opposite side of where you pan the piano or other keyboards.

 TIP

If the guitar was recorded with multiple mics (different distances from the amp or guitar itself), you'll need to carefully mix the sounds from the multiple sources to create the final guitar sound.

EQ and Effects

You compress electric and acoustic guitars slightly differently. For electrics, set the threshold in the −14 to −10 dB range; the ratio between 2:1 and 5:1 (higher if you want more sustain); and set a fast attack, medium release, and a hard knee. Acoustic guitar tracks may not need much compression, but if yours do, set the threshold in the −14 to −10 dB range, use a 2:1 to 5:1 ratio, and use a fast attack and medium release. Knee can be either hard or soft.

There's lots of EQ you can do to electric guitar tracks. I discussed most of them back in Chapter 14, so turn there for more. In general, you can cut the very low frequencies, boost the low-mids for more warmth and a fuller sound, boost the high-mids a bit to enhance the attack, and boost the highs (above 8,000 Hz) to add some high-end sparkle.

Acoustic guitars don't need much if any EQ, especially if they're recorded well. That said, you might want to roll off everything below 60 Hz to get rid of string squeaks and maybe even cut the 80 to 150 Hz range to reduce boominess. If the sound's a little harsh, try cutting 1,000 to 3,000 Hz or boosting in the 120 to 200 Hz range. You also can add more definition with a slight boost around 2,000 Hz and add a little sparkle with a boost between 5,000 and 10,000 Hz.

Both electric and acoustic guitars should benefit from a little reverb. Use a room reverb with a short delay time.

You probably don't need to add other effects to electric guitar tracks, assuming the guitarist shaped the recorded sound with his own pedals and effects—although a short delay might sound nice on lead lines. You might not need other effects on acoustic guitar tracks, either, although some engineers like to apply a subtle chorus effect to fill out the sound.

Mixing Bass Guitars

The bass guitar track is one of the key tracks in any type of music. You need the bass to anchor the entire recording—it needs to be solid and present without becoming dominant.

Levels and Panning

In terms of levels, bass needs to be fairly prominent but not too much so. Some engineers feel the bass is better felt than heard; others want to hear every thump and pluck. In other words, season to taste.

In terms of stereo placement, however, there is little debate. The bass needs to be panned direct center, along with the bass drum. Also, for a more spacious bass sound, you can duplicate the bass track and pan one far left and one far right. It still sounds in the center, even though it's coming from both sides.

EQ and Effects

Bass tracks need a fair amount of compression. Set the threshold between −20 and −2 dB; set the ratio between 4:1 and 10:1; and set fast attack, medium release, and a hard knee.

You can apply lots of equalization to bass guitar tracks, depending on the sound you want to achieve. I won't go through all of them here; turn to Chapter 14 to learn them.

You probably don't need or want to add a lot of other effects to the bass track. Reverb and delay are no-nos, and you don't need chorusing or other modulation effects. Just play with the compression and EQ, and you should end up with a solid bass track.

Mixing Pianos and Keyboards

In most rock and popular music, keyboards are used as backing instruments. Obviously, things are different in jazz and cabaret music, where the piano is second only to the vocal or lead instrument.

Levels and Panning

For rock/pop music, dial the keyboards back in the mix. For cabaret music, you can pull the piano back up, but be sure it doesn't overwhelm the vocalist. For jazz music, aim for a mix between all the instruments—but pull up the piano during solo passages.

When the keyboard is part of the rhythm section, pan the tracks to either the 11:00 or 1:00 position in the stereo soundfield, opposite where you pan the rhythm guitar. For cabaret music, pan a stereo piano hard left and right. For jazz, pick a place on the stereo soundstage, and drop it there.

EQ and Effects

If recorded properly, a good acoustic piano may not need any compression. If you do feel the need to compress, set a ratio in the 2:1 to 4:1 range and use a fast attack and a slow release.

Likewise, you probably don't need much if any EQ on your acoustic piano tracks. That said, you can add a bit more bottom by boosting the 60 to 120 Hz range, warm up the sound by boosting the 100 to 200 Hz range, improve clarity by boosting at 2,500 Hz, and add a little airiness by boosting high up in the 8,000 to 15,000 Hz range.

Solo piano can benefit from a judicious use of room reverb to give it that natural live sound. Other effects are probably unnecessary.

Mixing Horns

You might not have the opportunity to work much with horn sections (the heyday of bands like Chicago and Blood, Sweat and Tears is long gone), but horns can definitely add a lot to the mix.

In most instances, you need the horns back in the mix. You can bring up individual horns for solo instrumental parts, of course, but in most musical genres, horns stay in the background. (Jazz is an exception, where solo saxes and trumpets are as important—and as front and center—as every other instrument.)

If you want a horn section to sound as a single instrument (as with the horn hits in soul music), pan them to the same position either left or right of center. If you want to separate the individual horns in a section mix, spread their tracks left to right across the stereo soundstage. Obviously, solo horns can be panned directly or near center.

 TIP

If you're dealing with a small (two- or three-piece) horn section, make it sound fatter by duplicating the tracks and panning them hard right and left. Adding a slight distortion effect helps fatten them, too.

Mixing Strings

In most popular records, strings are used as sweetening. That means dialing them back in the mix unless you have specific instrumental sections.

Solo strings, such as violins and cellos, can be panned center or near center. Pan string sections hard left and right in stereo to emulate the live sound.

If you're dealing with classical recordings, your goal is to achieve the right balance for the entire ensemble. You're typically dealing with fewer mics and fewer tracks (like two), so pan the mics hard left and right and be sure everything's balanced properly. You probably don't need much if any compression and EQ.

The Least You Need to Know

- Use dynamic microphones for louder instruments and condensers for softer ones.
- You can record electric instruments by mic'ing an amplifier or via direct injection.
- Lead guitars need to be panned center and can benefit from a variety of effects.
- Acoustic guitars and pianos don't need a lot of EQ, compression, or other effects.
- Horns can be tracked and mixed either individually or as a section; you don't need a lot of postrecording processing.
- Mixing a string section is all about trying to capture the live sound.

CHAPTER 1

Mixing Drums

In Chapter 18, I discussed how to mic and mix all sorts of instruments, from guitars and keyboards to horns and strings. The only instrument I skipped was the drum set because it requires some very unique techniques.

Many engineers find that mixing drums is the most challenging part of the mixing (and recording!) process. Others pride themselves on their ability to capture and create killer drum sounds. In any case, you need to pay particular attention to the drums because they're important in the mix, of course, but also because they are challenging to work with.

In This Chapter

- How to record great-sounding drum tracks
- Setting levels and stereo placement
- A look at the best EQ settings and effects to use

Recording a Killer Drum Track

Confession: I'm a drummer. Getting the best drum sound is important to me. If the drums don't sound quite right on a recording, I'll let you know. Likewise, I've been known to gush about drum tracks that sound especially hot. Drums matter to me.

Drums should matter to you, too. Getting a killer drum sound takes time, effort, and skill—and it all starts with how they're recorded.

Secrets of Mic Placement

You can approach recording an entire drum set in a number of ways. You have to think of the kit as both a single instrument and a collection of individual drums and cymbals.

The most basic approach, often used in jazz music, puts two mics overhead and slightly in front of the kit to capture the total sound. This doesn't give you a lot of flexibility in the mixing process, however; you have to EQ and compress the kit as a whole rather than deal with individual elements.

Traditional two-mic approach to the drums, with optional bass drum and snare mics.

This basic approach is often augmented by a single mic positioned so it's pointing at the snare drum or between the snare and hi-hat to beef up the backbeat and another mic placed inside or in front of the bass drum to capture the basic pulse. This not only enhances the overall sound; it also gives you two specific tracks (snare and bass) you can punch up in the mixing process.

A variation of this approach is the one Abbey Road engineer Glyn Johns used on many legendary recordings in the 1960s, 1970s, and beyond. This four-mic approach uses separate snare and bass drum mics, but the "overheads" are positioned much differently. One is placed about 3 or 4 feet over the snare drum or slightly toward the middle of the kit. The second is placed to the drummer's right, just past the floor tom, the same distance from the snare as the other overhead and about 6 inches above the tom's rim. The resulting effect is surprisingly large, as witnessed in many recordings by The Beatles (Ringo Starr on drums) and Led Zeppelin (John Bonham on drums).

The Glyn Johns four-mic approach to the drums.

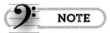 **NOTE**

Glyn Johns recorded and mixed many famous British artists, including The Beatles, The Rolling Stones, The Who, Led Zeppelin, Eric Clapton and Rod Stewart, as well as many American performers, such as Linda Ronstadt, Eagles, Steve Miller Band, Bob Dylan, and The Band. He's somewhat known for his big drum sound, as exemplified on multiple Led Zeppelin recordings.

All that said, most engineers today use a small arsenal of mics to record each drum separately. You'll put individual mics on the snare, bass, hi-hat, and each tom. You also can mic each cymbal separately or rely on a pair of overheads for that.

The thinking behind this approach is that if you capture each drum separately, you can mix, pan, EQ, and process each drum on its own as necessary. With a half-dozen or more drum tracks to work with, your job as a mixing engineer is both more complex, because that's a lot of tracks, and easier, because you can isolate each drum and apply whatever processing that drum needs without affecting the rest of the kit.

NOTE

Many pros use multiple mics on both the snare drum and the bass drum to capture the attack, resonance, and the overall drum sound separately. You might find three mics pointing at the snare (above, below, and in front) and two or more on the bass (on the batter head and either on the resonant head or inside the drum). You'll need to mix together all these mics to achieve the final drum sound.

Choosing the Right Drum Mics

What kinds of mics should you use to record your drum tracks? You definitely need dynamic mics because you're dealing with some very loud sound levels.

You don't have to spend a lot on drums mics; some of the most basic workhorses do just fine. I like the good old Shure SM57 for overhead, snare, and tom use, although other manufacturers' equivalents also work well. For the bass drum, you want a mic designed specifically for this purpose, such as the Shure Beta 52A (about $200).

Audix, Samson, Shure, and other microphone manufacturers sell complete kits of drum mics. A typical kit includes three or more small mics for snare and toms, a separate bass drum mic, and maybe two slightly different mics for overheads. You can find some kits for as low as $200, although better and bigger kits go for anywhere from $400 and up. Check out what's available; going the kit route can save you more than a few bucks.

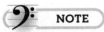

NOTE

You'll also need the proper hardware to position your drum mics. You can use various low-priced clips to attach mics to the snare and toms. You also can use boom stands, if you like, although too many booms present a logistical problem of sorts. Booms are necessary for overheads, of course, and probably for the bass drum—although various internal mic mounting systems are available for that.

The 7Kit drum mic set from Samson Technologies includes four tom/snare mics, two overheads, and a bass drum mic (samsontech.com).

Setting Levels and Panning

How you balance and pan the drums depends a lot on how they're recorded. If each drum was recorded on its own track, you have a lot more options available.

In general, drums need to be high in the mix, especially the bass drum (kick drum) and snare drum, which provides the two-and-four backbeat. Generally, the hi-hats and ride cymbal can be lower in the mix, as can crash cymbals. You want to hear the toms when they're hit, however, so creating a deep and present tom sound is imperative.

Balancing the Entire Kit

If you record the entire kit with just two overheads (or two mics placed in front of the kit), setting levels is pretty simple. Bring up the levels until the drums are present but not overwhelming—probably about the same level as the bass guitar (or acoustic bass).

With a two-mic setup, you want to pan the left and right channels hard to either side. This provides a nice stereo image with a defined, if virtual, center. It's your call on whether to reverse the track positioning; audiences will hear the hi-hat on their right and the large tom to the left, although traditional drummer-focused positioning puts the hats on the left and the tom on the right. I'd go with audience-focused positioning for jazz recordings and drummer-focused positioning for rock and pop stuff.

Balancing the Bass Drum

When you add a separate mic for the bass drum, it's time to get to work. You can spend a lot of time balancing the bass drum levels.

Most engineers consider the bass drum the second or third most important track in the mix. (Vocals are first; bass guitar is either number two or number three, depending.) The bass drum needs to punch through the rest of the mix, which means (along with all the EQ and effects I discuss later in this section) it needs to be fairly loud.

You should position the bass drum dead center, along with the bass guitar. You don't want that thumping coming only from one speaker; the low-frequency sound is nondirectional, so it needs to come from the center position.

Balancing the Snare Drum

Like the bass drum, the snare drum needs to be positioned in the center of the soundstage. It also needs to be mixed up high, almost as loud as the bass drum. You want the two-and-four backbeat hits to be really noticeable, with softer ghost notes just within the range of hearing.

Balancing the Toms

Most recordings today mic each tom individually, as mentioned earlier. Because the drummer doesn't play the toms as much as he does the bass and snare, they don't interfere with the mix very much. You will hear the toms when the drummer plays a fill at the end of a phrase and then you need to hear them in your gut. Everybody loves a nice, punchy tom sound.

As to positioning, you have multiple toms to work with. Place the smallest riding tom to the left and the largest floor tom to the right, and fill in all the other toms in between. In most instances, you'll use drummer-focused positioning. Avoid putting all the toms dead center; you want to fill up the soundstage during long fills.

Balancing the Cymbals (Overheads)

Finally, we come to the cymbals, most often captured by two overhead mics. If all you have are the overheads, pan them hard left and hard right, from the drummer's perspective. If you also have a separate mic on the hi-hat, pan it mid-left, around 10:30 on the clock dial.

As to levels, use your ears. You don't want the ride cymbal or hi-hat overwhelming the rest of the drum set and the other instruments, nor do you want the crashes clashing over the vocals. In general, pull back on the volume of these tracks, significantly below the level of the snare and bass tracks.

Applying the Right Effects

Close-mic'd drums benefit from a wealth of equalization, compression, and other effects. In fact, some of the more well-known drum sounds can only be achieved in the studio using the proper mixing effects.

Bass Drum

Bass drum first. Start by applying a noise gate with a high threshold level. You want to eliminate as much bleed-through as possible from the other drum mics; you don't want the snare drum or hi-hat triggering the bass drum gate, for example. Set a short attack time, which should work well. As to release, you want to be able to hear the full thump of the drum without running into the snare drum hit that follows.

Next comes compression. Start by setting the threshold around −15 dB. As to the compression ratio, something around 5:1 or 6:1 is good for most rock music; tap it down to the 3:1 to 4:1 range for softer songs. You'll want a fast attack, a medium-fast release, and a hard knee.

Equalize the bass drum with a slight boost between 80 to 100 Hz, a big cut between 200 to 500 Hz, and another slight boost at 2,500 Hz. If you want a punchier sound, boost even more between 80 to 100 Hz; if you want to hear more of the beater attack, boost the 2,000 to 4,000 Hz range instead.

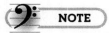 **NOTE**

Find more drum EQ tips in Chapter 14.

As to other effects, the less done the better. You don't want or need reverb or delay on the bass drum, nor are any modulation effects necessary. Just gating, compression, and EQ—and don't be subtle with 'em!

Snare Drum

Like the bass drum, the snare drum needs to be heavily gated. You want a high threshold level and a short attack time, to begin with. But it's the release time that most affects the sound of the snare. Use a shorter release for a dryer sound and a longer release if you want more ring.

Compression is also important for today's modern snare drum sound. Use a ratio in the 3:1 to 4:1 range for rock and other aggressive styles and in the 2:1 to 3:1 range for softer music. Use a fast attack unless you want a snappier sound; then go a little longer. In any case, experiment with medium-to-fast release times, and always use a hard knee.

You can create wildly different snare sounds by playing around with the EQ. Most drums benefit from slight boosts around 100 to 300 Hz, 1,000 to 3,000 Hz, 5,000 to 8,000 Hz, and 9,000 to 15,000 Hz.

If you want a fatter snare sound, boost even more (8 or 9 dB) at 200 Hz. For more crack, boost by 6 dB or so around 2,000 to 2,500 Hz. And if you have a lot of unwanted ring on the snare and can't get rid of it with gating, try a cut in the 400 to 800 Hz range. Cut too much here, however, and you'll end up with a dead drum sound.

Finally, you might want to consider adding a little reverb to the snare track. A lot of engineers like the snare a little drier, but a moderate amount of reverb can add necessary presence. Try to time the reverb to the tempo of the track—you don't want the reflections to run into the next snare hits.

Toms

To get that low and punchy tom sound, you need a lot of processing. Start by applying an aggressive noise gate with a high threshold and short attack. Then pay a lot of attention to the release time because that really shapes the tom's sound. For the punchiest sound, you'll want a relatively short release time with a sharp cutoff. Use a longer release if you want to capture more of the natural ring.

As to compression, set a high threshold (around −20 dB), a ratio in the 3:1 to 4:1 range, and a fast attack and release. Increase the ratio to 6:1 or so for an even more powerful sound.

EQ is also important in shaping the tom sound. Start by boosting the lows (between 80 and 100 Hz), cutting the mids (between 300 and 500 Hz), and boosting the highs (between 5,000 and 8,000 Hz and 9,000 and 12,500 Hz). Thicken the sound by boosting the lows and cutting the mids even more.

Finally, you can go dry or mix in a little small room reverb. Trust your ears on this one; too much reverb can muddy that wonderful punchy sound.

Cymbals and Overheads

You probably don't need gating for your overhead mics. The purpose is to capture a little bit of everything, so leave it wide open. Same thing with the hi-hat—it's pretty much in constant use, so gating isn't necessary.

> **TIP**
>
> If you only want to hear cymbals (not drums) from the overhead mics, apply a high-pass filter to cut out everything below about 500 Hz. If you don't need the toms or anything else in the overheads, this is a good way to go.

As to compression, a little goes a long way. Set a ratio in the 2:1 to 3:1 range, with a fast attack, a medium release, and a hard knee.

The overheads should sound fine with only minimal equalization. If you want to add some air to the sound, boost selectively above 6,000 Hz.

The hi-hats, however, can stand with some EQ. To start, cut big between 60 and 120 Hz and then boost slightly between 7,000 and 10,000 Hz. If the hats sound too bright, forgo the boost and instead cut at 9,000 Hz. If you want a louder "chink" sound from the foot, boost slightly around 200 to 300 Hz.

Bottom line: you can do a lot of shaping with your drum tracks. Take your time, do a little experimentation, and you'll be surprised by the results!

> **TIP**
>
> For a New York-style heavily compressed effect, employ what the pros call *parallel processing*. Send a copy of your drum tracks to a compressor, and apply the settings liberally. Now combine the compressed tracks with the original uncompressed tracks, and adjust the wet/dry mix until you get the desired punchy, in-your-face sound.

The Least You Need to Know

- Most drums today are recorded with mics on each drum and two overheads—although other approaches exist.
- You need to mix the drums both as a single instrument and as a collection of instruments, which means treating each drum and cymbal separately.

- Pan the bass drum and snare drum dead center, pan the hi-hat slightly to the left, pan the toms in a semicircle from left to right, and pan the overheads hard to each side.
- Apply noise gates to the snare, bass, and tom tracks, but not the cymbals.
- Apply appropriate compression and EQ to each individual drum and cymbal track.

Mastering the Final Mix

You've gathered all your recorded tracks and mixed them together. You've edited the tracks; set levels and panning; and applied EQ, reverb, compression, and other effects. What you have now is a perfect mix.

But that's not the end. When the mix is final, it's time to move on to the very last part of the recording process: mastering. During mastering, you (or a separate mastering engineer) take all the mixed tracks and apply any necessary master effects and equalization. (These are effects and EQ that are applied to the entire recording, not just a single track.) Finally, you export the final master as a stereo digital audio file, in whatever format is appropriate to your method of distribution. *Then* you're done.

In This Chapter

- Learning how mastering works—and how it differs from mixing
- How to know when your mix is ready for mastering
- Getting your mix ready for mastering
- Applying EQ and effects to create the perfect master
- Other options for mastering your recording

This process sounds fairly simple, and it can be. It also can be a tweaker's heaven, as the sign of a truly professional recording is the quality of the mastering. To this end, many home-brew musicians take their files to a professional recording or mastering studio for the final mastering. I talk about this option, as well as the rest of the process, as we move through this chapter.

Understanding the Mastering Process

Many novice engineers confuse the mixing and mastering processes in their minds. That's understandable; they both take place after the main recording and involve many of the same operations. But mixing and mastering are quite different, and it helps to know which is which—and why.

How Mastering Differs from Mixing

Mixing is all about dealing with individual tracks. You set levels and panning and apply EQ and effects, one track at a time. Yes, you do all this in service of the overall mix, but you do it by working with each track individually.

Mastering, on the other hand, is all about the whole. You don't fiddle with individual tracks; you listen to and apply EQ and effects to all the tracks together, not individually. The goal is the same—to create a final product that sounds exactly the way you want—but the process is completely different.

Think of it as if you're building a car: the first thing you do is manufacture or purchase all the individual parts—the doors, wheels, engine, and such. This is just like the recording part of our process, where you create each individual track.

The next thing you do is put all those parts together. You ensure the doors fit, the engine works, and all the wiring and gears are connected. You even paint the thing and put on the tires. This is just like the mixing part of our process, when you put all the individual tracks together.

The final thing you do is ensure the car looks good. You wash, buff, and detail it, and you ensure that the tires shine and the windows are squeaky clean. You even tweak the engine and the transmission so you get peak performance. This is just like the mastering part of our process, when you make the finished mix sound as good as it can.

So you have to mix before you master—and you have to master before you press your CDs or distribute your music through digital media.

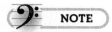 NOTE

> Some newbies might think that if they do a good enough job mixing, they don't need
> to master. That, unfortunately, is wrong. Many artists, even if they do all their own
> recording and mixing, lay out big bucks for professional mastering, and there's a
> reason for that. Even the best final mix in the world benefits from skilled mastering; a
> well-mastered mix simply sounds better than an unmastered one.

How Mastering Works

What exactly do you do in the mastering process? It's deceptively simple, at least compared to mixing. Here's what the mastering engineer does:

- Apply master equalization to all channels
- Apply any master effects to all channels
- Fade the recording in or out as necessary
- Save the final master to a two-channel WAV or AIFF format file for physical or digital distribution

That's it. Like I said, it looks fairly simple—even though it takes tremendous skill to turn the average mix into a superior master.

What Mastering Can Do

What exactly is it that mastering accomplishes? The difference between the sound of a raw mix and a professional master can be significant.

Here's just a sampling of what a good mastering engineer can accomplish:

- Make the song sound brighter or warmer or punchier or whatever by applying equalization
- Give the song more presence by applying reverb
- Make the song sound louder by applying compression
- Put the song in a wider soundstage by adjusting stereo panning
- Even out the volume levels across all the tracks on an album
- Ensure the final product is properly formatted, both in terms of levels and digital formats, for final distribution

It's difficult to define in words what a good master sounds like. You might describe the mastered mix as sounding more "alive" or brighter or more professional. It's a matter of fine-tuning and punching up the final mix as a whole and bringing out the best of what was created in the mixing process.

What Mastering *Can't* Do

Professional mastering can make a huge difference in how a project sounds. But there are limitations—mastering isn't the be-all and end-all for audio quality.

First, remember that mastering isn't mixing. You do not go back and set individual track levels, edit tracks, apply processing and EQ to individual tracks, or the like. Everything you do in the mastering process affects the entire sound, not the sound of individual tracks. If the balance or panning of your mix isn't quite right, you can't fix it in mastering—you have to go back and remix it.

Second, mastering can't fix a bad mix. If the vocals are too far in the background, a mastering engineer can't go back and turn them up. You can't change individual track EQ or unapply bad processing. The mastering engineer only has the two final stereo tracks to work with. He doesn't see the individual tracks; he only hears how they're fitted into the mix. So if the mix is bad, the mastering engineer can't fix it. Period.

Therefore, you should send your project to mastering only when you're positive the mix is as good as it can be. If something's wrong in the mix, it'll be wrong in the final master, too.

 **NOTE**

Just as you really can't fix a bad recording in the mix, you also can't fix a bad mix in mastering. Mastering can make any mix sound better, but the concept of garbage in, garbage out still applies. You have to do the best you can in the mixing room before you hand it off to be mastered.

Knowing When the Mix Is Done

If mastering takes place after mixing, how do you know when it's time to stop mixing and start mastering? This is a difficult question for some.

If you have any obsessive qualities at all, you can find yourself fussing over the details in a mix for days or weeks on end. Should you bring the bass line forward just a tad? Maybe try a different EQ on the snare drum? Use more reverb on the backing singers? Replace that guitar solo with something completely different?

You know how it goes. A mix is never perfect, so it's never finished. You always can go back and tweak something. Every time you listen to it, you hear something you want to do differently.

The problem is, at some point, the mix *has* to be finished. You can mix a single tune forever, but the artist and producer want to release it to their fans and you have other projects to engineer. At some point, you have to be done with it.

When, then, is a mix ready for mastering? Work through this checklist to know:

- ❑ Is the mix clean? Is there any unwanted noise? Are there any unexpected artifacts from effects or other processing?

- ❑ Can you hear the lead vocals throughout? Does any other voice or instrument interfere with the lead at any point? Can you understand the words?

- ❑ Does the song sound solid? Are there any weak spots? Does any part sound unprofessional at all? Are there any mistakes left in the mix?

- ❑ Does the song have a good flow? Does it go someplace, or does it just sit at a static level? Are there natural peaks and valleys?

- ❑ Does it have a good beat? Can you dance to it?

- ❑ Are the artist and producer happy with the sound?

- ❑ Can you live with the mix? Is there anything that's really bothering you that you need to change?

- ❑ Would any additional mixing make a big difference? Or would new tweaks go largely unnoticed?

- ❑ Is it just time to be done and move on?

If you can live with the mix as-is and the artist and producer like what they hear, the mix is ready for mastering. If anybody has any qualms, keep mixing. If there are still little things you'd like to tweak but nobody else hears them, it's time to move on.

 TIP

Sometimes you get too close to a mix to know when it's done. If you just can't decide, call in a fresh set of ears—either another engineer or the artist or producer. If they like where you are, you should feel more comfortable about letting go and moving on.

Preparing the Mix for Mastering

Whether you're doing your own mastering or passing it on to a different mastering engineer or mastering service, you need to prepare your project for mastering.

Here's a quick checklist on what you need to do:

- ❑ Be sure the mix is final and that the artist and the producer both have signed off on it.

- ❑ Mix down all your tracks to a final two-channel (stereo) mix. This may involve first converting MIDI tracks to audio tracks and then mixing those tracks along with your other tracks.

- ❑ Mix to the highest audio resolution possible. Do not mix down to a lower-quality format, and do not apply dithering or sample rate conversion. If you recorded and mixed at 24 bits/48 kilohertz (kHz), leave it at those settings for the mixdown.

 **NOTE**

> The standard bit depth for a final mix is 24 bits. The best sampling rate is 96 kHz, although 44.1 kHz is sometimes acceptable.

- ❑ Don't apply compression during the mixdown. If your client wants a louder mix, leave that for the mastering engineer.

- ❑ Be sure you select which region of your project you want to mix down. Leave a little space—but *clean* space—at the beginning and end for the mastering engineer to work with.

- ❑ Mix down to a stereo WAV or AIFF file.

- ❑ Use your DAW's controls to render the master mix.

The resulting two-channel WAV file can then be sent to the mastering engineer.

 **NOTE**

> WAV has pretty much become the industry standard for professional audio files, although some Mac users still prefer the similar AIFF format.

Making the Perfect Master

What makes for a superbly mastered recording? Mastering is a subtle art, but there are some key points to keep in mind.

First, remember that mastering is not the same as mixing. Mastering happens after the mixing process, so don't try to fix any mix problems at this stage. If the mix is bad, go back and remix it—before you begin the mastering process.

It's important to enter the mastering process with your ears as fresh as possible. You're used to listening to track-oriented details during mixing; during mastering, you should be listening to the whole recording, not individual tracks. Sometimes it helps to put some real time (days, if not weeks) between the mixing and mastering operations. It also may help to do your mastering at a different facility (or even just a different room) than where you did your mixing. It certainly pays to listen to your master on a different set of speakers, not only to freshen your ears but also to get a different perspective on the sound of the thing.

TIP

You want to be sure your final master sounds good through headphones and earbuds, but you shouldn't attempt to do your mastering through headphones. You *might* be able to record and mix with headphones (not that I'd advise it, mind you), but you definitely need a good set of monitor speakers to hear the subtleties in the master recording. Speakers, yes; headphones, no.

When mastering, keep the entire album in mind. That is, you want the individual songs to fit comfortably with one another, in terms of volume level, equalization, and general tonal quality. This is where you pull out your master insert effects and master EQ to create the best sonic match among all the songs.

That said, any changes you make during the mastering process should be subtle ones—tweaks rather than dramatic changes. You don't want to alter your mix; you just want to improve upon it. That means giving the bass just a hair more definition or making the high end just a tad crisper. This is not the point to decide to change the entire sound of a song. If you don't like what you're hearing, stop mastering and do a remix instead.

Applying Master Effects and EQ

Now we come to the subject of master effects and equalization. As noted previously, these are effects and EQ you apply to your entire mix, not just to individual tracks. Why would you want to apply effects and EQ globally like this? There are a few good reasons.

First, you might want to apply a specific effect to the entire recording. Maybe you want your songs to sound as if they were recorded in a concert hall. The simple solution is to apply reverb as a master effect.

Second, EQ'ing the entire mix lets you tweak the sonic qualities of the entire recording. If you want your songs to sound bright and poppy, add some EQ on the top end. Want a boomier bass sound? Add some EQ to the low end. You get the picture.

Which effects can you apply? Not a lot, really. You don't use gating or flanging or even limiting during the mastering process. Compression and reverb are pretty much all you need—and you need to be judicious in using either of these effects.

Using—and Abusing—Compression

Dynamic compression is arguably the most-used master effect in today's music. Compression is typically applied to the entire recording to make it louder and "hotter." Compress the entire recording, and you make the soft parts louder and guard against unwanted transients—which lets you pump up the volume. When every other recording on the air is compressed within an inch of its life, you need to play in the same ballpark. Even though I personally don't like overcompressed recordings, master compression is necessary to compete in the loudness wars.

The problem is, at least to my ears, much of today's popular music overuses compression. When you overcompress your final mix, there's little or no difference between the softest and loudest sections of the song. The volume level stays pretty much in one place from the start to the finish.

This type of single-level recording might be fine for the dance floor, and radio programmers also like it, but it's just one more way to dehumanize modern music. When you listen to musicians performing live—electric or acoustic, it doesn't matter—you hear a broad range of dynamics. Great musicians use dynamics for effect, contrasting whisper-quiet sections against full-on attacks. When you compress a recording, you lose this contrast; everything sounds the same.

Of course, there are good reasons to employ some degree of compression. As noted, radio programmers like compressed recordings because much of their audience is listening in an automotive environment full of ambient noise (the car's engine, other passengers, even the sound of the outdoors filtering in through an open window). If a station plays music that's too soft, listeners will simply switch stations. In this situation, some degree of volume normalization is a necessity.

In the home, however, especially on a quality audio system, this degree of compression is uncalled for. Unfortunately, many engineers, producers, and even musicians are fooled into thinking that an overly compressed recording sounds "hotter" to the listener. (This false impression comes from the fact that the recording can be mastered louder, knowing there won't be any transient highs to worry about.) When a fine recording is overcompressed, however, it's the listener—particularly the audiophile listener with a high-quality audio system—who is cheated.

Yes, heavily compressing your master mix will get you noticed on the radio. It'll even make for a slightly more pleasant experience for those listening to music on the go via the omnipresent earbuds. But not everyone listens to music on a smartphone or car stereo system. Should you compromise your recording by playing to the lowest common denominator?

It may be too late to step back from this overuse of mastering compression, but if the genie isn't fully out of the bottle yet, let's consider trying to put the cap back on. A little compression is fine, but too much makes everything sound the same. And that's not good.

Exporting for Distribution

When you've applied your master EQ and effects, tweaked the master levels, and maybe adjusted the separation between the two stereo tracks, it's time to export the final master to a final audio file.

It's this audio file that you'll use to distribute your music. If you're making a CD, you'll send the audio file to the disc pressing plant or import it into the CD creation software on your own PC. If you're distributing your song over the internet, you'll upload the audio file to online music stores and streaming services.

The final audio file is the end result of the entire recording process.

Other Options for Mastering Your Recording

Pro Tools, Cubase, and most other DAW programs make it relatively easy for you to turn your multitrack recording into a two-channel stereo file. You can use these programs to apply basic effects and EQ to the final two-channel mix to make your recording sound as good as possible for distribution on CD or over the internet.

As good as all that is, however, it might not be good enough. Many professional musicians, even those who make their recordings in home studios, hand off the mastering process to other programs (or other people) that provide more mastering options than offered by the typical DAW program.

Third-Party Mastering Programs

Cubase and Pro Tools are digital recording and mixing programs. They aren't dedicated mastering programs. As such, they're limited to some degree in how they process two-channel audio files.

Not to fear, however. Numerous manufacturers offer dedicated mastering programs and plug-ins. These let you perform all sorts of audio tweaking on your stereo files, or in many cases offer almost-magical one-button mastering solutions. These programs make it easy to punch up the sound of your stereo master files or perform any fine editing that may be necessary.

Here are the most popular of these mastering programs:

- iZotope Ozone (izotope.com)

- Sony Sound Forge and Audio Master Suite (sonymediasoftware.com)

- Steinberg WaveLab (steinberg.net)

- T-RackS (t-racks.com)

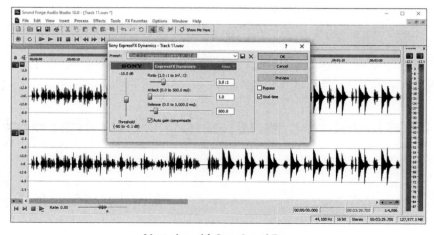

Mastering with Sony Sound Forge.

Professional Mastering

Mixing a recording is one thing; creating a master is another. Many musicians gladly pay a few hundred (or thousand) bucks to let a professional mastering studio turn their tracks into professional recordings. A professional mastering engineer does this sort of thing for a living and knows exactly how to punch up and prepare a recording to best effect. Most professional recording studios offer mastering services, and many studios specialize in mastering work.

Depending on the studio, you might need to provide your entire DAW project or just your exported stereo WAV/AIFF files. Consult with the mastering engineer beforehand so you know what they need—and maybe save yourself a little work in the process.

And Now You're Done ...

When the mastering is complete, your project is done. You've recorded all the vocals and instruments, mixed and processed all the tracks, and created the final master file, which can now be distributed to consumers.

Congratulations! I hope the process hasn't been too challenging and that you've not only created a great-sounding recording but also learned a little in the process. I also hope this book has helped you become a better mixing engineer.

Don't rest on your laurels, though. Take a deep breath, grab a cup of coffee, and get back to your mixing console. More projects await!

The Least You Need to Know

- Mastering is applied to the entire mix, not to single tracks individually.
- When you're done with the mixing process, mix everything down to a final two-channel mix.
- During mastering, EQ and compression (along with some other effects) are applied, and the track is saved to a high-resolution WAV or AIFF file for distribution.
- Several mastering-only software programs are available, or you can use your standard DAW software for mastering. You also can employ professional mastering services.

Interview with a Professional Mixing Engineer

If you've gotten this far, you've read about a lot of essential techniques and skills you need to develop in order to be a successful mixing engineer. But how do those techniques and skills apply in the real world? Let's talk with a professional mixing engineer to get his take on how things work.

In This Chapter

- Meeting mixing engineer Corey Miller

- A look at The Lodge Recording Studios

- Understanding what a professional mixing engineer does

Introducing Corey Miller of The Lodge Recording Studios

Corey Miller (no relation to the author) is an engineer/producer at The Lodge Recording Studios in Indianapolis, Indiana. The Lodge is unique in that it does lots of work with the music publishing industry, recording orchestras, choirs, concert bands, and the like, playing the latest compositions and arrangements for schools and other organizations. This is in addition to recording local and regional bands and solo artists of all genres. This diverse combination of clients keeps The Lodge really busy throughout the year and gives its staff a wealth of experiences in all types of recording and mixing.

Corey has been in the industry (and with The Lodge) since 1995. He's a graduate of The Recording Workshop in Chillicothe, Ohio, and he currently teaches a music technology course for Indiana University–Purdue University Indianapolis focusing on recording techniques.

Corey is part of a production team known as "The Mix Up" that works with local and regional artists in the pop/rock and hip-hop genres. Their music has been featured on NBC's *The Voice* and MTV's *The Real World* and *Catfish*, along with being placed with several other major television networks. In 2013, Corey received a platinum record for his engineering on B.o.B.'s single "So Good" from the *Strange Clouds* album.

With his 21 years in the business, Corey obviously has a lot of experience under his belt. I felt he could add some real-world advice to what you've read so far in this book.

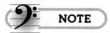 **NOTE**

> The Lodge Recording Studios is located in Indianapolis, Indiana. Learn more (and book studio time!) at thelodgestudios.com.

Interview with Corey Miller

I interviewed Corey in June 2016. It was tough getting on his schedule; he's a very busy engineer working at a very busy studio. But we managed to carve out an hour over the phone on a sunny summer afternoon between his many projects.

Getting Started

Michael Miller (MM): How did you get started in the business?

Corey Miller (CM): I went to the Recording Workshop over in Chillicothe, Ohio, and once I got out of there, I went out to New York for a while, to try to find a job. I had a lot of studios offer me an internship, but, of course, most internships are unpaid. So I decided, since I'm originally from Indiana, my family lives like an hour north of Indianapolis, figured I'd come back to Indiana where it's a little bit cheaper to live and look for a job here. I thought, if I'm gonna work for free then I'd rather be in a place where the cost of living is a lot lower.

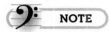

> **NOTE**
>
> The Recording Workshop is a well-known school in Ohio that teaches music recording, mixing, and production. Learn more at recordingworkshop.com.

So I came back to Indiana. Gosh, back then in '95, the accessibility that you have now thanks to the internet, being able to contact studios wasn't as good as it is now. I was just making cold calls, trying to find out what I could.

Probably a month or two after that, the Recording Workshop actually called me and said that there was a studio in Indianapolis, called The Lodge, that was looking for possible interns. So I drove down to Indy, interviewed, and got the internship. I did that for 6 months, unpaid. Then right at the tail end of my internship, I didn't think they were going to hire me on, just because work fluctuates—sometimes the studios are really busy, sometimes it's kind of slow. So it was kind of tapering off around the end of my internship. Then, just a few days before, it just got crazy busy. They said, well, we'll pay you just to stay on temporarily, maybe for a month or so, just until it kind of dies down again. And 21 years later, I'm still there.

MM: It hasn't died down that much, then, huh?

CM: Exactly. *(laughs)*

MM: That's a little unusual, though, with all the people doing recording and mixing in their home studios now. That's affected a lot of the big studios. But The Lodge still seems to keep busy. Why is that?

CM: Well, one of the major things that we do, and this is kind of crazy, but Indianapolis is kind of a mecca for (music) publishing. What I mean is we do a lot of stuff for school programs. A lot of the bigger publishers like Hal Leonard, Alfred Music Publishing, Shawnee Press—there are quite a few of them out there. We do consistent work with a lot of the big publishers throughout the year. We'll do orchestra recordings for them; we'll do choirs; we'll do their pop catalogs, concert bands. So there's a lot of work in that alone.

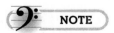

> **NOTE**
>
> The educational music publishing industry produces music arrangements for middle school, high school, and college bands, orchestras, and choirs. The publishers typically supply CDs or streaming tracks of the new music they offer each school season and, thus, need to record performances of their music—many of which are recorded at The Lodge.

Really, it's the combination of the publishing companies that we work with and the local and regional original music, the bands that are from the area.

Working with Different Types of Projects

MM: That's a pretty big variety. How is it different when you're working with, say, a choir or an orchestra, concert band, something like that, and working with a typical rock group or pop group?

CM: From a mixing standpoint, if I'm working on, say, a rock or a pop record, I'm generally using a lot more compression. I'm a lot more aggressive with my EQ'ing. Because, especially those two genres, I'm pretty much at home with pop and rock. I would say if there are two styles that I really dive into and feel at home with, it would be those two styles of music.

It's a lot more manipulation of the sound and the mix, compared to if you're doing an orchestral session, or mixing a choir. Those styles of music, and even a lot of styles of jazz or folk music or acoustic music, you're trying to keep a lot more natural. So I'll generally use a lot less compression. I'll ride the faders more. My EQs will be a lot more broad strokes. I'm not getting very surgical with the EQ. I'm not doing a lot of, like, notch filtering and that kind of stuff that I would use in pop and rock.

MM: When you're dealing with a big group recording, orchestra, concert band, whatever, how many tracks are you generally working with?

CM: Let's say with an orchestra session, you're usually dealing with, in the mixing process, if it's just the orchestra with no vocals on top of it, we run about maybe 48 tracks. If you put vocals on it, and it's choral-style vocals, you're sometimes looking at 70 or 80 tracks by that point in time.

MM: So you're using a lot of mics to record this, then?

CM: Yeah. I'd still say that a lot of the blend in the mix for orchestral music—and honestly for the choral music, too—it's a fair amount of just the room mics. I would say I try to mix in about 75 percent of the room mics. Even though we've got mics on every single section of the orchestra, it's mainly just to give it a little bit of presence. Also, it's a good backup or safety net to have those tracks, just in case the producer says, "Hey, I want to hear a little bit more of this section here," or "I really want to bring these guys up over here." Then you've at least got that spot mic you can kind of blend in a little bit more.

MM: That makes a lot of sense. How much time is involved mixing a project like that, as opposed to, say, a rock band album?

CM: I would say, with the orchestral tracks that we do, a lot of the tracks that we do for the publishers, we're pretty efficient. Mixing a single piece that's, say, 4 or 5 minutes long, if it's an orchestra piece, this probably sounds crazy, we can usually get it mixed in like an hour and a half.

A lot of that's room mics, too, so you're not necessarily going through and soloing every single track and EQ'ing it and doing compression with it like you would on a rock record. If you have 12 mics on a drum kit on a rock record, you're really trying to make sure that everything is in phase in the mix, it's tight, and you're getting the sound that you want. So even though it's got a lot more tracks, it still doesn't take that long to mix.

Now, for rock records, I find that it's a little bit different. If I have the luxury and bands let me do this—because a lot of times it comes down to budget—I love spending, like, 4 hours on a rock track. Anywhere in that vicinity, where I'm mixing, like, two songs a day. Usually I don't get that, but I can still mix a rock track in, say, 2 to 2½ hours, somewhere in there.

MM: Would it be fair to say that with the orchestral and concert stuff, you're really capturing a performance, but with a rock band, pop record, you're also participating in the creative part of the process?

CM: Oh yeah, for sure. I feel like, on rock and pop records, you're not dealing necessarily with realistic sounds. You might be dealing with over-the-top synthesizer sounds or guitar tracks that don't necessarily sound like traditional guitar tracks. Drums that are acoustic but you're trying to make them sound a little edgier, maybe closer to an electronic sound or whatever. There are so many directions you can go in trying to get all those sounds to fit together.

The goal in mixing anything, you're trying to bring out the energy or the emotion that the writer or the artist was trying to portray. You're trying to translate that over to whatever the target audience is.

That's what I love about rock and pop—there's really no rules. You can take it in any direction you want, as long as you still maintain whatever the message of that piece is by the time you're done with it.

Working with People

MM: Now, when you're doing the mixing part of the process, who's in the room with you? Are you dealing with the artist? Are you dealing with the producers? How much free rein do you have?

CM: You know, most artists kind of let me make that call. I actually prefer to have the artist with me, especially when I'm working with singer-songwriters. If it's a situation where there's one main writer and we've hired in session players to put their songs together, I like the singer-songwriter there. Especially if they've recorded before, with me or at another studio, they have that experience, and they pretty much have a vision of what they're looking for. When I'm mixing, like I said, in pop and rock, you can take it in so many different directions, and I might have a bunch of ideas, but I don't know if those are necessarily in line with what they're thinking. So I tell them, "Hey, if you can be at the studio to mix this, that'd be great." I really enjoy that the most, because then I can sit there and we can discuss, even down to each section of the song, what we're trying to achieve with each one of those sections.

In a band scenario, I still like the band to be there, but my approach with a band is a little bit different. Because if I have like four or five guys in the control room with me, when I start to mix a rock or pop record, if I start soloing tracks, those players will immediately start having input, even though I just literally started mixing the tracks. I might be EQ'ing a vocal, and it's dry, no effect, and the singer is going, "Oh man, that sounds terrible. We gotta recut that. I don't like the sound of that." They're kind of freaking out, because they're hearing it as a finished thing, even though we just started mixing.

What I do in that case is I tell the band, "Yeah, it'd be great if you guys could be here," but I usually send them down to the kitchen for about an hour. Or I tell them, "Hey, go get lunch or something, go get something to eat." I just get 'em out of the room and mix by myself for about an hour. That gives me enough time to get basic EQs in place, compression, maybe some effects pulled up, and panning done. Then what I do is have them come back down to the room where they can actually hear a blend of the instruments.

On top of that, what I also do—if you just leave it at that, you're still gonna get the drummer saying, "Oh, I want the drums louder." And the bass player says, "Oh yeah, make my bass louder." And the guitar player says, "Yeah, yeah, make me loud, too." Everybody wants to be loud, loud, loud. So what I do is I tell them beforehand, "Before you guys come back down to the room, I pretty much need one spokesperson from the band. So you guys talk amongst yourselves, listen to the preliminary mix that I have going on, then you guys discuss; you guys need to decide. So if the drummer's saying the drums need to come up, you guys all discuss it and see if you all agree. If you do, then let me know." So I'm not just getting feedback from individual players who are really concerned about their part.

That kind of keeps it a little less, I guess, chaotic in the studio. It also keeps me from being the bad guy. If the band has to collectively make a decision on something, I can make the adjustments from there.

MM: You touched upon something here I think is important: part of your job is obviously the engineering skills, but it seems like another big part of the job is personal skills, dealing with the musicians and the producers and whatnot who, obviously, can be a little flakey sometimes, right?

CM: Sure, sure. *(laughs)*

MM: So what does a good engineer bring into this, in terms of personal skills, in dealing with these folks?

CM: They told us in school: there's a lot of psychology that goes into working on a project. You always have to keep in mind that you're working with somebody's music, whether that's a band collectively or just a singer-songwriter—especially in the case of a singer-songwriter—you're dealing with something that is pretty personal to most people. And it's in a state when you're working on it that's pretty vulnerable, because they haven't let too many people listen to it yet. They're not always sure if something's good, or if it's bad, or how people are going to react to it. So you really have to approach a lot of projects with kid gloves on.

The biggest thing is you definitely have to get the artist to trust you.

One of the ways I do that is I always have a meeting with the singer-songwriter or band, even before we start anything on the recording or the mixing end of it. I sit down and lay everything out on the table. I make sure everything is clear-cut in terms of what my role is. I try to figure out, especially if they've recorded before, how they like to record. I kind of let them in on some of the ways that I like to work. And like I said, I make sure that they know, and that I know, what my role is. "Do you want me to co-produce this with you?" "Do you want me to just be the guy that pushes 'record'?" "Are you going to be very active in the mixing, or do you want me to mix it?" We get all those things out of the way.

I also tell them, especially in the recording phase, that it's ultimately about the music. It's about the song. It's about the record that we're working on. It's never anything personal. So, for example, we're cutting a guitar solo and I think that it could be better, and I tell the guitar player, "Hey, let's try that again," I'm not picking on the guitar player or saying he's a bad player. I'm just feeling that we could have a better solo for the record.

I think that once you explain those concepts to the band or to the singer-songwriter, they kind of loosen up a little bit. They relax. They trust you. Because you've discussed where those lines are.

I also let them know, I say, "Ultimately, it's your music. It is not my music. So as long as you're okay with it, I am going to speak up when I have ideas, and I'm going to speak up when I think something is not right. But ultimately, you have the veto power. You can take my ideas and run with them, and that's great, but if you shoot 'em down, I'm not going to be hurt by that, either."

That's probably the biggest part of it, establishing that trust. Then people generally open up and the session goes pretty smooth for the most part, relaxed as they should be. And hopefully everybody's having a good time.

Working with Today's Technology

MM: You've been doing this since 1995. How have things changed since you've been in the business, the past 21 years or so?

CM: When I started out, everything was on analog tape. When you recorded a project, you went through the recording process, you went through the overdub process, and then you had a set time set aside for mixing that song or mixing an album. And, obviously, that stage was always at the end, after the overdubs were done.

In this day and age, a lot of projects are being done "inside the box," which is the way I like to work. I'm doing everything entirely inside Pro Tools, in terms of mixing. I'm still using a lot of outboard gear when I'm tracking, but once everything gets inside Pro Tools it stays in there. I process everything with either stock Pro Tools plug-ins or third-party plug-ins.

The mixing board in Studio B at The Lodge Recording Studios.

Really, one of the biggest changes has been that I'm kind of mixing as I'm going. What I've found is it gives the artist a better idea of the direction that the song is headed in. Maybe in between vocal takes or the guitar player's getting set up, I'm not just sitting there at the board twiddling my thumbs. I'm rolling back and sticking an EQ on something, or I'm compressing something. I'm kind of building the mix as I go.

So by the time we get to what would normally be the time to mix, after the last overdub, sometimes there's not a whole lot of mixing time involved past that. Maybe to set up, like, parallel compression and bus compression, stuff I'm not going to necessarily set up during tracking. But it's a lot of fine-tuning at that point in time, adding a couple of extra effects you were planning on doing in the last stages of the game.

The line's really blurred between recording and mixing.

The other thing that's really changed is—and this goes back to what you mentioned before— back then, when I was doing everything on tape, people obviously didn't have that kind of equipment at home to do their own records. And if you did have equipment to do your own records, four-track and eight-track tapes, or very early digital machines that didn't have good pre-amps or good A-to-D converters, if you did stuff at home it just sounded like a demo. Whereas now, if you've got some fairly decent microphones, and you've got a decent interface, and you kind of know what you're doing, you can easily make records at home.

What happens now is I get a lot of bands and a lot of singer-songwriters who will record their own albums. Or they might go to another studio or smaller studio and have an engineer record their album. Then they'll bring it to me because they don't know how to mix. They don't have the time for it; they don't have the patience for it. They're seeking out somebody with experience in that. They've been careful with the recording process, but they want somebody else to take it to the next level.

How that's really made a change, not only in my mixing projects that I maybe didn't start from scratch with the band or the singer-songwriter—and this kind of circles back to what you were talking about with pop and rock, especially—is sometimes I'll get tracks from bands that the guitar is just a DI track and they want me to process it and figure what kind of sound it's supposed to have. Maybe they were monitoring with some kind of distortion, but they don't really know if it was a good enough amp or what. So they just give me a DI track. Or maybe they give me 20 different takes of a guitar solo. Or in the bridge there's eight different instruments playing, and they're all playing different things—because the band didn't have a producer.

So a lot of the role of the producer, by saying "Yes, guys, we need to do this," or "We need to take it in this direction," the band's thrown out a lot of ideas. You get these sessions that have a crazy amount of tracks. Even with a laptop, I mean, you can easily record 70 or 80 tracks if you want.

MM: As many as you want.

CM: Yeah. So a mixer, in this day and age, a lot of times, if you haven't been part of the production or the recording process, and you're just solely the mixing engineer, you have to develop the skills that a producer would. You have to be able to go in there and figure out what's gonna be a better arrangement of a song or which parts need to be stripped out.

And a lot of times it's not just subtracting parts. Maybe you feel like it would have sounded so much better if there were a keyboard part in the bridge—it just feels like it's lacking that. If you're a musician yourself and you can play that part, I have no problem going in and adding a keyboard part or adding a guitar part if I feel like that's what it needs.

Sometimes I'll listen to a track and rather than just dive into the mix, I'm thinking in terms of production and saying, "Does the song have everything it needs?" If it does, I need to start stripping away some of these elements that I feel are getting in the way. But if I feel like it's empty in spots, I'm putting back on the engineer or the producer hat and adding parts before I actually mix the song.

So a lot of it now is going through and editing the songs, condensing it down to what I feel like are the right elements that need to be there before I even dive into equalization or compression or any of that stuff.

MM: Working in that way, is that more fun for you or more challenging for you? Or both?

CM: It's both. I mean, definitely if it's a style of music that I really connect with, and I can really get into the songs in an emotional sense, or I feel like I can really gravitate to what the song is talking about, or I love the energy of it or whatever, I feel it's a lot easier for me in that aspect. You know how they've always said that George Martin was the fifth Beatle? You kind of feel like you're another member of the band at that point, if you feel like you can connect to the music.

Like I said, most bands that I work with, especially some of these people I'm on their fourth or fifth record over the last 20 years, they trust me enough. I might send them an email or call them ahead of time and say, "You know, I was thinking it might be cool to add this keyboard part in there somewhere." And most of the time, if I've worked with them before, they're like, "Yeah, yeah, do whatever you think and just let me listen to it."

A lot of times they just give me that free reign to add what I think. Then, when they hear it, no different than if I was just mixing the song and let them hear it, and they go, "Yeah, well, that's close but it's not quite what I was thinking." That part that I worked on, that instrument I added might stay or it might go. Or it might trigger them to hear something else and go, "Oh, if you're gonna put that in there, can you add this or this or this?" They might ask me to add in other parts. Or we might even go back and have a guitar player add something or the bass player add something or the vocalist do something. Just because it's kind of triggered other ideas that weren't initially there.

Yeah, it's fun. It's a challenge to come up with the parts, sometimes.

It's definitely a lot tougher if it's music that is a lot harder to connect with. Usually in that scenario, I tend to be a little bit more conservative. I'm not trying to change any elements or sounds that the band has. I'm utilizing their parts that they've recorded, with another engineer or themselves at home. I'm just trying to take those recorded elements and figure out how the puzzle pieces need to go together to still achieve what they're going for.

Wrapping Things Up

MM: Especially when you're in this creative part of it, how do you know when you're done? You could mix all day long if you wanted to. How do you know when you've got the final mix?

CM: That can be tough, especially for artists. With the digital technology now and being able to save every single setting you do and go back and tweak things to the nth degree, that can get a little out of control sometimes.

The way that I'm able to put something to rest or when I feel like it's done, I do one thing that I think is really, really important. I can't stress enough to people out there. You know, I've taught some audio classes for a couple of the colleges in the area, and one thing that I've always stressed to students is you need to be able to have a lot of different systems or ways of monitoring your mix. Don't just buy a set of studio monitors and listen 100 percent of the time that you're mixing on that one set of monitors and then, when you think you're done, call it a day. Yeah, it might sound good on those monitors, but does it translate to headphones, does it translate to somebody's car stereo, boom box, that kind of stuff?

So after I've gone through and I've checked the mix on my main studio monitors, I've got a $15 Walmart boom box that I bought years ago that I use that's got an aux in. I have a mirrored feed out of Pro Tools going into that boom box, so I can just reach over and turn up the volume on the boom box and there's the mix. Whereas back in the day you had to burn a CD, run out to the car, that kind of stuff. So it's easy now to take a WAV file, throw it on my phone, run out to my car, and listen to it. I'm not burning a lot of CDs or anything.

What I'm doing, from a technical standpoint, is I'm using headphones; I'm using my main monitors; I'm using a cheap boom box; I'm using Auratone speakers. I'm listening in mono. I'm walking around the room, getting out of the chair. I'm doing all these kinds of different tests to get the balances to where I feel they should be. I'm tweaking it out per system so that it sounds good on all the systems.

 **NOTE**

Auratone is a company that sells relatively low-cost, small-footprint studio monitors. Learn more at auratonesoundcubes.com.

Then, when I feel like I've got the balances in place for the song, the true test for me to know when the song is done is I will then sit right between my main monitors that I probably use, say, 75 percent of the time. Then I will turn up the music to a fairly good volume—85 to 90 dB. Not too low but not too loud at the same time. I will close my eyes—because I feel if you cut out the visual aspect of it you're not distracted by looking at the wave form or where the cursor is on the screen. So I close my eyes, I hit the spacebar in Pro Tools, run it from the beginning, and I switch out of that mode.

Now I'm not thinking of, well, was that reverb on that vocal too much? Or does the bass need to come up a little bit? I'm not thinking in terms of the detail that I just put into it. I'm trying to switch my brain into that mode of, if I'm listening to that song for the first time, can I relate to it? Is it pulling me into that world that the artist is trying to create?

And as I'm playing along, if there's ever a spot in the song that takes me out of that illusion or brings me back to the real world, makes me think, "Oh, something's not right there," I'll just immediately stop it. I'll figure out what pulled me out of the song, fix it, then not just pick it up from there but I'll rewind back to the beginning again and do the same process.

Once I can make it through the song and I'm not stopping it to fix something that's kind of jarring me, and I feel I can listen all the way from the top of the song to the end, get pulled into the artist's world for four or five minutes, then I know it's done.

The Studio B control room at The Lodge—including a comfy couch for clients and a spare keyboard for overdubbing.

MM: One last thing: what advice do you have for somebody getting started with mixing, maybe as an intern or on his or her own home system? What do they need to know?

CM: One of the biggest things is—and I know a lot of guys out there are probably going to say this, but it's definitely something I feel like is pretty tried and true—when you're mixing a song, you've got to use reference mixes. Especially starting out, you don't want to just mix in isolation, where all you're listening to is the song you're working on and you have no reference point to the outside world, in terms of where your kick drum level is, or how loud the vocals are compared to the music, and that kind of stuff. You need to pick songs that you're familiar with. Of course this is very subjective, but songs that you're really drawn toward in that genre. If you're mixing a pop song, pick a handful of pop songs—5 to 10 pop tracks by different artists that you really like, and you love the sound of, and you like how they're mixed. Or maybe even for specific elements— you love how the snare sounds, or you love the vocal effect on a certain song. Load those up in iTunes, or get them on your computer somehow so that you can import those into your mixing session and you can actually do some A-B comparison as you go.

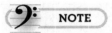

NOTE

A reference track, or reference mix, is an existing recording from another artist you listen to for inspiration and ideas.

Not that you're trying to mimic that song and try to copy it exact. But you might find that you're going along, and you're mixing, and you're an hour into it, and you switch over to a reference track, and you go, "Oh, wow. My vocal's totally buried. I didn't even realize that." Compared to these other 5 or 10 pop songs that you've got on your computer. So then you're thinking, "Oh, gosh, I should turn the vocal up." By doing that, you're kind of in the beginning stages of training your brain to hear that the next time you mix, or get a better reference point as to where your vocals should be, where your drums should be, that kind of stuff. So reference mixes are a big thing.

The other thing, too—and this doesn't require a whole lot of money, either—is try to listen to it on different systems. And make sure you're making changes that translate to each of those systems. Going to Target or Walmart and buying a $20 or $25 boom box that's got an aux in on it, to me, that's kind of my secret weapon sometimes. Trying to make it sound good on a cheap boom box, then it's probably going to translate pretty well on a lot of other systems, too.

Having different reference points, not just sitting between the same set of speakers the whole time, is important. You know, walk around the room, or turn it up loud and go into a different room. Go into the kitchen and do dishes while you're listening to the mix from another room. Even though you're not hearing all the details, if the vocals are sticking out really loud, you're gonna hear it from another room.

I grew up in the '70s and listening to vinyl records where you sit between the speakers and it was an experience, all the way through. You kind of sat there 'til the record was done. In this day and age, people have music on in the background. They're walking around the house; they're doing other stuff. You need to put yourself in the position of how are people listening to it? They might not be sitting right between the speakers. You need to get another perspective of where they might be in relation to the system, also, that they're listening to it on.

So having different reference tracks to compare your work to, I feel, that makes you strive to be better. Some people don't use reference tracks because they're scared that when they switch over to it, they're gonna realize their stuff doesn't sound as good. But to me, it made me work so much harder. While there was a little frustration in the beginning—why doesn't my stuff sound as good? Why aren't my mixes coming out as well as this record that I just bought last week?—it made me work harder. It made me figure out, tear it down, instrument by instrument over time. Say, "Okay, how can I get my kick to sound as good as that?" And I would do whatever it took to try to achieve that, whether it was talking to other engineers about what they do in the mix to the kick drum, or what kind of vocal effects they like to add, to reading *Mix* magazine or *Tape Op*. You know, just trying to figure out where your weaknesses are and focus on those when you're mixing.

Final Thoughts

Corey reinforced a lot of ideas I've tried to get across throughout this book—the importance of listening through different speaker systems, the need to develop strong people skills, putting the music first, and more. I also like his emphasis, at least when you're first starting out, on comparing your work to various reference recordings. You should never mix in a vacuum; it's good to listen to other recordings to figure out how you want things to sound.

Bottom line: becoming a successful mixing engineer requires a mixture of technical and interpersonal skills. Having a musical background is also good because it helps you better understand the music you're mixing and communicate more efficiently with the musicians you're working with. (For what it's worth, Corey plays guitar with several local bands—a definite plus.)

The Least You Need to Know

- A good mixing engineer can work in a variety of genres, with a variety of different artists.
- The goal in mixing a project is to bring out the energy and emotion in the music, as envisioned by the artist.
- It's important to meet with the artists beforehand, to establish your role in the project—and get the artists to trust you.
- Use reference recordings to help establish the sounds you want to achieve.
- Listen to your mix through a variety of speaker systems to simulate how real-world listeners hear the music.
- Keep learning—listen to a variety of music, talk to other engineers, read industry magazines, and more.

Glossary

0 dB   Zero decibels, a common reference point for discussing sound levels. Levels above 0 dB are expressed as positive (+1 dB); levels below 0 dB are expressed as negative (−1 dB).

acoustic instrument   An instrument without pickups or built-in electronics that requires a microphone for recording.

acoustical foam   A type of sound-absorbing foam used to deaden recording studios.

acoustics   The science that deals with sound and its physical properties.

active speaker   A loudspeaker with a self-contained power amplifier. Most studio monitors (and all computer speakers) are active speakers.

AIFF (Audio Interchange File Format)   A type of digital audio file used on the Macintosh operating system. AIFF files (along with Windows WAV files) deliver the best-quality sound and are used to export final recordings in Cubase.

ambience   The acoustics, reverberation, and reflections of a room or other space.

ambient noise   The natural background noise of a room or space.

amplitude   The height of a sound wave. The larger the amplitude, the louder the sound.

analog recording   A traditional form of recording in which the recorded waveform maintains the general shape of the original waveform.

arrangement   How instruments and voices present a composition.

attack   The very beginning of a note or sound.

attack time   When using a compressor or similar plug-in, the time it takes for gain reduction to occur in response to the attack of a note.

attenuate   To reduce the level of a signal.

audio engineer   One of several individuals who record, mix, or master an audio recording.

audio interface   An outboard box or internal card that connects microphones and instruments to a computer, often replacing the computer's built-in sound card functionality.

Auto-Tune   The most popular pitch correction plug-in used to correct the pitch of vocal and other tracks.

automation   A feature that lets a mixing engineer program control changes made to a track, so that on playback, these changes happen automatically.

baffle   A sound-absorbing panel used to prevent sound from entering or leaving a certain space. Baffles are used in recording studios to isolate certain acoustic instruments or vocalists.

balance   The relative volume levels of various instruments, tracks, or channels.

bandwidth   A range of audio frequencies.

bidirectional microphone   Sometimes called a "figure-eight microphone," a microphone with a pickup pattern to sound arriving at the front and rear of the microphone but not at the sides.

bit depth   *See* bit rate.

bit rate   Also known as the *bit depth* or *sample depth,* the number of bits transferred in 1 second by a digital audio device. The higher the bit rate, the higher quality the recording.

bleeding   When the sound of one instrument or track unintentionally mixes in with another.

board   *See* mixer.

boomy   A sound or mix that emphasizes lower frequencies.

bottom   Another term for low frequencies, typically those below 125 Hz.

bouncing   The process of saving one or more tracks as a separate audio file. (In the analog tape recording era, bouncing involved playing multiple tracks on one recorder and recording them as a single track on a second recorder.)

boxy   A sound or mix that emphasizes mid frequencies.

bright   A sound or mix that emphasizes higher frequencies.

bus   A signal path that feeds into or out of a program or device, such as a mixer. An input bus feeds into the device; an output bus feeds out of the device.

cardioid microphone   A microphone with a pickup pattern that is strongest from the front, less strong from the sides, and weakest from the rear.

channel   (1) A signal path. (2) An individual track within a recording project. (3) In the final audio file, it's one of the sides of a stereo recording.

channel strip   That part of a mixer or DAW that consolidates all mixing controls for a given channel, including volume fader, EQ, sends, and inserts.

chorus   An audio effect in which a single sound source is made to sound like several through the use of time delay and modulation.

clean   A sound that is free of noise, distortion, and other effects.

click   (1) The sound made by a *click track*. (2) In some forms of music, such as death or speed metal, the nonboomy part of a bass drum sound.

click track   A metronome-like click that sounds on every beat of each measure, in time to the selected tempo. Click tracks are used during recording to help all the musicians play to the same steady beat.

clipping   The introduction of distortion into an audio signal by playing it too loud—above the 0 dB level.

close mic'ing   A recording technique in which the microphone is placed very close to the instrument being mic'd. This technique yields a great deal of presence and detail while avoiding leakage from other sound sources and minimizing the room's natural acoustics.

closed back   A type of headphone, typically used in recording, that surrounds the ear and provides maximum isolation.

composition   The melody, chords, and lyrics of a song.

compressed   An audio recording with a restricted dynamic range.

compression   The process of reducing the dynamic range of a recording to create a punchier sound. Typically achieved via use of a compressor or limiter.

compressor   Also known as a *dynamic compressor*, this is a device or plug-in that compresses the dynamic range of a program by limiting the volume peaks and boosting the lowest volume levels.

condenser microphone   A type of microphone that is powered by an outboard power source (called *phantom power*). Condenser mics are more sensitive than dynamic mics and are particularly suited to recording vocals.

console   *See* mixer.

control surface   An outboard mixing board that connects to a computer and interfaces with the DAW software program.

cross-fade   The process of fading out the sound on one clip as it fades into the sound on the following clip.

DAW   *See* digital audio workstation (DAW).

dB   *See* decibel (dB).

dead   Having little or no reverberation; *dry*.

decay   The trailing section of a waveform; the last sounding part of a note.

decibel (dB)   A means of measuring sound levels. The decibel scale is not linear; raising the level by 1 dB increases volume by 10 percent, while raising the level by 6 dB results in a 200 percent increase (doubles the volume).

de-esser   A device or plug-in that removes excessive sibilant sounds (S's, CH's, and so on) by compressing frequencies in the 5,000 to 10,000 Hz range.

delay   (1) The time interval between a signal and its repetition. (2) An audio processing effect that creates a copy of the original sound, positioned slightly after the original.

DI   *See* direct injection (DI).

diaphragm   In a microphone, the thin, flexible membrane that vibrates in response to sound waves to produce electrical signals.

digital audio workstation (DAW)   A type of software program that offers audio recording and mixing capabilities.

digital recording   A form of audio recording in which the original analog waveform is represented by a series of digital 1s and 0s. With digital recording, the recorded signals can be easily edited and processed using DAW programs.

digital signal processing   The act of somehow altering the original recorded signal using digital techniques.

direct injection (DI)   The process of recording an electric instrument, such as an electric guitar or bass, directly to the mixing board without using an instrument amplifier.

distortion   A change to the original audio waveform, typically caused by overloading the input signal, that causes a raspy or unclear sound quality.

double-track   The process of combining the original audio signal with a copy of the signal, sometimes delayed by 15 to 25 milliseconds, to produce a fatter sound than a pure signal.

doubling   *See* double-track.

driver   A separate speaker within a larger speaker enclosure.

dry   A sound or track without any effects or reverberation; the opposite of *wet*.

dynamic compressor   *See* compressor.

dynamic effect   A plug-in that affects a track's dynamics, or volume levels.

dynamic microphone   A type of microphone that records via electromagnetic induction using a small diaphragm that vibrates under sound pressure.

dynamic range   The loudness spectrum of a recording (or the ability to handle a given loudness spectrum), from the softest passage to the loudest.

echo   The delayed repetition of a sound or signal, usually at least 50 milliseconds after the original sound. Echo is typically cleaner than reverb because it doesn't include any unwanted reflections in the sound.

edit   To modify, copy, or delete sections or parts from a recording.

effect   In general, any device or plug-in that changes or processes the sound of a recording in any way other than equalization or volume level. Reverb, delay, and compression are all audio effects.

engineer   *See* audio engineer.

EQ   *See* equalization (EQ).

EQ hole   A frequency range that is deliberately cut to make room for a similar-sounding voice or instrument in the mix.

equalization (EQ)   A means of shaping a recorded tone by boosting or cutting specific frequencies or frequency bands.

equalizer   A device or plug-in that changes the frequency of a recorded signal.

event   A distinct recorded part, typically from a single instrument or microphone.

fade in   The process of gradually increasing the volume of a signal from 0 to the desired level.

fade out   The process of gradually decreasing the volume of a signal from the starting level to 0.

fader   A slider that typically controls volume level.

fat   A warm, full sound. This is sometimes accomplished by doubling.

file format   The type of audio file used to save recorded tracks.

filter   A device or plug-in that removes frequencies from a sound or waveform above or below a certain frequency.

flanging   A plug-in that modulates and delays a copy of the original sound to create a whooshing or swishing effect.

frequency   The number of cycles per second of a sound wave, measured in hertz. High frequencies have higher pitches, and low frequencies have lower pitches.

frequency response   A measure of the sonic properties of a signal, typically represented as a graph.

gain   (1) Also known as *amplification,* the ratio between the input power and the output power, typically expressed in decibels. (2) Sometimes used to refer to an increase or decrease in volume level.

gain staging   The process of setting the initial gain or levels in each stage of the project workflow to optimal levels in order to prevent noise and distortion.

gate   *See* noise gate.

harsh   An unpleasant sound that peaks in the upper midrange area, typically between 2,000 and 6,000 kHz.

headroom   A margin of safety between the current signal level and the maximum signal level before clipping occurs.

hertz (Hz)   A measure of frequency or pitch that describes the vibrations of an audio signal in cycles per second.

hot   Recording audio signals at a high level, at or slightly above the 0 dB clipping point, causing a mild distortion to occur.

hum   An undesired low-pitched sound, typically around 60 Hz, that is heard along with the audio signal.

Hz   Abbreviation for hertz.

input bus   The signal path that feeds into a program or device.

input insert effect   A plug-in or audio effect inserted into the signal path of the input bus as a recording is being made.

insert   *See* insert effect.

insert effect   A plug-in or audio effect inserted into the signal path after the original input and before equalization and volume are applied.

kHz   Abbreviation for kilohertz.

kilohertz (kHz)   A measure of frequency or pitch that describes the vibrations of an audio signal in thousands of cycles per second; 1 kHz is equal to 1,000 Hz.

latency   The amount of time between a signal arriving at a sound card and when it comes out of the speakers. Low latency results in almost immediate response to any input; high latency means that what you play and what you hear are separated by a noticeable period of time.

leakage   The spill of one instrument's sound into another instrument's microphone.

level   The strength or volume of an audio signal, typically measured in decibels.

limiter   Also known as a *peak limiter,* a device or plug-in that dictates a maximum volume level; any sounds louder than this level are automatically lowered in volume to match (but not exceed) the peak level.

live   A sound or recording that has reverberation.

loop   A short audio sample, typically repeated multiple times to create a longer track in a recording.

loop-based recording   A recording constructed primarily from repeated audio loops.

low-pass filter   A filter that passes frequencies below a given frequency and cuts all frequencies above that level.

magnetic tape   A medium for audio or video recording that incorporates a thin magnetic coating on a narrow strip of plastic film.

master EQ   Equalization applied to the entire recording via the output bus.

master insert effect   A plug-in or audio effect inserted into the master output bus during the mastering process, after the individual tracks have been mixed down to a stereo signal.

mastering   The process of readying a final mix for distribution on other media.

mastering engineer   A recording engineer who specializes in the mastering process.

mastering studio   A small recording studio—often just a recording booth—devoted to the mastering process.

meter A device that indicates signal level. In Cubase's mixer, meters display the current volume level.

mic *See* microphone (mic).

microphone (mic) A device that converts acoustic sound waves into electronic form.

MIDI (musical instrument digital interface) A standard that dictates how various electronic instruments (such as synthesizers) communicate with each other, with computers, and with computerized mixers.

MIDI instrument A synthesizer or synthesizer program (*soft synth*) that reproduces the sounds of one or more acoustic or electric instruments. A MIDI recording must be fed through a MIDI instrument to play a sound.

midrange That range of frequencies between 200 and 2,000 Hz.

Mike The author's first name. (The short form of microphone is *mic*, not Mike.)

mixer (1) A hardware device that accepts multiple microphone and audio inputs, mixes the sound from these inputs, and sends the signals to a recording device. Also known as a *board, console, mixing board,* or *mixing console.* (2) That part of a DAW program that functions as a virtual mixer.

mixing The process of putting together all the tracks in a recording project to make a pleasing overall recording.

mixing board *See* mixer.

mixing console *See* mixer.

mixing down *See* mixing.

mixing engineer The person who supervises the mixing process.

modulation effect A plug-in that modulates low-frequency notches on copies of the original signal.

monitor Another name for the small powered speakers used in most recording studios.

MP3 Short for MPEG layer 3, a type of digital audio file that uses compression technology to create smaller-size files. It's the most common file format for internet music downloads.

muddy A sound or mix that lacks clarity.

multitrack recording The process of recording on multiple channels within a single recording.

mute   To silence a track or signal.

nearfield monitor   A small speaker designed for listeners located very close to the speaker, as in a recording booth.

noise   Unwanted sound.

noise gate   A device or plug-in that shuts down a signal when its volume falls below a given level. It's typically used to eliminate unwanted noise between notes.

offline processing   Audio processing that takes place offline, before playback or mixing. Offline processing is applied to individual audio events.

omnidirectional microphone   A microphone that is equally sensitive to sounds coming from all directions.

open back   A type of headphone, typically used by mixing engineers, that sit on top of the ear.

outboard equipment   Signal processors or other devices not software based.

output bus   The signal path that feeds out of a program or device.

overdub   To record a new musical part on an unused track, or to replace an existing section of a recorded track.

pan   To place an audio element along the width of the stereo soundstage.

parametric equalizer   A type of equalizer in which the range of frequencies affected by level boosts/cuts is adjustable.

passive speaker   A loudspeaker that requires external amplification. Almost all home audio speakers are passive speakers.

patch   A particular instrument sound produced by a synthesizer or sampler.

peak limiter   *See* limiter.

phantom center   A virtual center channel created by duplicating a mono signal and positioning the two tracks hard left and right in the stereo soundstage.

phantom power   The outboard power supplied to condenser microphones.

phase shifter   *See* phaser.

phaser   A plug-in that modulates a copy of the original signal with little or no delay.

pitch correction   The process of altering the pitch of a voice or instrument. It's typically used to correct off-key vocals.

plug-in   A device or software program that inserts into the signal path and performs some useful function.

pop filter   *See* windscreen.

port   A small opening in a speaker cabinet designed to enhance bass response.

presence   The aural characteristic of an instrument being "up front" in the listening environment.

Pro Tools   One of the most popular DAW programs in use today, especially in professional recording studios.

processing   The act of somehow altering an audio signal or track.

processor   *See* signal processor.

producer   In a traditional recording environment, the person in charge of the recording session. Not to be confused with the recording engineer, who actually makes the recording.

project   All the tracks that make up a complete recording, song, or soundtrack.

project window   The part of a DAW interface that displays the track list, track inspector, and event display.

Q   The means of defining the width of a frequency band affected by equalization.

RAM (random access memory)   The memory capacity of a personal computer, typically measured in gigabytes (GB).

record   (1) To store an audio or MIDI event in a permanent form. (2) As a noun, those old vinyl discs that preceded CDs.

recording engineer   The person who runs the recording board and captures the recording during a recording session.

recording studio   A room where musicians sing and play their instruments during the recording process. Recording studios can be any size, from a spare bedroom to a large dedicated hall.

reflected sound   Sound waves that reach the listener after being reflected from one or more surfaces (walls, ceilings, and so on).

reflection   *See* reflected sound.

release   The final portion of a sound's envelope, where the sound falls from its sustain level back to silence.

release time   In a signal processor, the time it takes for the gain to return to normal from its processed level.

reverb   (1) The persistence of sound in a room or other space, after the original sound has ended, caused by sound reflections that decrease in intensity over time. (2) An audio processing effect that artificially creates the sound of natural reverb.

reverb time   The time it takes for reverb to decay to 60 dB below the original level.

reverberation   *See* reverb.

rhythm tracks   The collective name for the recorded tracks of the rhythm section—drums, bass, rhythm guitar, keyboards, and other percussion.

ribbon microphone   A type of microphone in which the conductor is a long, metallic ribbon, similar to a filament in a lightbulb, suspended in a magnetic field. Ribbon mics are very fragile and sensitive to loud sound pressure levels.

sample depth   *See* bit rate.

sample rate   The frequency at which bits of data are recorded in digitizing a sound. Higher sample rates result in more accurate digital reproduction of the original signal.

sampling   The process of digitally encoding a sound.

send effect   A plug-in or audio effect added to the end of the signal path as a separate effects track. The final audio is routed to the effects track as the final step in the process.

sends   *See* send effect.

sibilance   In a vocal recording, excessive peaks in the frequency response in the 6,000 to 10,000 Hz range, typically due to an overemphasis of S, SH, and CH sounds. A vocal recording with excessive sibilance is referred to as "essy" and can be corrected with a "de-esser" plug-in.

signal   A varying electronic voltage that represents sound.

signal path   The route a signal travels from input to output in the recording process.

signal processor   A device or plug-in used to deliberately alter a signal in a controlled manner.

sound wave   A physical wave that pulses through the air, the changing pressure of which creates a distinct sound.

soundfield   *See* soundstage.

soundstage   The physical or virtual space in which sounds reside. The stereo soundstage defines the left-to-right presence of played or recorded sounds.

stereo   An audio recording with distinct left and right channels.

studio   *See* recording studio.

subwoofer   A freestanding speaker designed to reproduce very low bass notes.

surround sound   A multichannel audio format that envelops the listener from speakers positioned both in front of and behind the audience.

sustain   (1) That portion of the envelope of a sound in which the level is constant. (2) The ability of a sound to continue without noticeably decaying.

synthesizer   A musical instrument that generates sound electronically and allows changes to the sound parameters (via filters, oscillators, and so forth) to create new sounds.

take   One recorded performance of a song or part. Many recording sessions consist of multiple takes, the best of which is used for the final recording.

tempo   The speed of the beat in a song or composition.

three-way speaker   A speaker system that includes three drivers—tweeter, midrange, and woofer.

threshold   (1) In a compressor or limiter, the level above which compression or limiting takes place. (2) In a noise gate or expander, the level below which gating or expansion takes place.

timbre   The character or quality of a given voice or instrument, separate from its pitch and frequency range.

track   (1) An individual recorded channel or part in a recording project. (2) An individual song on a compact disc. (3) As a verb, the process of making a recording, as in "tracking the band."

track group   An assemblage of related tracks that can be worked on together as a single item.

track list   The part of the DAW interface that lists all the tracks available in the current project.

transient   An unusually high amplitude, rapidly decaying, peak signal level.

tweeter   A small speaker driver designed to reproduce high frequencies.

two-way speaker   A speaker system that includes two drivers, a tweeter and a woofer.

unidirectional microphone   *See* bidirectional microphone.

upper midrange   That range of frequencies between 2,000 and 6,000 Hz.

virtual instrument   A software program that emulates a physical instrument.

vocoder   A device that combines a vocal signal with an instrument signal to create a mechanical-sounding vocal.

warm   (1) A mix or track with good bass and sufficient low frequencies. (2) A mix or track that sounds spacious, with good reverberation.

warp   A feature in many DAW programs that enables the shrinking or stretching of an event or track, or of individual notes within an event, without changing the song's pitch.

watt   A measurement of power in electrical systems and devices.

WAV   A type of digital audio file used on the Windows operating system. WAV files (along with the Macintosh AIFF files) deliver the best-quality sound and are used to export final recordings during the mastering process.

waveform   A graph of an audio signal's sound pressure over time.

wet   A sound or track that contains reverberation or ambience.

windscreen   Also known as a *pop filter*, a screen placed between a vocalist and a microphone that filters out pop or wind disturbances before they strike the microphone diaphragm.

woofer   A larger speaker driver designed to reproduce low frequencies.

Resources

Throughout this book, I've discussed various products from numerous manufacturers. Use this handy guide to find more information about those products in which you're interested.

DAW Software

Ableton Live (Ableton)
ableton.com

ACID Pro (Sony Creative Software)
sonycreativesoftware.com

Bitwig Studio (Bitwig)
bitwig.com

Cubase (Steinberg)
steinberg.net

Digital Performer (MOTU)
motu.com

Logic Pro (Apple)
apple.com

Nuendo (Steinberg)
steinberg.net

Pro Tools (Avid)
avid.com

REAPER (Cockos Incorporated)
reaper.fm

Reason (Propellerhead Software)
propellerheads.se

SONAR (Cakewalk)
cakewalk.com

Studio One (PreSonus)
studioone.presonus.com

Plug-Ins and Effects

Antares Audio Technologies
antarestech.com

Celemony
celemony.com

Eventide
eventideaudio.com

IK Multimedia
ikmultimedia.com

iZotope
izotope.com

Mu Technologies
mu-technologies.com

Native Instruments
native-instruments.com

Slate Digital
slatedigital.com

Softube
softube.com

Soundtoys
soundtoys.com

Toontrack
toontrack.com

Waves
waves.com

zplane
zplane.de

Audio Interfaces

Allen and Heath
allen-heath.com

Apogee Electronics
apogeedigital.com

Audient
audient.com

Behringer
behringer.com

Focusrite
us.focusrite.com

Lexicon
lexiconpro.com

Mackie
mackie.com

MOTU
motu.com

Native Instruments
native-instruments.com

PreSonus
presonus.com

Universal Audio
uaudio.com

Mixing Consoles and Control Surfaces

Allen and Heath
allen-heath.com

Avid
avid.com

Behringer
behringer.com

KORG
korg.com

Mackie
mackie.com

Nektar
nektartech.com

Novation
us.novationmusic.com

PreSonus
presonus.com

QSC Audio Products
qsc.com

Roland
proav.roland.com

Slate Media Technology
slatemt.com

Soundcraft
soundcraft.com

TASCAM
tascam.com

Yamaha Pro Audio
yamahaproaudio.com

Studio Monitor Speakers

ADAM Audio
adam-audio.com

Alesis
alesis.com

Behringer
behringer.com

Event Electronics
eventelectronics.com

Genelec
genelec.com

JBL Professional
jbl.com

KRK Systems
krksys.com

Mackie
mackie.com

M-Audio
m-audio.com

PreSonus
presonus.com

Roland
proav.roland.com

Samson Technologies
samsontech.com

Yamaha Pro Audio
yamahaproaudio.com

Studio Furniture

Argosy Console
argosyconsole.com

Malone Design Works
malonedesignworks.com

Middle Atlantic Products
middleatlantic.com

Omnirax
omnirax.com

On-Stage Stands
on-stage.com

RAB Audio
rabaudio.com

Sound Construction and Supply
soundconstructionsupply.com

Pro Audio Retailers

Full Compass
fullcompass.com

Musician's Friend
musiciansfriend.com

Pro Audio Solutions
proaudiosolutions.com

ProAudio
proaudio.com

Sweetwater Sound
sweetwater.com

zZounds
zzounds.com

Index

Q